WHEN PARTNERS BECOME PARENTS

CAROLYN PAPE COWAN
and PHILIP A. COWAN

When
Partners
Become
Parents

The Big Life Change
for Couples

BasicBooks
A Division of HarperCollins*Publishers*

Library of Congress Cataloging-in-Publication Data
Cowan, Carolyn Pape.
    When partners become parents: the big life change for
couples / by Carolyn Pape Cowan and Philip A. Cowan.
        p.   cm.
    Includes bibliographical references and index.
    ISBN 0–465–01595–6 : $24.00
    1. Parents—United States—Longitudinal studies.
    2. Parenthood—Longitudinal studies.   I. Cowan, Philip A.
    II. Title.
    HQ755.8.C68   1992
    306.87—dc20   91–55457
                                                          CIP

With our love and appreciation to our parents and children—
Norman Cowan, Lee Pape
Joanna Cowan White, Dena Cowan, Jonathan Cowan
Kennen White, and Jennifer Cowan

and in loving memory of
Bertha Cowan, Grace Pape, and Ben Pape

CONTENTS

PREFACE

BABIES ARE GETTING a bad press these days. Newspaper and magazine articles warn that the cost of raising a child from birth to adulthood is now hundreds of thousands of dollars. Television news recounts tragic stories of mothers who have harmed their babies while suffering from severe postpartum depression. Health professionals caution that child abuse has become a problem throughout our nation. Several books on how to "survive" parenthood suggest that couples must struggle to keep their marriage alive once they become parents. In fact, according to recent demographic studies, more than 40 percent of the children born to two parents can expect to live in a single-parent family by the time they are eighteen (Glick and Lin 1986). The once-happy endings to family beginnings seem clouded with strain, violence, disenchantment, and divorce.

What is so difficult about becoming a family today? What does it mean that some couples are choosing to remain "child-free" because they fear that a child might threaten their well-established careers or disturb the intimacy of their marriage? Is keeping a family together harder than it used to be?

Over the last three decades, sociologists, psychologists, and psychiatrists have begun to search for answers to these questions. Results of the most recent studies, including our own, show that partners who become parents describe an ideology of more equal work and family roles than their mothers and fathers had; actual role arrangements in which husbands and wives are sharing family work and care of the baby less than either of them expected; more conflict and disagreement after the baby is born than they had reported before; and increasing disenchantment with their overall relationship as a couple.

To add to these disquieting trends, psychiatrists' and obstetricians' studies of emotional distress in new parents suggest that women, and possibly men, are more vulnerable to depression in the early months after having a child, and that mothers with children under five and without a supportive partner are at greater risk for becoming clinically depressed than any other group of adults.

Finally, in the United States, close to 50 percent of couples who marry will ultimately divorce. In our longitudinal study of relatively well functioning couples having a first baby, 12.5 percent of the parents had separated or divorced by the time their first baby was one and a half years old. If this figure were to hold up in larger studies, it would mean that at least one-quarter of American divorces occur in households with children who are not old enough to retain the memory of living with two parents.

We believe that children are getting an unfair share of the blame for their parents' distress. Based on fifteen years of research that includes a three-year pilot study, a ten-year study following seventy-two expectant couples and twenty-four comparable couples without children, and ongoing work with couples in distress, we are convinced that the seeds of new parents' individual and marital problems are sown long before their first baby arrives.

Our conviction is bolstered by two findings from our studies: The couples who report the most marital difficulty after having a baby tend to be the ones who were experiencing the most strain in their relationships before they became parents; and the couples who feel that they have productive ways of working out the differences and difficulties that confront them report the least dissatisfaction and distress in the first few years of parenthood.

Our concern about the high incidence of marital distress and divorce among the parents of young children led us to study systematically what happens to partners as they become parents. Rather than simply add to the mounting documentation of family problems, we created and evaluated a new preventive program, the Becoming a Family Project, in which mental health professionals worked with couples during their transition to parenthood, trying to help them get off to a healthy start. Then we followed the families as the first children progressed from infancy to the preschool period to the first year of elementary school, to get a fuller picture of how the parents' well-being or distress affected their children's development at home and at school.

What we have learned from our Project is more troubling than surprising: The majority of husbands and wives become more disenchanted with their relationships as couples as they make the transition to parenthood. Most new mothers struggle with the question of whether and when to return to work. For those who do go back, the impact on their families depends both on what mothers do at work and on what fathers do at home. The more unhappy mothers and fathers feel about their marriage, the more anger and competitiveness and the less warmth and responsiveness we observe in the family during the preschool period—between the parents as a couple and between each parent and the child. The cycle continues as the children of parents with more tension during the preschool years have a harder time adjusting to the challenges of kindergarten two years later.

On the positive side, becoming a family provides a challenge that for some men and women leads to growth—as individuals, as couples, and as parents. For couples who work to maintain or improve the quality of their marriage as they become parents, with or without help, having a baby can lead to a revitalized relationship. Couples with more satisfying marriages work together more effectively with their children in the preschool period, and their children tend to have an easier time adapting to the academic and social demands of elementary school.

When Partners Become Parents describes what happens to men and women, and especially to their relationships as couples, when they have their first baby. In an introductory chapter, we describe how our personal history led to the creation of the Becoming a Family Project, our study examining both stability and change in five major aspects of a couple's life on their journey to parenthood. In part I we begin with a discussion of why the transition to parenthood is stressful even for well-functioning couples. We then explore a couple's preparation for the excursion: their decision-making process about whether and when to have a baby and the issues they face during pregnancy and childbirth.

Part II begins where childbirth preparation classes end. The men and women in our study talk about the changes they experience after their babies are born in their sense of self, in the "who does what?" of family life, in their work outside the family, and in their relationships with their parents and in-laws. We demonstrate that what is happening in the marriage provides a context for the relationship that each parent establishes with the child, and that the preschooler's family environment is influential in his or her academic and social adjustment to elementary school. It becomes very clear that for new parents to maintain the quality of their relationships as partners, they must strike a delicate balance among these competing but essential aspects of their lives.

In the service of stimulating more preventive work with developing families, we focus in part III on the reactions of a randomly chosen set of parents in our study. These couples met once a week throughout the last three months of pregnancy and the first three months of parenthood in small groups led by couples who are trained mental health professionals. Our results show that when sensitive group leaders help men and women focus on what is happening to them as individuals and as a couple during their transition to parenthood, it buffers them from turning their strain into dissatisfaction with each other and seems to keep them from resorting to early separation and divorce. We show how the typical difficulties of keeping marital communication open and intimate can easily become more problematic in the hectic period around the birth of a first child. Finally, we talk about who is most at risk for distress in the early family years, spelling out the implications of our findings for new parents, for health professionals, for family researchers, and for those who make the policy decisions that affect both parents and children.

This book is addressed to several audiences. It is for couples thinking about having a baby as well as for those who have started their families but want to know more about the parts of family making that friends and researchers rarely discuss: Why does becoming a parent have such a powerful impact on a marriage? What can couples do to make the family formation period a time of development rather than decline? From our couples groups we have learned that one of the most difficult aspects of becoming a family is that so much of what happens is unexpected. At the risk of sounding alarmist, we provide some warnings about the dangers that seem to sidetrack couples from the wonderful side of having babies and nurturing their development. We find that helping couples anticipate how they might handle the potentially stressful aspects of becoming a family can leave them feeling less vulnerable, less likely to blame each other for the hard parts, and more likely to decide that they can work it out together.

We believe that our findings have something to say to researchers from various disciplines who study what goes on in families. We want to urge family sociologists, developmental psychologists, and psychiatrists who study the family to look beyond the relationships between mothers and children—to accord fathers their full due as family members and to pay more attention to the effects of parents' marital quality on their children's early development.

In addition to parents and family researchers, this book is addressed to health professionals who are involved with family matters. The experiences of the parents in our study should convince obstetricians, pediatricians, nurse practitioners, and physicians in family practice to be more active in attending to the health of the whole family. If doctors and nurses were to ask more about the well-being of both parents during checkups in the early family years—for example, by asking "How are *the two of you* doing?"—they could encourage parents to seek help for moderately troubling problems before they feel insurmountable.

We hope to begin a dialogue with mental health professionals about the prevention and treatment of family distress. Throughout the book, we demonstrate that our assessments of how the partners are doing during pregnancy as individuals and as a couple can identify a substantial number who are at risk for later distress. We are eager to involve more health professionals in this venture in order to give parents at greater risk a chance to beat the odds before their distress permeates all of the relationships in the family.

We conclude by highlighting our picture of the delicate balance: what it takes for today's fathers and mothers to feel satisfied with themselves as individuals, as parents, and as couples. In the virtual absence of comprehensive government policies to support the development of families, contemporary couples are forced to be pioneers, making the arduous trek to parenthood on their own. Men and women push on, wondering when they will feel less alone, trying to find better ways to take care of themselves, their babies, their work inside and outside the family, and their relationships as partners and parents. How parents approach the rough spots and how satisfied they are with the outcome of their efforts can have profound effects on how they feel about themselves, what happens to their marriage, and how well their children do as they meet the challenges of elementary school.

When Partners Become Parents is not so much a "how-to" book as a "why-it's-so-hard-to" book. Whether you are a new parent, an old hand, a grandparent, or a researcher or clinician who works with families, we hope that the ideas here will help you make more sense of the difficult parts of becoming a family and suggest some new ways to search for the delicate balance that contemporary family making seems to require.

ACKNOWLEDGMENTS

A STUDY AS LONG AND COMPLEX as the Becoming a Family Project can be accomplished only with extremely dedicated and loyal colleagues, and we have had the good fortune to work with many. First, we pay tribute to Trudie Heming, who served as data manager for the entire ten years of the study. In addition to her exceptional ability to keep us and the data on track, Trudie has made invaluable contributions to our thinking about statistical analysis and our conceptualization of the project's direction.

The data set for a longitudinal study is the backbone of the enterprise. We are indebted to Dena Cowan, who entered a major portion of the data into the computer and conducted some of the analyses with patience and a keen eye for detail. Others contributed their time and skill to the painstaking work of entering data as each follow-up of the families was completed: Barbara Epperson, Beth Schoenberger, and Karen Whitmer. Marc Schulz also conducted some of the recent statistical analyses.

For their early collaboration, support, and friendship, we give special thanks to John and Lynne Coie. Together, the four of us developed the initial interviews and questionnaires, interviewed couples in a dozen obstetrical practices, and led the first couples group in the pilot study. During the next five years, we had the good fortune to work with three other wonderful staff couples. Harriet Curtis-Boles and Abner Boles III, and Ellen Garrett and Bill

Coysh, the other interviewers and leaders of the couples groups throughout the first four years of the longitudinal study, met together regularly with us to monitor the process of the groups and refine our ideas about the intervention. When these two couples moved on to begin their personal family projects, Laura Mason Gordon and David Gordon joined us to complete the final follow-ups of the study families. The sensitivity and warmth of these staff couples kept the participants working with us well beyond the two years we envisioned when we recruited them.

We are most grateful for the enthusiastic cooperation of a number of obstetrician-gynecologists and their staff members for believing enough in the project to help us get the word out to potential participants for our studies. Special thanks go to Joe Weick, Linda Robrecht, Hank Streitfeld, Max Bynum, Elijah Hill, Joseph Washington, Ed Blumenstock, Louis Klein, Jeffrey Waldman, and the dedicated staff of each of their practices.

The playroom visits with the children in the preschool and kindergarten periods were conducted with empathy and skill by Sacha Bunge, Michael Blum, Julia Levine, David Chavez, and Marc Schulz. The parent-child and family visits were conducted and rated by Linda Kastelowitz and Victor Lieberman, who helped to develop the rating scales, and Marsha Kline and Charles Soulé, who were instrumental in revising them for the later follow-ups. As the children completed kindergarten, Joanna Cowan White met with each one, administering an individual achievement test and talking with them about their families, their friends, and their experiences at school. The children's delightful responses are a tribute to her skill and sensitivity.

Incredible resourcefulness in convincing kindergarten teachers to rate each child in their classrooms was shown by Elaine Ransom and Laurie Leventhal-Belfer. A new set of rating scales for the family visits when the children were three and a half was constructed under the guidance of Yona Teichman by Joanna Self, Nancy Miller, Christina Whitney, and Juanita Dimas. The family scale items were revised and the kindergarten year visits coded by Jennifer Berland, Eric Gortner, Gwen Lai, and Reni Szczepanski under the able supervision of Elizabeth Owens. Yo Elberbaum, Eve Cumberbatch, Stacy Miller, Karen Spangenberg, and Barbara Zachary devoted hours to searching different aspects of our interviews with the couples for patterns of change and stability, and Isabel Bradburn and Joan Kaplan prepared detailed case studies of two of the families. Thanks also to Jamie McHale and Juanita Dimas for additional help in reviewing the literature on the family-to-school transition.

A number of graduate student researchers have contributed to our understanding of the early family-making period. Using the data to make in-depth explorations of some aspect of the becoming a family period, fourteen team members completed studies, a number of them already published: doctoral dissertations by Trudie Heming, Jessica Ball, Abner Boles III, Bill Coysh, Marsha Kline, Julia Levine, Pat Kerig, Elaine Ransom, and Laurie Leventhal-Belfer; Master's theses by Rachel Conrad, Joan Kaplan, Marc Schulz, and Dan Silver; and an undergraduate honors thesis by Barbara Epperson.

We have been most fortunate in having the collaboration of a number of colleagues from afar over the past ten years. Nancy Miller, now at the University of Akron, and Deborah Cohn, now at the University of Virginia, served as Postdoctoral Fellows with us, sponsored by a grant from the National Institute of Mental Health to the Family Research Consortium. In addition to their contributions to data analyses and publication, they contributed a great deal to the life of the project during their two-year tenure. Michael Pratt, from Wilfred Laurier University in Canada, has collaborated with us for a number of years, taking us in new directions with his ideas about children's and adults' cognitive development. Yona Teichman, from Tel Aviv University in Israel, has stimulated our thinking about how to assess family dynamics.

For help with the daily organization and secretarial support of the project, we thank Julia Babcock, Joanna Self, and Bonita Thoreson. Especially during the crunch of preparing grant proposals or conference papers, Jonathan Cowan and Jennifer Cowan offered their considerable talents to do timely editing, reference checking, and data preparation.

We are indebted to the National Institute of Mental Health for ongoing financial and collegial support throughout the ten-year longitudinal study, and to the Spencer Foundation for a year of crucial support as we completed our analysis of the data on the family-to-school transition.

The members of the Family Research Consortium, brought into being by Joy Schulterbrandt at the National Institute of Mental Health, have made ongoing and valuable contributions to our conceptualization of this work. At their regular meetings and summer institutes, we received encouragement combined with the kind of critical feedback that was essential to refining our ideas. The second phase of the project especially shows the influence of discussions with David Reiss, Mavis Hetherington, John Gottman, Irv Sigel, Ross Parke, Shep Kellam, Bob Cole, Elaine Blechman, and Gerry Patterson.

The Institute of Human Development at U.C. Berkeley has supported our work with allocations of research space and video equipment to record the family visits. Over a period of five years, the Interdisciplinary Faculty Study Group in Family Dynamics, initiated by Ed Swanson, met monthly at the Institute. Our regular discussions of both professional and personal experiences of family life stimulated our thinking and broadened our horizons.

Joanne Wile made helpful comments on an earlier draft of this manuscript. Dan Wile and Hilde Burton provided detailed critiques that contributed immeasurably to the final version. In the early years of the project, Hilde Burton also served as our consultant, helping us to sort out all of the couples' issues—our own, those of the group leaders, and those raised by the couples in the study. We are most appreciative of her warmth, her insightful observations, and her ongoing support of our work over the years. For their patience and encouragement as we completed this project, warm thanks to Audrey Cole, David Burton, Gene Rosenberg, Pat Miles, Kit Naftzger, Naomi Lowinsky, Rhona Weinstein, Harvey Weinstein, R. Jay Engel, and Pam Hamilton.

The people at Basic Books have been wonderful to us. Judy Greissman initially signed us on and encouraged us. Susan Arellano served as Senior Editor, taking us through the evolution of the manuscript, and going beyond the call of duty by initiating her own family project. Linda Carbone, Development Editor, understood what we were trying to say and, with the deft surgical strokes of her blue pencil, helped us say it more economically. It has been our pleasure to have Senior Editor Jo Ann Miller shepherd us through the last phase of the project. Her knowledge of the ropes and her unswerving support have been invaluable.

And, finally, we owe our greatest debt to the devoted families who have participated in the Becoming a Family Project. By giving us so many hours of your time—talking to us in the interviews, visiting our project playroom, completing our questionnaires year after year—you have made it possible for us to take an inside look at what it means to be partners and parents today. It has been a truly humbling and inspiring experience for us and our staff to have the opportunity to get to know so many wonderful families in the making.

WHEN PARTNERS BECOME PARENTS

INTRODUCTION

Becoming a Family

O UR DECISION to undertake a study of what happens when partners become parents was triggered by the collision of events in our personal and professional lives. We met as teenagers in the mid-1950s and, like many of our contemporaries, were still young when we married, four years later. Carolyn was nineteen and had just signed her first contract to teach elementary school. Phil, twenty-one, was completing his undergraduate degree in psychology. Having worked and gone to school throughout our teenage years, we felt ready to take on the responsibilities of the adult world we had entered.

We began trying to start a family two years after we were married. Carolyn's desire to have a baby was powerful. Because Phil felt unable to articulate his feeling that he was not yet ready to become a father, Carolyn's expressed feelings governed the decision about timing. Over the next few years we would learn the painful lessons taught by making decisions that affect both partners without thoroughly exploring or talking about them.

Carolyn did not become pregnant for eighteen months, by which time both of us were more than eager to expand our family. Joanna was born in 1961, followed by Dena in 1963 and Jonathan in 1965. We felt extremely lucky. All three children were healthy, different from one another in many ways, and a total delight to their parents and grandparents. These were times when a majority of women stayed home to look after the children, and, despite loving her work and having earned a permanent teaching credential, Carolyn eagerly left her position to become a full-time mother.

We spent the early years of parenthood trying to juggle everything so that our lives as parents and partners would match our dreams. We were totally absorbed by the parenting part and worked hard to make everything else in our lives fit around it. With our first child not quite two years old and our second about to be born, Phil's offer of a position at the University of California at Berkeley triggered our move there from Canada.

In our naïveté, we did not consider that moving three thousand miles from our family and friends to a new country and a new job might bring stresses that would challenge our relationship as a couple. In the years that followed, when our children were out of diapers and we began to sort out what had happened to us, one thing became abundantly clear: We had not been prepared for the shifts that had occurred in almost every aspect of our lives—especially in our relationship as a couple. In the midst of the family adventure we had embarked upon, our ten-year marriage began to feel precarious for the first time.

We had expected to feel differently about ourselves once we became parents, but we were startled by what felt like a major upheaval in our sense of ourselves. We had assumed, naturally, that there would be some changes in the "who does what" of our life, but had given little thought to how those shifts might actually feel. We hadn't known that becoming parents might lead us to feel more distant from each other based on our different levels of involvement in work inside and outside the family. We hadn't anticipated that having a baby could revive long-buried feelings of gratitude or disappointment about how loved we had felt as children, or realized that our disagreements about whether the baby needed to be picked up and comforted or left alone to "cry it out" would actually have more to do with our own needs than they did with the baby's. And, having always viewed the important issues of life similarly, we certainly did not anticipate how differently we could see the "same" things. Not only were we unprepared for these conflicts inside or between us but we found ourselves unable to talk about them productively once they surfaced.

By the time our children were in elementary school, there was no avoiding the issue: Our relationship was very strained. The task of dealing with our stress felt all the more daunting because suddenly we were surrounded by friends and neighbors who were looking up after ten or fifteen years of marriage and saying, in effect, "This isn't what I dreamed it would be. I want out!" Couples who had once been full of hopes and plans were dismantling families they had been building for decades. Announcements of separations and divorces became so frequent that a friend joked wryly that someone must have been tampering with the local water supply.

As we listened to the pain and disenchantment that other husbands and wives described in their relationships and struggled to make sense of our own, we began to hear a common refrain. We were experiencing distress now in our relationships as couples, but almost all of us could trace the beginning of our difficulties back to those early years of becoming a family. Our dreams had gotten lost somewhere between our starry-eyed pictures of intimate couples with cuddly babies and the stark reality of juggling the competing needs of growing children and parents.

In our professional roles, too, we realized that we were hearing over and over that when things start to feel shaky, few husbands and wives know how to tell anyone, especially each other, that they feel disappointed or frightened. "This is supposed to be the best time of our lives; what's the matter with me?" a wife might say through her tears. Or a husband would ask: "How can I talk about how scary it feels to have so much responsibility when I convinced her that we could manage our work, our relationship, *and* kids? When she's upset, I feel *I* have to be strong." Without discussing these worrisome thoughts and feelings with others, parents don't get to discover how widely their experiences are shared. They can't see that some of their tension may be attributable to the conflicting demands of this very complex stage of life, not simply to a suddenly stubborn, selfish, or unresponsive spouse.

As we talked with others about what seemed to be happening to contemporary families, we continued to work at getting our marriage back on track. We came to see that becoming parents had not so much raised new problems as it had brought old unconscious or unresolved issues to the surface. For example, we had grown up in qualitatively different family atmospheres, but we both came to our relationship determined to avoid conflict and fighting. Before children come along, it is possible for a couple to deal with differences or disagreements by avoiding them or by simply accepting the fact that each partner has a different view. But once children are part of the family, most of us discover, certain disagreements have to be resolved on the spot. Crying infants will not wait tolerantly while their parents engage in long-winded discussions about how to respond to them. And, somehow, in these years with so much vulnerability and so much to take care of, differences that have nothing to do with the children can take on a greater urgency.

After some trying and painful struggles, we slowly began to regain some of our balance and our sense of humor—with the help of each other, therapy, some good friends, and the sheer wonder of life with three active, inquiring children. We began to learn how to work out our differences or impasses more productively, which led paradoxically to our feeling both closer *and* more separate. This difficult work took a number of years. We now believe that most couples must undertake this kind of rebalancing of their relationship at certain points in their lives, to accommodate their individual and family growth and change.

We emerged with a stronger marriage and a resolve to "do something" about the stress that so many couples seem to experience in the early family-making years. We wondered whether we could encourage couples to confront their early difficulties rather than sweep them under the proverbial carpet. By this time we were into the 1970s, and had begun to hear about childbirth preparation classes for expectant mothers *and* fathers. In six- to eight-week classes, childbirth educators were instructing couples to use exercises and breathing techniques to cope with the pain of labor and delivery without medication. One of the best parts of this experience, couples told us, was that they attended these sessions together and "went through it" with other couples.

We were struck by a certain irony in this wonderful new intervention. Meeting with calming experts and other expectant couples was clearly reassuring for men and women as they approached first-time parenthood. But the work and support in these groups focus on preparing the couple for one day, the day of their baby's birth, after which they are completely on their own to manage the rigors of the next twenty years. Carolyn began to wonder whether we could create groups for expectant couples in which they could begin meeting with mental health professionals before the birth of their babies and continue talking with them after the babies were born. Not parenting groups and not merely support groups, these would be settings in which professionals could help men and women talk about the disappointments and impasses that we had found so difficult to discuss. Phil had been initiating some preventive programs in local elementary schools to spot some of the problems children were having before they felt overwhelming to the children, their parents, and their teachers. In addition to creating and systematically evaluating our couples groups for expectant and new parents, he suggested that we encase the preventive program in a more comprehensive study, following a larger group of expectant couples who would not take part in groups. We hoped that with this combined longitudinal and intervention study, we would be able to learn more about what happens to men, women, and marriage as families are beginning.

Much of our initial thinking about the question of what to study was stimulated by the preparation for our pilot study with two friends and colleagues from North Carolina, Lynne Coie, then an obstetrical nurse, and John Coie, a professor of psychology at Duke University. They agreed to work on the pilot study with us in 1974–75 while in Berkeley on sabbatical (Cowan et al. 1978). The four of us met regularly for several months, reviewing the existing research literature and talking about our own lives as partners and parents. Slowly, we pieced together a picture of what to look at based on the scant research literature at the time (see Cowan and Cowan 1988) and on what we felt had made a difference to our doing well or feeling under stress as individuals and as couples when we began our own families. We then selected or developed interviews and questionnaires to tap what we believed to be the key aspects of family life for men and women during this major transition.

Over the next few years, we made a number of additions to what we asked about the lives of the study participants, based on our ongoing reading of the relevant research and on influential consultations with a number of colleagues, particularly Gertrude Heming on our own research team, Jay Belsky at Pennsylvania State University, Frances Grossman at Boston University, Christoph Heinicke at UCLA, Shirley Feldman at Stanford University, Joy

Osofsky and Howard Osofsky, now at Tulane University, Susan McHale at Pennsylvania State University, Ted Huston at the University of Texas at Austin, Martha Cox, now at the Western Carolina Center, Mavis Hetherington at the University of Virginia, Ross Parke and Barbara Tinsley, now at the University of California at Riverside, and the members of the Family Research Consortium sponsored by the National Institute of Mental Health (see Patterson 1990; Cowan and Hetherington 1991).

What emerged from this conceptual work is a model describing five central aspects of family life that we expect will affect what happens when partners become parents (see Cowan and Cowan 1990):

1. The inner life of both parents and the first child, with special emphasis on each one's sense of self, view of the world, and emotional well-being or distress;
2. The quality of the relationship between the husband and wife, with special emphasis on their family roles and patterns of communication;
3. The quality of the relationships among the grandparents, parents, and grandchildren;
4. The relationship between the nuclear family members and key individuals or institutions outside the family (work, friends, child care), with special emphasis on the stress and support that these people and institutions provide;
5. The quality of the relationship between each parent and their first child.

We think of this model as a map of five separate but interrelated aspects or "territories" that partners encounter on their journey to becoming a family. As they make their way along the path from pregnancy to parenthood, they cross and recross the borders that mark off their inner lives, their relationship as a couple, their links to other generations, their connections with the world outside the family, and their relationships with their child.

We followed Urie Bronfenbrenner's (1979) admonition to study families in their ecological context. Our model directs us to look for change in family life at different levels, from the small details to the big picture. We zoom in for a close-up by asking what is happening to each individual family member. We move back for a mid-level view of what is happening in the immediate family by examining each of the relationships within it (mother-father, mother-child, father-child, sibling-sibling) and the dynamics of the family as a whole. For a longer shot, we step back to examine the links between family members and key people and institutions in the world outside the family.

Even with all of this information about the critical parts of family life, static snapshots of each of these separate domains of family life miss some essential ingredients of the larger scenario. What we need is a moving picture of how change in any one family domain affects all the individuals and relationships in the family. We use the metaphor of spillover at various points in the book to illustrate the idea that distress in any of these central areas of family life can seep into any of the other areas. Think, for example, of a man who feels anxious about becoming a new father (inner life) and wants to be more involved with his child than his father was with him (quality of relationships in family of origin) but feels pressured by the demands of his job (stress outside the family). Once the baby is born, he may have difficulty negotiating new family roles and decisions with his wife (quality of the marriage). He may begin to attribute the distress he feels at home to problems in his marriage. Although the partners may not be aware that he is experiencing distress in a number of these aspects of his life, both are likely to experience tension *between* them, with the result that one or both feel less confident and more vulnerable about themselves and their relationship as a couple.

Fortunately, spillover can be positive too. When a parent has a wonderful day with the baby or accomplishes a great deal at work, both partners may reap the benefit later when they are together. Support from one spouse who feels satisfied can provide encouragement and energy for the other—to try a new tack with the baby, to think in a different way about a problem at work or with a parent or in-law, or to arrange to spend time together as a couple. Our assumption has been that if we can discover some of the crucial links among the five domains of family life, we will understand more about what leads to progress or difficulties in parents' and children's development.

The design of our study is based on a number of assumptions about families and how they develop over time. Our five-domain model is consistent with the premise of family therapists that the family is a "system" and that we cannot make sense of the well-being or distress of individual family members until we understand something about the characteristics of the system as a whole (Bateson et al. 1956; Bowen 1978; Framo 1981; Haley 1976; Minuchin and Fishman 1981). In other words, to understand more about the children's development we must go beyond observing the relationship between the mother and the child to look at the relationship between the father and the child and at the *combined* influence of both parents and their relationship on the child. We give special attention to the question of how the quality of the parents' marriage may be affecting their child's adjustment, both by influencing the kind of relationship each parent establishes with the child and by providing the child with a model of how to behave in relationships.

In 1957, the sociologist E. E. LeMasters concluded that the transition to parenthood can produce a "crisis" for couples. Although our results are consistent with this notion, we do not view crisis as inevitably destructive in the long run. One of the fathers in our study taught us that the Chinese ideograph for "crisis" combines characters that represent danger *and* opportunity, a particularly fitting way to think of the becoming-a-family period. The transition to parenthood can increase the tension within or between new mothers and fathers, or between either of them and their child, and this can feel very frightening to already vulnerable new parents. But it is equally plausible that becoming a parent will provide the kind of challenge that pushes men and women to develop new insights, more effective ways of solving their problems, and greater feelings of maturity, which can result in their feeling particularly strong and triumphant (P. Cowan 1988a).

Who the Couples Are

For a three-year pilot study of our Becoming a Family Project, we followed sixteen couples becoming parents in 1975 (Cowan et al. 1978). For our ten-year study, we recruited ninety-six couples: seventy-two expectant couples and twenty-four nonparent couples from a range of obstetrics and gynecology practices, both private and clinic, and from announcements in several newsletters in the San Francisco Bay Area.* We followed them from their pregnancies in 1979 or 1980 through their child's kindergarten year (Cowan et al., in press).

Most of the couples (94 percent) were married—anywhere from eight months to twelve years, with an average length of relationship of four years— and several married after they joined the study. They lived in twenty-eight different cities and towns in Northern California within a forty-mile radius of the University of California at Berkeley. Their backgrounds and education ranged widely: All had completed high school and some had extensive training beyond. Over the ten years, we talked with carpenters, teachers, architects, writers, housewives, doctors, nurses, postal workers, professors, lawyers, retail store clerks, mental health professionals, electricians, an airline mechanic, a clothes designer and seamstress, a caterer, and a cable car driver. Their family incomes ranged from $7,000 to $72,500 per year, with an average family income of $22,500 at the beginning of the study in 1979–80. Fifteen percent of the participants were black, Asian American, or Hispanic; 85 percent were Caucasian.

When we first met them, the men and women ranged in age from twenty-one to forty-nine; on the average, the expectant mothers were twenty-nine years old and the fathers were thirty. The average age of the partners not yet decided about having children was one year younger. The age of the expectant parents seemed somewhat high to us for couples expecting a first baby, but it is consistent with the ages of men and women in the other recent longitudinal studies of the transition to parenthood (Belsky, Lang, and Rovine 1985; Grossman, Eichler, and Winickoff 1980; Heinicke et al. 1986; Lewis, Owen, and Cox 1988).

Just how far can we generalize our conclusions based on these ninety-six couples? Certainly, the sample we recruited is not representative of all new families in the United States. It consists of volunteers from a wide, though not randomly sampled, array of communities in Northern California. Our announcements attracted two expectant mothers under twenty years of age, but

*The names and identifying characteristics of the study participants have been changed to respect their privacy.

we decided to limit the sample to women who were at least twenty years old, reasoning that the issues and stresses for teenage parents might be quite distinct from those of adults in their twenties to forties. In addition, we could accommodate only those participants who spoke and wrote English. We did not turn people away based on socioeconomic status, but families on welfare did not tend to volunteer, nor did families from the upper class.

We believe that what we describe in the following chapters applies to a large segment of the population of couples becoming first-time parents, for two main reasons. First, the couples span a wide range of demographic and psychological characteristics. The income differential between the lowest and highest earners is immense. Men's and women's scores on a widely used marital satisfaction measure (the Locke-Wallace Brief Marital Adjustment Test, Locke and Wallace 1959) indicate that their marriages ranged from very happy to seriously distressed. Similarly, men's and women's scores on a symptoms-of-depression scale developed for use in nonclinical populations (Center for Epidemiological Study of Depression Scale, CES-D, Radloff 1977) indicate that at least one-quarter to one-third of the parents in our study were in the clinically distressed range when their children were in preschool and kindergarten. The proportion of couples at risk in our study may vary from the proportion in a large national sample, but the range from well-being to dysfunction in our study families makes it clear that we are describing a wide spectrum of men and women creating new families.

Second, our central findings about what happens to couples' satisfaction with marriage are consistent with those of many other investigators. Scores on the Locke-Wallace marital satisfaction scale typically range from about 40, which indicates serious dissatisfaction, to about 140, which suggests very high satisfaction; average scores are expected to be around 100. In the beginning, the expectant spouses' average marital satisfaction scores were well above 100—121 for the men and 123 for the women—as we would expect from a majority of partners about to have a first baby. Five to six years later, however, when their first children were in kindergarten, the parents' average scores were close to the average score of 100 reported in studies of couples across the entire marital life span.

Over the past ten years, the results of other studies in other locales—Southern California, Texas, Kansas, Pennsylvania—have conveyed similar pictures of couples making the transition to parenthood. At a talk he gave in Toronto in 1990, Jay Belsky, a researcher from Pennsylvania State University who has published a great deal on this topic, said in reference to our study that finding such similar results in working-class parents in the middle of Pennsylvania and working- to middle-class parents in California gives us a pretty solid indication that what we're saying about the transition to parenthood can be taken seriously.

The couples in our study were invited to participate in one of four ways: in groups of couples, as individual couples before and after childbirth, as individual couples after childbirth only, and as couples who have not yet decided whether to have children. We followed the expectant couples from late pregnancy until their children were eighteen months old and tracked the nonparent couples over the same number of months in Phase 1.

COUPLES GROUPS

One of our central goals was to create and evaluate a couples group intervention designed to strengthen the parents' relationship as a couple while they are making the transition from couple to family (discussed at length in chapter 9). We randomly selected one-third of the expectant couples and invited them to take part in a couples group with us or with leaders whom we trained. We set up six groups of four couples with similar due dates to meet with their staff couple every week during the last three months of pregnancy and the first three months after the baby arrived.* Over the course of six months, we talked with these men and women about their dreams and their difficulties as they made the journey to first-time parenthood.

The couples groups provided an experience that we wish we could have had as we became parents fifteen years earlier. In the last few months of pregnancy, the group leaders helped couples take a look at their current lives, anticipate what their lives would be like once the baby arrived, and make explicit some of their unexplored pictures of life as a family. The staff couples provided a safe setting in which husbands and wives could begin to discover where they differed or disagreed, and how they could work together to get their relationship on a more solid base before the babies arrived. The babies joined us in the groups in the first week or two after they were born. It did not take long for us to see how every couple's conversations got interrupted regularly, and how easy it was for partners to get out of touch. Through the tears and the laughter, couples began to see that despite many differences in background, outlook, personality, and economic circumstance, they were experiencing very similar shifts in their relationships. Along with our encouragement to modify the patterns that felt unsatisfying, this feeling of being in the same boat had a powerful impact on the participants.

EXPECTANT PARENTS: BEFORE AND AFTER

A second randomly chosen set of twenty-four expectant couples was interviewed and filled out questionnaires just as the group participants had (during pregnancy and six and eighteen months after birth), but did not take part in our group intervention. We were concerned initially that we were offering less help to these couples than to the group participants, but the couples in our control group in our pilot study (Cowan et al. 1978) told us that thinking and talking about the issues we raised in our regular interviews

*Of the first couples we randomly chose for the groups, 85 percent agreed to participate in a group. We continued to invite every third expectant couple entering the study until we had enough couples to fill six groups, with four participating couples and one staff couple in each group. The two other staff couples were Ellen Garrett and Bill Coysh and Harriet Curtis-Boles and Abner Boles.

and questionnaires proved very helpful to their adjustment to parenthood. Apparently the regular follow-up format with questionnaires and interviews with mental health professionals was operating as an intervention in its own right.

EXPECTANT PARENTS: AFTER ONLY

The third set of twenty-four randomly chosen expectant couples met with us for our standard interview during pregnancy but did not fill out questionnaires until six and eighteen months after their babies were born. By comparing these couples with those who filled out questionnaires before and after they became parents, we had an opportunity to evaluate whether the experience of looking at their lives in detail with our questionnaires before and after having a baby acted as an intervention in itself.*

NONPARENTS

Finally, using the same obstetrics/gynecology practices and community newsletters with which we recruited the expectant parents, we recruited twenty-four couples who had not yet decided whether to have children. These couples had not closed off their options about having children and were not, to their knowledge, infertile. We interviewed each of these couples, too, and asked them to complete our questionnaires at the beginning of the study (comparable to late pregnancy for the expectant couples) and at intervals that correspond to the six- and eighteen-month postpartum follow-ups with the new parents. In the first two years of the study, fifteen of the original twenty-four nonparent couples remained childless. The patterns they described help us distinguish between changes that occur in couple relationships over time and those that are apparently attributable to having a baby.

Couple Relationships and Children's Development

The first two years of the study comprised Phase I, in which we concentrated on the period from late pregnancy until eighteen months after the baby is born. Since we were focusing on men's and women's perceptions and evaluations of their lives, our analysis of the results from Phase I relied heavily on what they told us in the interviews and questionnaires. During Phase II, as we

*We did *not* find that the couples who were interviewed and filled out questionnaires in pregnancy were any better off after their babies were born than those who filled out only postbirth questionnaires. However, the couples who did the prebirth questionnaires were more loyal to the study. All of them continued with us at least to the eighteen-months-after-birth follow-up, whereas only 63 percent of the couples who filled out the questionnaires for the first time after they had given birth agreed to do them again one year later.

attempted to understand how the dynamics of family interaction were affecting the children's development and adaptation, we began to rely increasingly on information from our observations of the parents and children to supplement their self-reports.

When we returned to interview the parents of eighteen-month-olds, we saw that many had recovered from the disequilibrium of being the parents of new babies, but now they faced the new challenges of an independent toddler.

Most of the couples were enjoying their babies' development, but a few appeared seriously stressed. Although we did not conduct systematic observations in Phase I, our impression was that there was a strong similarity between how parents handled the dilemmas and strains of the early months of becoming a family and how they responded to their children as toddlers. We noticed that parents who talked about having very conflicted relationships with their own parents described more conflicted relationships with their children. Parents who fought more as a couple said that they were having more difficulty in handling their children. By contrast, parents who got along well with each other tended to describe their relationships with their children in more positive terms.

We also noticed that parents who described positive relationships with each other and their children tended to describe their children's development as proceeding well. They did not spontaneously characterize their children as having or posing severe problems. The idea that parents influence their children's development is not new, of course. Nor is the idea that parenting is influenced by what we carry over and reject from the families we grew up in or by our children's temperaments and how they affect us. What is news, we think, is that the relationship *between* the parents seems to act as a crucible in which their relationships with their children take shape.

When we were interviewing the parents, we could not know whether they were describing their children's development or the parent-child relationship accurately. Virtually all studies of how families socialize children begin after children are born, making it impossible to tease out which parts of the parent-child relationship come from the parents and which from the temperament or personality of the child. Because we had come to know these couples before they had children, we were in a unique position to shed some light on the question of how adaptation in the family before the child is born influences the nature and quality of the relationships between parents and their children. Clearly, eighteen months after becoming a family was not the time to end our investigation of adaptation to family life.

We conducted two more intensive follow-ups of each family, gathering information about the children and parents in the preschool and kindergarten years. To this new round of interviews and questionnaires we added visits to our laboratory playroom in the Institute of Human Development at the University of California at Berkeley. In these visits, members of our research staff worked and played with the children to get a sense of their level of cognitive and social adaptation. We invited each parent separately and then together to work and play with their son or daughter using structured and unstructured tasks and games so that we could observe the range of responses in parents and children.

When the children were in kindergarten, we incorporated their teachers' views of them by asking them to describe every child in the classroom, using a checklist of behaviors that reflect academic, social, and emotional adjustment. This gave us an indication of how the child was doing in relation to his or her classmates. By combining this information from Phase II with the information the parents had given us before their children were born, we could begin to trace the links from how couples adapted to parenthood, to their family patterns during the preschool period, to how the children met the academic, emotional, and social challenges of their lives at home and at school.

Our study is not simply to demonstrate that the transition to parenthood can leave men and women feeling vulnerable about their marriage. We must try to understand why, at such a potentially hopeful time of life, tension and distress tend to intrude on the stability of the parents' relationship as a couple. Our study could not address the special circumstances of parents dealing with abortion, adoption, or single parenthood, although some of the issues we address will be relevant to their lives.

There are warnings here that we hope will help some readers find ways to reduce the tension and distress they are experiencing in their lives as individuals, couples, or parents. Perhaps some of the examples from the couples we interviewed will suggest ways to modify the arrangements in your life to make it more satisfying. Even if the story sounds a little grim at times, we encourage you to read on. Some of the couples' experiences will let you know that you are not alone if your life feels stressful.

It is certainly clear from our own lives, from what our study participants tell us, and from the results of large-scale national surveys of men and women (Fawcett 1988) that despite the strain, most parents are thrilled that they have had children and would make the same decision if they were starting again. Nothing can substitute for the wonders of seeing the world anew through the eyes of a child or watching a tiny human being develop into a curious, independent, self-motivated young person and adult. And the strain that partners experience on becoming parents can propel them to work out some of their unresolved difficulties, either on their own or with help. We have provided examples in each chapter of couples who managed to overcome the unexpected obstacles in their path and to respond to the challenge of being partners and parents with creativity, growth, and a renewed sense of humor and purpose. We hope that they will inspire you with their optimism, as they have inspired us.

PART I

The New Pioneers

CHAPTER 1

Changing Families in a Changing World

SHARON: I did a home pregnancy test. I felt really crummy that day, and I stayed home from work. I set the container with the urine sample on a bookcase and managed to stay out of the room until the last few minutes. Finally, I walked in and it looked positive. And I went to check the information on the box and, sure enough, it *was* positive. I was so excited. Then I went back to look and see if maybe it had disappeared; you know, maybe the test was false. Then I just sat down on the sofa and kept thinking, "I'm pregnant. I'm really pregnant. I'm going to have a baby!"

DANIEL: I knew she was pregnant. She didn't need the test as far as I was concerned. I was excited too, at first, but then I started to worry. I don't know how I'm going to handle being there at the birth, especially if anything goes wrong. And Sharon's going to quit work soon. I don't know when she's going to go back, and we're barely making it as it is.

SHARON: My mom never worked a day in her life for pay. She was home all the time, looking after *her* mother, and us, and cleaning the house. My dad left all of that to her. We're not going to do it that way. But I don't know how we're supposed to manage it all. Daniel promised that he's going to pitch in right along with me in taking care of the baby, but I don't know whether that's realistic. If he doesn't come through, I'm going to be a real bear about it. If I put all my energy into Daniel and the marriage and something happens, then I'll have to start all over again and that scares the hell out of me.

Sharon is beginning the third trimester of her first pregnancy. If her grandmother were to listen in on our conversation with Sharon and her husband, Daniel, and try to make sense of it, given the experience of her own pregnancy fifty years ago, she would surely have a lot of questions. Home pregnancy tests? Why would a woman with a newborn infant *want* to work if she didn't have to? What husband would share the housework and care of the baby? Why would Sharon and Daniel worry about their marriage not surviving after they have a baby? Understandable questions for someone who made the transition to parenthood five decades ago, in a qualitatively different world. Unfortunately, the old trail maps are outmoded, and there are as yet no new ones to describe the final destination. They may not need covered wagons for their journey, but Sharon and Daniel are true pioneers.

Like many modern couples, they have two different fantasies about their journey. The first has them embarking on an exciting adventure to bring a new human being into the world, fill their lives with delight and wonder, and enrich their feeling of closeness as a couple. In the second, their path from couple to family is strewn with unexpected obstacles, hazardous conditions, and potential marital strife. Our work suggests that, like most fantasy scenarios, these represent extreme and somewhat exaggerated versions of what really happens when partners become parents. Our goal in this book is to tell the story behind both the fantasy and the reality of changing families in our changing world.

The Five Domains of Family Life

The responses of one couple to our interview questions offer a preview of how the five domains in our model capture the changes that most couples contend with as they make their transition to parenthood.* Natalie and Victor have lived in the San Francisco Bay Area most of their lives. At the time of their initial interview, Natalie, age twenty-nine, is in her fifth month of pregnancy. Victor, her husband of six years, is thirty-four. When their daughter, Kim, is six months old, they visit us again for a follow-up interview. Arranged around each of the five domains, the following excerpts from our second interview reveal some universal themes of early parenthood.

CHANGES IN IDENTITY AND INNER LIFE

After settling comfortably with cups of coffee and tea, we ask both Natalie and Victor whether they feel that their sense of self has shifted in any way

---

*An extended description of this couple's transition to parenthood can be found in Bradburn and Kaplan (in press).

since Kim was born. As would be typical in our interviews, Mother and Father focus on different aspects of personal change:

NATALIE: There's not much "me" left to think about right now. Most of the time, even when I'm not nursing, I see myself as attached to this little being with only the milk flowing between us.

VICTOR: I've earned money since I was sixteen, but being a father means that I've become the family breadwinner. I've got this new sense of myself as having to go out there in the world to make sure that my wife and daughter are going to be safe and looked after. I mean, I'm concerned about advancing in my job—and we've even bought insurance policies for the first time! This "protector" role feels exciting *and* frightening.

Another change that often occurs in partners' inner lives during a major life transition is a shift in what C. Murray Parkes (1971) describes as our "assumptive world." Men's and women's assumptions about how the world works or how families operate sometimes change radically during the transition from couple to family.

NATALIE: I used to be completely apathetic about political things. I wasn't sure of my congressman's name. Now I'm writing him about once a month because I feel I need to help clean up some of the mess this country is in before Kim grows up.

VICTOR: What's changed for me is what I think families and fathers are all about. When we were pregnant, I had these pictures of coming home each night as the tired warrior, playing with the baby for a little while and putting my feet up for the rest of the evening. It's not just that there's more work to do than I ever imagined, but I'm so much more a part of the action every night.

Clearly, Natalie and Victor are experiencing qualitatively different shifts in their sense of self and in how vulnerable or safe each feels in the world. These shifts are tied not only to their new life as parents but also to a new sense of their identities as providers and protectors. Even though most of these changes are positive, they can lead to moments when the couple's relationship feels a bit shaky.

SHIFTS IN THE ROLES AND RELATIONSHIPS WITHIN THE MARRIAGE

VICTOR: After Kim was born, I noticed that something was bugging Natalie, and I kept saying, "What is bothering you?" Finally we went out to dinner without the baby and it came out. And it was because of small things that I never even think about. Like I always used to leave my running shorts in the bathroom . . .

NATALIE: He'd just undress and drop everything!

VICTOR: . . . and Nat never made a fuss. In fact she *used to* just pick them up and put them in the hamper. And then that night at dinner she said, "When you leave your shorts there, or your wet towel, and don't pick them up—I get furious." At first I didn't believe what she was saying because it never used to bother her at all, but now I say, "OK, fine, no problem. I'll pick up the shorts and hang them up. I'll be very conscientious." And I have been trying.

NATALIE: You have, but you still don't quite get it. I think my quick trigger has something to do with my feeling so dependent on you and having the baby so dependent on me—and my being stuck here day in and day out. You at least get to go out to do your work, and you bring home a paycheck to show for it. I work here all day long and by the end of the day I feel that all I have to show for it is my exhaustion.

In addition to their distinctive inner changes, men's and women's roles change in very different ways when partners become parents. The division of labor in taking care of the baby, the household, the meals, the laundry, the shopping, calling parents and friends, and earning the money to keep the family fed, clothed, and sheltered is a hot topic for couples (C. Cowan and P. Cowan 1988; Hochschild 1989). It seems to come as a great surprise to most of them that changes in some of their major roles affect their feelings about their overall relationship.

In a domino effect, both partners have to make major adjustments of time and energy as individuals during a period when they are getting less sleep and fewer opportunities to be together. As with Natalie and Victor, they are apt to find that they have less patience with things that didn't seem annoying before. Their frustration often focuses on each other. For couples who thought that having a baby was going to bring them closer together, this is especially confusing and disappointing.

NATALIE: It's strange. I feel that we're much closer *and* more distant than we have ever been. I think we communicate more, because there's so much to work out, especially about Kim, but it doesn't always feel very good. And we're both so busy that we're not getting much snuggling or loving time.

VICTOR: We're fighting more too. But I'm still not sure why.

Victor and Natalie are so involved in what is happening to them that even though they can identify some of the sources of their disenchantment, they cannot really make sense of all of it. They are playing out a scenario that was very common for the couples in our study during the first year of parenthood. Both men and women are experiencing a changing sense of self *and* a shift in the atmosphere in the relationship between them. The nurturance that partners might ordinarily get from one another is in very short supply. As if this were not enough to adjust to, almost all of the new parents in our study say that their other key relationships are shifting too.

SHIFTS IN THE THREE-GENERATIONAL ROLES AND RELATIONSHIPS

VICTOR: It was really weird to see my father's reaction to Kim's birth. The week before Natalie's due date, my father all of a sudden decided that he was going to Seattle, and he took off with my mom and some other people. Well, the next day Natalie went into labor and we had the baby, and my mother kept calling, saying she wanted to get back here. But my dad seemed to be playing games and made it stretch out for two or three days.

Finally, when they came back and the whole period was past, it turned out that my father was *jealous* of my mother's relationship with the baby. He didn't want my mother to take time away from him to be with Kim! He's gotten over it now. He holds Kim and plays with her, and doesn't want to go home after a visit. But my dad and me, we're still sort of recovering from what happened. And when things don't go well with me and Dad, Natalie sometimes gets it in the neck.

NATALIE: I'll say.

For Victor's father, becoming a first-time grandfather is something that is happening *to* him. His son and daughter-in-law are having a baby and he is becoming a grandfather, ready or not. Many men and women in Victor's parents' position have mixed feelings about becoming grandparents (Lowe 1991), but rarely know how to deal with them. As Victor searches for ways to become comfortable with his new identity as a father, like so many of the men we spoke to, he is desperately hoping that it will bring him closer to his father.

As father and son struggle with these separate inner changes, they feel a strain in the relationship between them, a strain they feel they cannot mention. Some of it spills over into the relationship between Victor and Natalie: After a visit with his parents, they realize, they are much more likely to get into a fight.

CHANGING ROLES AND RELATIONSHIPS OUTSIDE THE FAMILY

NATALIE: While Victor has been dealing with his dad, I've been struggling with my boss. After a long set of negotiations on the phone, he reluctantly agreed to let me come back four days a week instead of full-time. I haven't gone back officially yet, but I dropped in to see him. He always used to have time for me, but this week, after just a few minutes of small talk, he told me that he had a meeting and practically bolted out of the room. He as much as said that he figured I wasn't serious about my job anymore.

VICTOR: Natalie's not getting much support from her friends, either. None of them has kids and they just don't seem to understand what she's going through. Who ever thought how lonely it can be to have a baby?

Although the burden of the shifts in roles and relationships outside the family affects both parents, it tends to fall more heavily on new mothers. It is women who tend to put their jobs and careers on hold, at least temporarily, after they have babies (Daniels and Weingarten 1982, 1988), and even though they may have more close friends than their husbands do, they find it difficult to make contact with them in the early months of new parenthood. It takes all of the energy new mothers have to cope with the ongoing care and feeding that a newborn requires and to replenish the energy spent undergoing labor or cesarean delivery. The unanticipated loss of support from friends and co-workers can leave new mothers feeling surprisingly isolated and vulnerable. New fathers' energies are on double duty too. Because they are the sole earners when their wives stop working or take maternity leave, men often work longer hours or take on extra jobs. Fatigue and limited availability means that fathers too get less support or comfort from co-workers or friends. This is one of many aspects of family life in which becoming a parent seems to involve more *loss* than either spouse anticipated—especially because they have been focused on the gain of the baby. Although it is not difficult for us to see how these shifts and losses might catch two tired parents off guard, most husbands and wives fail to recognize that these changes are affecting them as individuals and as a couple.

NEW PARENTING ROLES AND RELATIONSHIPS

Natalie and Victor, unlike most of the other couples, had worked out a shared approach to household tasks from the time they moved in together. Whoever was available to do something would do it. And when Kim was born, they just continued that. During the week, Victor would get the baby up in the morning and then take over when he got home from work. Natalie put her to bed at night. During the weekends the responsibilities were reversed.

It was not surprising that Natalie and Victor expected their egalitarian system—a rare arrangement—to carry over to the care of their baby. What is surprising to us is that a majority of the couples predicted that they would share the care of their baby much more equally than they were sharing their housework and family tasks *before* they became parents. Even though they are unusually collaborative in their care of Kim, Natalie and Victor are not protected from the fact that, like most couples, their different ideas about what a baby needs create some conflict and disagreement:

VICTOR: I tend to be a little more . . . what would you say?
NATALIE: Crazy.

VICTOR: A little more crazy with Kim. I like to put her on my bicycle and go for a ride real fast. I like the thought of the wind blowing on her and her eyes watering. I want her to feel the rain hitting her face. Natalie would cover her head, put a thick jacket on her, you know, make sure she's warm and dry.

NATALIE: At the beginning, we argued a lot about things like that. More than we ever did. Some of them seemed trivial at the time. The argument wouldn't last more than a day. It would all build up, explode, and then be over. One night, though, Victor simply walked out. He took a long drive, and then came back. It was a bad day for both of us. We just had to get it out, regardless of the fact that it was three A.M.

VICTOR: I think it was at that point that I realized that couples who start off with a bad relationship would really be in trouble. As it was, it wasn't too pleasant for us, but we got through it.

Despite the fact that their emotional focus had been on the baby during pregnancy and the early months of parenthood, Victor and Natalie were not prepared for the way their relationship with the baby affected and was affected by the changes they had been experiencing all along as individuals, at work, in their marriage, and in their relationships with their parents, friends, and co-workers—the spillover effects. They sometimes have new and serious disagreements, but both of them convey a sense that they have the ability to prevent their occasional blowups from escalating into serious and long-lasting tensions.

As we follow them over time, Victor and Natalie describe periods in which their goodwill toward each other wears thin, but their down periods are typically followed by genuine ups. It seems that one of them always finds a way to come back to discuss the painful issues when they are not in so much distress. In subsequent visits, for example, the shorts-in-the-bathroom episode, retold with much laughter, becomes a shorthand symbol for the times when tensions erupt between them. They give themselves time to cool down, they come back to talk about what was so upsetting, and having heard each other out, they go on to find a solution to the problem that satisfies both of their needs. This, we know, is the key to a couple's stable and satisfying relationship (Gottman and Krokoff 1989).

Compared to the other couples, one of the unusual strengths in Natalie and Victor's life together is their ability to come back to problem issues after they have calmed down. Many couples are afraid to rock the boat once their heated feelings have cooled down. Even more unusual is their trust that they will both be listened to sympathetically when they try to sort out what happened. Because Natalie and Victor each dare to raise issues that concern them, they end up feeling that they are on the same side when it comes to the most important things in life (cf. Ball 1984). This is what makes it possible for them to engage in conflict and yet maintain their positive feelings about their relationship.

Most important, perhaps, for the long-term outcome of their journey to parenthood is that the good feeling between Victor and Natalie spills over to their daughter. Throughout Kim's preschool years and into her first year of kindergarten, we see the threesome as an active, involved family in which the members are fully engaged with one another in both serious and playful activities.

What Makes Parenthood Harder Now

Natalie and Victor are charting new territory. They are trying to create a family based on the new, egalitarian ideology in which both of them work *and* share the tasks of managing the household and caring for their daughter. They have already embraced less traditional roles than most of the couples in our study. Although the world they live in has changed a great deal since they were children, it has not shifted sufficiently to support them in realizing their ideals easily. Their journey seems to require heroic effort.

Would a more traditional version of family life be less stressful? Couples who arrange things so that the woman tends the hearth and baby and the man provides the income to support them are also showing signs of strain. They struggle financially because it often takes more than one parent's income to maintain a family. They feel drained emotionally because they rely almost entirely on their relationship to satisfy most of their psychological needs. Contemporary parents find themselves in double jeopardy. Significant historical shifts in the family landscape of the last century, particularly of the last few decades, have created additional burdens for them. As couples set foot on the trails of this challenging journey, they become disoriented because society's map of the territory has been redrawn. Becoming a family today is more difficult than it used to be.

In recent decades there has been a steady ripple of revolutionary social change. Birth control technology has been transformed. Small nuclear families live more isolated lives in crowded cities, often feeling cut off from extended family and friends. Mothers of young children are entering the work force earlier and in ever larger numbers. Choices about how to create life as a family are much greater than they used to be. Men and women are having a difficult time regaining their balance as couples after they have babies, in part because the radical shifts in the circumstances surrounding family life in America demand new arrangements to accommodate the increasing demands on parents of young children. But new social arrangements and roles have simply not kept pace with these changes, leaving couples on their own to manage the demands of work and family.

MORE CHOICE

Compared with the experiences of their parents and grandparents, couples today have many more choices about whether and when to bring a child into their lives. New forms of birth control have given most couples the means to engage in an active sex life with some confidence, though no guarantee, that they can avoid unwanted pregnancy. In addition, despite recent challenges in American courts and legislatures, the 1973 Supreme Court decision legalizing abortion has given couples a second chance to decide whether to become parents if birth control fails or is not used.

But along with modern birth control techniques come reports of newly discovered hazards. We now know that using birth control pills, intrauterine devices, the cervical cap, the sponge, and even the diaphragm poses some risk to a woman's health. The decision to abort a fetus brings with it both public controversy and the private anguish of the physical, psychological, and moral consequences of ending a pregnancy (see Nathanson 1989). Men and women today may enjoy more choice about parenthood than any previous generation, but the couples in our studies are finding it quite difficult to navigate this new family-making terrain.

Sharon, who was eagerly awaiting the results of her home pregnancy test when we met her at the beginning of this chapter, had not been nearly as eager to become a mother three years earlier.

> SHARON: Actually, we fought about it a lot. Daniel already had a child, Hallie, from his first marriage. "Let's have one of our own. It'll be easy," he said. And I said, "Yeah, and what happened before Hallie was two? You were out the door."
>
> DANIEL: I told you, that had nothing to do with Hallie. She was great. It was my ex that was the problem. I just knew that for us a baby would be right.
>
> SHARON: I wasn't sure. What was I going to do about a career? What was I going to do about me? I wasn't ready to put things on hold. I wasn't even convinced, then, that I wanted to become a mother. It wouldn't have been good for me, and it sure wouldn't have been good for the baby, to go ahead and give in to Daniel when I was feeling that way.

In past times, fewer choices meant less conflict between spouses, at least at the outset. Now, with each partner expecting to have a free choice in the matter, planning a family can become the occasion for sensitive and delicate treaty negotiations. First, couples who want to live together must decide whether they want to get married. One partner may be for it, the other not. Second, the timing of childbirth has changed. For couples married in 1950–54, the majority (60 percent) would have a baby within two years. Now, almost one-third of couples are marrying *after* having a child, and those who marry before becoming parents are marrying later in life. Only a minority of them have their first child within two years. Some delay parenthood for more than a decade (Teachman, Polonko, and Scanzoni 1987).

Couples are also having smaller families. The decline in fertility has for the first time reduced the birthrate below the replacement level of zero population growth—less than two children per family.* And because couples are having fewer children and having them later, more seems to be at stake in each decision about whether and when to have a child. What was once a natural progression has become a series of choice points, each with a potential for serious disagreement between the partners.

Alice is in the last trimester of her pregnancy. In our initial interview, she and Andy described a profound struggle between them that is not over yet.

> ALICE: This pregnancy was a life and death issue for me. I'd already had two abortions with a man I'd lived with before, because it was very clear that we could not deal with raising a child. Although I'd known Andy for years, we had been together only four months when I became pregnant unexpectedly. I loved him, I was thirty-four years old, and I wasn't going to risk the possibility of another abortion and maybe never being able to have children. So when I became pregnant this time, I said, "I'm having this baby with you or without you. But I'd much rather have it with you."
>
> ANDY: Well, I'm only twenty-seven and I haven't gotten on track with my own life. Alice was using a diaphragm and I thought it was safe. For months after she became pregnant, I was just pissed off that this was happening to me, to us, but I gradually calmed down. If it was just up to me, I'd wait for a number of years yet because I don't feel ready, but I want to be with her, and you can hear that she's determined to have this baby.

Clearly, more choice has not necessarily made life easier for couples who are becoming a family.

ISOLATION

The living environments of families with children have changed dramatically. In 1850, 75 percent of American families lived in rural settings. By 1970, 75 percent were living in urban or suburban environments, and the migration from farm to city is continuing.

We began our own family in Toronto, Canada, the city we had grown up in, with both sets of parents living nearby. Today we live some distance from our parents, relatives, and childhood friends, as do the majority of couples in North America. Increasingly, at least in the middle- and upper-income brackets, couples are living in unfamiliar surroundings, bringing newborns home to be reared in single-family apartments or houses, where their neighbors are strangers. Becoming a parent, then, can quickly result in social isolation, especially for the parent who stays at home with the baby.

John and Shannon are one of the younger couples in our study. He is twenty-four and she is twenty-three.

*There are indications, however, that the birthrate in the United States is now on the rise.

JOHN: My sister in Dallas lives down the block from our mother. Whenever she and her husband want a night out, they just call up and either they take the baby over to Mom's house or Mom comes right over to my sister's. Our friends help us out once in a while, but you have to reach out and ask them and a lot of times they aren't in a position to respond. Some of them don't have kids, so they don't really understand what it's like for us. They keep calling us and suggesting that we go for a picnic or out for pizza, and we have to remind them that we have this baby to take care of.

SHANNON: All the uncles, aunts, and cousins in my family used to get together every Sunday. Most of the time I don't miss that because they were intrusive and gossipy and into everybody else's business. But sometimes it would be nice to have someone to talk to who cares about me, and who lived through all the baby throw-up and ear infections and lack of sleep, and could just say, "Don't worry, Shannon, it's going to get better soon."

WOMEN'S ROLES

Since we began our family thirty years ago, mothers have been joining the labor force in ever-increasing numbers, even when they have young babies. Women have always worked, but economic necessity in the middle as well as the working classes, and increased training and education among women, propelled them into the work force in record numbers. In 1960, 18 percent of mothers with children under six were working at least part-time outside the home. By 1970, that figure had grown to 30 percent, and by 1980 it was 45 percent. Today, the majority of women with children under *three* work at least part-time, and recent research suggests that this figure will soon extend to a majority of mothers of one-year-olds (Teachman, Polonko, and Scanzoni 1987).

With the enormous increase in women's choices and opportunities in the work world, many women are caught between traditional and modern conceptions of how they should be living their lives. It is a common refrain in our couples groups.

JOAN: It's ironic. My mother knew that she was supposed to be a mom and not a career woman. But she suffered from that. She was a capable woman with more business sense than my dad, but she felt it was her job to stay home with us kids. And she was *very* depressed some of the time. But I'm *supposed* to be a career woman. I feel that I just need to stay home right now. I'm really happy with that decision, but I struggled with it for months.

TANYA: I know what Joan means, but it's the opposite for me. I'm doing what I want, going back to work, but it's driving me crazy. All day as I'm working, I'm wondering what's happening to Kevin. Is he OK, is he doing some new thing that I'm missing, is he getting enough individual

attention? And when I get home, I'm tired, Jackson's tired, Kevin's tired.
I have to get dinner on the table and Kevin ready for bed. And then I'm
exhausted and Jackson's exhausted and I just hit the pillow and I'm out.
We haven't made love in three months. I know Jackson's frustrated. *I'm*
frustrated. I didn't know it was going to be like this.

News media accounts of family-oriented men imply that as mothers have
taken on more of a role in the world of paid work, fathers have taken on a
comparable load of family work. But this simply hasn't happened. As Arlie
Hochschild (1989) demonstrates, working mothers are coming home to face
a "second shift"—running the household and caring for the children. Although there are studies suggesting that fathers are taking on a little more
housework and care of the children than they used to (Pleck 1985), mothers
who are employed full-time still have far greater responsibility for managing
the family work and child rearing than their husbands do (C. Cowan 1988).
It is not simply that men's and women's roles are unequal that seems to be
causing distress for couples, but rather that they are so clearly discrepant
from what both spouses expected them to be.

Women are getting the short end of what Hochschild calls the "stalled
revolution": Their work roles have changed but their family roles have not.
Well-intentioned and confused husbands feel guilty, while their overburdened wives feel angry. It does not take much imagination to see how these
emotions can fuel the fires of marital conflict.

SOCIAL POLICY

The stress that Joan and Tanya talk about comes not only from internal
conflicts and from difficulties in coping with life inside the family but from
factors outside the family as well. Joan might consider working part-time if
she felt that she and her husband could get high-quality, affordable child care
for their son. Tanya might consider working different shifts or part-time if
her company had more flexible working arrangements for parents of young
children. But few of the business and government policies that affect parents
and children are supportive of anything beyond the most traditional family
arrangements.

We see a few couples, like Natalie and Victor, who strike out on their own
to make their ideology of more balanced roles a reality. These couples believe
that they and their children will reap the rewards of their innovation, but they
are exhausted from bucking the strong winds of opposition—from parents,
from bosses, from co-workers. Six months after the birth of her daughter,
Natalie mentioned receiving a lukewarm reception from her boss after negotiating a four-day work week.

NATALIE: He made me feel terrible. I'm going to have to work *very* hard to
make things go, but I think I can do it. What worries me, though, is that
the people I used to supervise aren't very supportive either. They keep

raising these issues, "Well, what if so-and-so happens, and you're not there?" Well, sometimes I wasn't there before because I was traveling for the company, and nobody got in a snit. Now that I've got a baby, somehow my being away from the office at a particular moment is a problem.

VICTOR: My boss is flexible about when I come in and when I leave, but he keeps asking me questions. He can't understand why I want to be at home with Kim some of the time that Natalie's at work.

It would seem to be in the interest of business and government to develop policies that are supportive of the family. Satisfied workers are more productive. Healthy families drain scarce economic resources less than unhealthy ones, and make more of a contribution to the welfare of society at large. Yet, the United States is the only country in the Western world without a semblance of explicit family policy. This lack is felt most severely by parents of young children. There are no resources to help new parents deal with their anxieties about child rearing (such as the visiting public health nurses in England), unless the situation is serious enough to warrant medical or psychiatric attention. If both parents want or need to work, they would be less conflicted if they could expect to have adequate parental leave when their babies are born (as in Sweden and other countries), flexible work hours to accommodate the needs of young children, and access to reasonably priced, competent child care. These policies and provisions are simply not available in most American businesses and communities (Catalyst 1988).

The absence of family policy also takes its toll on traditional family arrangements, which are not supported by income supplements or family allowances (as they are in Canada and Britain) as a financial cushion for the single-earner family. The lack of supportive policy and family-oriented resources results in increased stress on new parents just when their energies are needed to care for their children. It is almost inevitable that this kind of stress spills over into the couple's negotiations and conflicts about how they will divide the housework and care of the children.

THE NEED FOR NEW ROLE MODELS

Based on recent statistics, the modern family norm is neither the Norman Rockwell *Saturday Evening Post* cover family nor the "Leave It to Beaver" scenario with Dad going out to work and Mom staying at home to look after the children. Only about 6 percent of all American households today have a husband as the sole breadwinner and a wife and two or more children at home—"the typical American family" of earlier times. Patterns from earlier generations are often irrelevant to the challenges faced by dual-worker couples in today's marketplace.

After setting out on the family journey, partners often discover that they have conflicting values, needs, expectations, and plans for their destination.

This may not be an altogether new phenomenon, but it creates additional strain for a couple.

> JAMES: My parents were old-school Swedes who settled in Minnesota on a farm. It was cold outside in the winters, but it was cold inside too. Nobody said anything unless they had to. My mom was home all the time. She worked hard to support my dad and keep the farm going, but she never really had anything of her own. I'm determined to support Cindy going back to school as soon as she's ready.
>
> CINDY: My parents were as different from James's as any two parents could be. When they were home with us, they were all touchy-feely, but they were hardly ever around. During the days my mom and dad both worked. At night, they went out with their friends. I really don't want that to happen to Eddie. So, James and I are having a thing about it now. He wants me to go back to school. I don't want to. I'm working about ten hours a week, partly because he nags at me so much. If it were just up to me, I'd stay home until Eddie gets into first grade.

Cindy and James each feel that they have the freedom to do things differently than their parents did. The problem is that the things each of them wants to be different are on a collision course. James is trying to be supportive of Cindy's educational ambitions so his new family will feel different than the one he grew up in. Given her history, Cindy does not experience this as support. Her picture of the family she wanted to create and James's picture do not match. Like so many of the couples in our study, both partners are finding it difficult to establish a new pattern because the models from the families they grew up in are so different from the families they want to create.

INCREASED EMOTIONAL BURDEN

The historical changes we have been describing have increased the burden on both men and women with respect to the emotional side of married life. Not quite the equal sharers of breadwinning and family management they hoped to be, husbands and wives now expect to be each other's major suppliers of emotional warmth and support. Especially in the early months as a family, they look to their marriage as a "haven in a heartless world." Deprived of regular daily contact with extended family members and lifelong friends, wives and husbands look to each other to "be there" for them—to pick up the slack when energies flag, to work collaboratively on solving problems, to provide comfort when it is needed, and to share the highs and lows of life inside and outside the family. While this mutual expectation may sound reasonable to modern couples, it is very difficult to live up to in an intimate relationship that is already vulnerable to disappointment from within and pressure from without.

The greatest emotional pressure on the couple, we believe, comes from the culture's increasing emphasis on self-fulfillment and self-development (Bellah et al. 1985). The vocabulary of individualism, endemic to American society from its beginnings, has become even more pervasive in recent decades. It is increasingly difficult for two people to make a commitment to each other if they believe that ultimately they are alone, and that personal development and success in life must be achieved through individual efforts. As this individualistic vocabulary plays out within the family, it makes it even more difficult for partners to subordinate some of their personal interests to the common good of the relationship. When "my needs" and "your needs" appear to be in conflict, partners can wind up feeling more like adversaries than family collaborators.

The vocabulary of individualism also makes it likely that today's parents will be blamed for any disarray in American families. In the spirit of Ben Franklin and Horatio Alger, new parents feel that they ought to be able to make it on their own, without help. Couples are quick to blame themselves if something goes wrong. When the expectable tensions increase as partners become parents, their tendency is to blame each other for not doing a better job. We believe that pioneers will inevitably find themselves in difficulty at some points on a strenuous journey. If societal policies do not become more responsive to parents and children, many of them will lose their way.

A HAZARDOUS JOURNEY

Unfortunately there are no historical comparative studies to substantiate our claim that the transition to parenthood is more difficult now than it used to be, but the evidence of risks to the parents' marriage and the children's well-being continues to mount. When we began the Becoming a Family Project in 1974, several studies suggested that the early child-rearing years could be stressful, but no one had studied the transition to parenthood by following *couples* from before to after they had their first baby. Today there is a large body of data to suggest that the transition to parenthood is disequilibrating for a majority of men, women, and marriages (see Cowan and Cowan 1988). Edward E. LeMasters's (1957) claim that a majority of new-parent couples experience "moderate or severe crisis" may be a slight overstatement of the case (see Hobbs and Cole 1977), but it is clear that both mothers and fathers are at increased risk for disenchantment or distress in the early years of parenthood. We can expect to find that one in a thousand new mothers will have a full-blown postpartum psychosis, that 7 percent to 15 percent will be diagnosed as clinically depressed, and that 30 percent to 50 percent (some claim as high as 80 percent) will experience "the blues" (Kumar and Robson 1984; O'Hara 1986). Because there are no epidemiological studies of new fathers, we do not have estimates of how many men becoming parents suffer from disabling psychological distress (Zaslow et al. 1981).*

---

*It was sobering to find that in our own study of ninety-six couples, one of the seventy-two men who became a father and one of the seventy-two women who became a mother during

There is consistent evidence from a number of careful longitudinal studies that couples' conflict and disagreement increases after they have a baby (Cowan et al. 1985) and that, on the average, men's and women's dissatisfaction with marriage tends to increase from pregnancy into the early child-rearing years (Belsky, Lang, and Rovine 1985; Cowan et al. 1985; Grossman et al. 1980).

Living in changing families in a changing world, pioneering couples find the trek to parenthood exciting, but surprisingly lonely, stormy, and frightening. Given the mixed messages from the family frontier, couples considering whether or when to become parents face a difficult decision.

---

the first two years of the study experienced a severe emotional breakdown requiring psychiatric care in the first three months after the birth of their first babies.

CHAPTER 2

To Be or Not to Be a Parent

ROB: We thought and thought about whether we should have kids and when would be a good time—a time that wouldn't somehow take away what we've worked so hard to build between us. And the more we thought, and the more we went back and forth about it, the more we discovered that there wasn't a clear answer or a perfect time. So I said, "Let's stop using birth control and see what happens."

JOAN: I was more committed than he was. At first, I was content to let it ride, because I was building my career, but I couldn't let it go forever. I always knew I wanted a child, so if he hadn't at least agreed to try, our marriage would have been in serious difficulty. I mean, I love Rob but I don't know if I could have just given in on this one. I was relieved when he said that I should stop taking the pill. He didn't really agree to "go for it" but at least he was willing to let it happen.

The decision to have a child has been described as the most fateful (Whelan 1975) or important (Bombardieri 1981) choice a couple can make, especially because its consequences are so far-reaching financially and psychologically (LaRossa 1986). There is no question that children are expensive. One husband in our study referred to his and his wife's debate about whether to have a baby as the "million-dollar decision." It was estimated about a decade ago that raising a male child from birth to twenty-five years of age cost at least $214,956 (Olson 1983), and a daughter cost even more (LaRossa 1986). Considering inflation and the state of the economy, not to mention the fact that these days children stay in college or professional training beyond the age of twenty-five, a seven-figure estimate may not be too far off.

The psychological aspects of having children add greater complexity to the debate. Unlike some other family decisions, becoming a parent is irrevocable. This provides a high incentive for couples to make the "right" decision.

As we listened to men and women talk about the choices they made, we heard both the reasons they wanted to have or not to have babies and the process—or the absence of a process—by which they decided what kind of family theirs would be. We began to discover just how important this process can be in determining how couples cope with the consequences of their baby decisions, especially if they fail to resolve serious disagreements between them.

At the time of our initial interview at six or seven months into the pregnancy, nine of the seventy-two expectant couples (14 percent) are still voicing strongly contrasting views about whether they are ready to have a child. In two couples, the husbands are eager to have a baby, but their wives are still facing parenthood reluctantly. Over the next six years these two couples experience serious marital crises but they stay together. In seven couples, the wives are feeling enthusiastic but their husbands have serious reservations about becoming fathers. These seven couples all separate and divorce by the time their first child is six years old.

This startling finding, which we will return to, reinforces one of our central themes. The birth of a baby does not suddenly convert a well-functioning couple relationship into one that is fraught with difficulty. Much of what happens after the birth of a baby is shaped by what is happening in couples' lives before the baby comes along. And one of the most important things that happens in the prebaby period is the way the couple goes about deciding whether to become parents in the first place.

My Choice, Your Choice, Our Choice

Rob and Joan touch on some of the most salient baby-maybe dilemmas that contemporary couples face. Quoted at the beginning of the chapter, they are in their early thirties and have been married for eight years. Like most of the participants in our study, they were initially somewhat ambivalent about becoming parents—if not about whether, at least about when. When two partners agree to live together or get married, they rarely make a firm agreement about whether to have children or when to begin a family (Daniels and Weingarten 1982). Even couples who discuss their family-making timetable before they make a long-term commitment to each other often find that changing circumstances, like career moves or parents who become ill and need to be taken care of, can alter the plans of one or both partners and throw their timetables into conflict. Because couples have to cope with both predictable dilemmas and unexpected events *for each partner,* it is a wonder that they ever arrive at the same conclusion at the same time about this major life step.

By the time we come to conduct our initial interview, about half of the couples have discussed the issues at length, come to a mutual decision, and entered into a deliberate plan that they will or will not have children. By contrast, the other half of the couples seems to have been involved in a rather inarticulate process in which both partners have been teetering between individual soul searching and meaningful conversation. For them, the process of deciding seems muddier and the outcome of their deliberations much less clear-cut. Peggy and Bill, in their mid-twenties, are talking with us in the living room of their small suburban apartment. Peggy is six months pregnant and feeling uncomfortable. Bill is telling us about how they came to be having a baby at this time.

BILL: Well, you know, we've been talking about it on and off, and it was always, "Do you want one?" "I don't know, do you want one?" And I didn't want to say, "I want one," because I don't want my wife to go through the tremendous changes if she doesn't really want one. And she was afraid to say she wanted one because I might not really want one.

PEGGY: I don't know how we finally decided, really. I got a new job last year, and I felt that it was not right to say "Let's have children" my first year on the job. And Bill was just getting his roofing business going, so we thought we'd probably start next year. And that's why we were so surprised to find we were pregnant.

I wouldn't have minded having children sooner. It's just that I didn't know if he really wanted—you know, if he could put up with the noise they would make. Like, we'd go out to lunch, and there would be kids screaming, "Mommy, mommy, I want . . ." and I could tell by looking at Bill that he was not very happy about all the noise these kids were making. So I didn't really push the matter. To me, it was OK if he didn't want any.

Only a few of the expectant couples describe themselves as having had a consistent stance over time; most report that each partner has shifted positions at least once before meeting with us at our initial interview. We find four patterns in how couples come to be—or not to be—having a baby:

Planners. These couples actively discuss the question and come to an agreement about becoming pregnant.

Acceptance-of-Fate Couples. These partners acquiesce or are pleasantly surprised when they discover that a baby is on the way.

Ambivalent Couples. They have strong feelings pro and con before and after conception and well into the pregnancy.

Yes-No Couples. By late pregnancy, these couples are still struggling, with each other and with the consequences of deciding to go ahead with the pregnancy.

Three of these patterns—Planners, Ambivalent, and Yes-No—are also present in the couples who are not having babies when we meet them at the beginning of the study.

To illustrate how couples in each of the four patterns handle the parenthood decision, we focus on a few representative couples. We show how the partners' reasons for wanting or not wanting to have a child are influenced by who they are, what routes they have taken to arrive at this time of life, and how they feel about their relationship. That is, their histories as individuals and as couples set the stage for whether their family-making discussions will be smooth or rough sailing.

Especially because we do not meet the expectant couples in our study until the seventh month of pregnancy, we are under no illusion that what they describe provides a complete picture of their motivations. What the interviews do reveal, we think, is what couples expect to happen if or when they have children—Will it be wonderful, problematic, or both?—and how they think and feel about making major life decisions when they agree or disagree on a course of action.

Four Decision-Making Patterns

One assumption that seems to be shared by most of the couples in our study, whether they wish passionately to have children or resolve firmly to remain child-free, is that babies will bring change: more closeness, excitement, and joy according to some couples; more distance, frustration, and tension, say others. Almost all of the reasons men and women gave for or against having children focused on one or more of the aspects of family life we had set out to study. Couples who are becoming parents expect their relationship with the child to change their lifestyle; alter their sense of themselves; affect their friendships, work lives, and stress levels; promote a reworking of their relationships with their parents; and have a profound impact on their marriage.

THE PLANNERS

Fifty-two percent of *both* nonparents and expectant couples in our study approached family making in a very deliberate way. By the time they try to conceive, the Planners who want a child have agreed that they do, and most have waited until both spouses agree on when. After extensive discussions, the Planners who are not expecting had decided (1) probably, but not now

(32 percent), or (2) definitely no for now, but the future is unclear (20 percent).

Clearly No   Marty and Evelyn, both twenty-eight, live in a small, comfortably furnished home, which they own. Marty is self-employed as a lawyer with an office nearby. Evelyn is a therapist who also works close to home. After ongoing, serious discussion, they have made a mutual decision not to have children.

> MARTY: The more I think about it, the clearer I get. I don't know if I can love another little being unselfishly. Most of the kids I know are unmanageable, and I don't think I have the patience to deal with that. I just don't have my shit together. Growing up in my family was like being in the middle of a perpetual shouting match. There's no way I can guarantee that it would be different with Evelyn and me.
>
> EVELYN: Well, my family didn't get the "Little House on the Prairie" award either. I know from what I did when I was growing up that kids can make their parents miserable. I might still be OK as a mother, I guess, but at this point babies would seriously interfere with where I am going in my work.

Wanting to avoid what happened in the families they grew up in is one of the most frequently mentioned reasons men and women give for deciding not have children. Yet, other couples with similarly troubled childhoods feel challenged to make their peace with their pasts by creating new, better-functioning families of their own.

The issues that Evelyn raises about work and career advancement play a major role in both men's and women's decisions about parenthood, but the consequences of the decision appear to be much more serious for women. Studies of women and careers document the fact that those occupying top positions in business and industry tend disproportionately to be single and/or childless (Baum and Cope 1980). It is little wonder, then, that many women are apprehensive about what will happen to their jobs if they become mothers. Since women still maintain primary responsibility for home and child care, even if they work full-time (see chapters 5 and 6 and Hochschild 1989), they wonder how they will be able to handle the demands of work and family without losing professional ground. As Evelyn says, "I'm afraid that I'd be torn in both directions, and not do justice to either one." Men are rarely asked by researchers about this work-family balance, and they rarely raise the issue spontaneously.

Not surprisingly, Marty and Evelyn believe that parenthood would have a negative effect on their marriage, too.

> EVELYN: We've worked very hard to get our marriage where it is. At the beginning, we were scrapping all the time. I hated it. He hated it. We got some help, and it got a little better.

MARTY: But it still wasn't better enough. Finally, we went camping for a week and talked maybe sixteen hours a day. I said that I wanted to be with her, but things would have to change. I'd have to give up some of my critical, angry stuff, and she'd have to pay more attention to me.

EVELYN: And I said I'd be willing to try if he would, and it really has been getting better ever since. I worry that a kid would shake us up, and I'm not willing to risk it.

At the time of our interview, Marty and Evelyn are both clear about their individual choices, and in agreement. Furthermore, they are able to talk about their emotions directly, without having to hold back on potentially controversial feelings, such as their fear about what effect children might have on the solidity of their marriage.

Clearly Yes Marty and Evelyn raise issues that are familiar to John and Shannon, but John and Shannon have a very different view of them. John is a twenty-four-year-old, energetic sports enthusiast who works in a small auto parts firm. His boss, whom he describes as "crusty," has promised John a share of the business if he stays on for a few years. Shannon, six months pregnant, is a year younger than John and works as a secretary in a community college. They can hardly wait to become parents, a goal they worked toward for more than a year. As they talk to us about why they decided to have a baby now, their eyes get misty:

SHANNON: Having a child will give me someone to love—someone who will love me back in a special way. It'll be unlike any other relationship I've ever had, even with John. I've always wanted to be a mother, whatever else I do. It's a very important part of me. It's giving me a greater purpose in life; I don't know how to describe it, but I know it's going to make my life more meaningful. I'd have been crushed if we couldn't conceive (*patting her stomach tenderly*). I was even a little worried when it didn't happen the first month we tried.

John focuses more on the influence he will have:

JOHN: I see having a child as a chance to shape the life of another human being—someone who will be very important to me and who I can teach about my view of the world.

The most frequent reason both men and women gave us for becoming a parent was their desire for an intimate and special relationship with their children. Watching them grow and develop would bring parents fulfillment. Being with them would give grownups a chance to be childish or playful, and to look at the world anew through the eyes of a child.

The second most frequent reason men and women gave for having a baby, or for remaining childless, had to do with changes they thought parenthood would make in their sense of themselves. As John says, "Becoming a dad now has something to do with my personal development. At twenty-four, I'm running out of ways to be adolescent gracefully."

The idea that having babies means being a "grownup" led about half the couples in our study to decide that it was not wise to become parents until they had reached an appropriate place in their life journey. Lois and Martin Hoffman found this to be true two decades ago: "More than finishing school, going to work, or even getting married, parenthood establishes a person as a truly mature, stable, and acceptable member of the community and provides him access to other institutions of adult society" (1973, p. 47).

Men's and women's relationships with their friends, their jobs, and the larger communities in which they live are the third most frequently mentioned issues. Some couples' decisions about having children are heavily influenced by whether their friends have babies, although friends can also be a source of pressure against having children. When John and Shannon first started talking about having a baby, he was shocked to find that their friends actively tried to discourage them, warning them that it would interfere with their friendship: "They said that we wouldn't be able to go to dinner or play softball or just hang out with them. Some even upped the ante by telling us about couples they knew whose marriages were falling apart now that they have children!"

Neither partner feels that work ambitions will interfere with his or her family plans. Shannon likes her job but is not emotionally invested in it right now. She thinks she will be able to return to a secretarial job in the college if and when she is ready to go back to work. John has the fantasy that his boss may see him as more serious and responsible once he becomes a father, and thus more disposed to offer him a share in the business.

They do not share Marty and Evelyn's assumption that life with children will be full of conflict. Shannon and John expect to have fun with their children. They expect parenthood to enhance their views of themselves and their work. Not surprisingly, their childhood family memories are mostly warm and positive, and their own relationship has been solid since they met.

A number of couples cite their marriage as the reason they want to go ahead and have a child. Beth and Paul are both thirty-four when they decide to have a baby. He is finishing up his doctoral degree, and she is a drama teacher and coach at a local high school. It took him a bit longer than her to make the decision. As he explains it, the change came when he realized that "over time our relationship, which has always been good, has been getting better and better. We've learned so much from each other in the past few years that I feel we're in a really good place to bring a child into the world."

Beth had been more eager to go ahead but felt like she had to wait: "He was willing to keep on talking about it, and I felt that he heard me out even though he wasn't ready to go along. He's really behind it now—I know he didn't just give in. I don't know what would have happened if Paul wanted even more time, what with the biological clock ticking away." She feels that bringing up a baby will give them something special to work on together.

Clearly, Planners do not always begin with unambivalent feelings about having a baby, nor do the partners always agree at the outset. Their conclusion that their relationship is now on good enough footing to handle bringing a child into the world flows naturally from their style of working things out. Each seems to assume that the other is "on the same side." They describe themselves as ready to negotiate, although Beth hints that she might not have been able to accommodate to Paul's timetable much longer. Perhaps the most important aspect of their style of working on this major decision is that both of them have been willing to keep talking about it.

As we follow Paul and Beth over the years of the study, we continue to be impressed with their engaged and thoughtful stance toward their life together. They work very long hours and love their jobs. They travel regularly to visit their parents in another state, where they originally met, and even more often since they learned that Paul's mother has a terminal illness. They continue to work at their relationships with their parents and with each other, and we see them struggling gently over the things they want to change. Beth and Paul's is a very well functioning and satisfying marriage. We rarely found couples like them, who could continue to sail the stormy seas after someone had rocked the boat. Planners as a group have developed a more effective process of problem solving and more satisfying relationships than the couples in the other three groups, whether they remain childless or become parents.

Frustrated Plans: Due Date Surprises and Infertility   Planner couples tend to proceed as if the world were predictable and under their control, but even the most elaborate plans do not always work out. One of our academic colleagues attempted to become pregnant in August so that the baby would be born late the following May, at the end of the spring semester, giving her all summer to be home with the baby. Her carefully thought out timetable began perfectly, but a surprise was in store: She did become pregnant in August, but "the baby" turned out to be twins. The boys arrived early, just before she needed to grade final exams, and the new mother never did complete that academic year.

A much more serious deterrent to family planning is the inability to conceive for months or years after deciding to begin a family. Problems with fertility, which increase the longer a couple waits, remind us that nature can thwart the best-laid plans.

Four of the thirty-seven Planners in our study took at least two years to become pregnant. By the time we interviewed Seth and Karen, their infertility problem had been resolved, but its consequences lingered. Over three years of attempting to conceive had left them careworn from continually coping with the uncertainties and with the monthly evidence that their efforts had failed. They had to face the possibility that they would never be able to have their own biological child. Because the inability to conceive is often experienced by men and women as a failure of their basic masculinity or femininity, infertility can pose a serious psychological challenge. The evidence is beginning to show that those who do not mourn or cope with this loss may suffer serious long-term consequences to their well-being as individuals and as couples (Menning 1977; Shapiro 1982).

Along with scientific advances in the field of reproduction come unforeseen problems. What we hear from couples who have struggled with problems of fertility is that today's high-tech medical procedures, designed to help them have babies, actually bring a combination of possibly false hope and intrusion into what used to be a private and delicate matter. Rigidly scheduling sexual intercourse almost inevitably decreases partners' spontaneity and enthusiasm for lovemaking. After months or years of preoccupation with getting pregnant, many couples say they never get back to normal. Forever trying to catch up with themselves, with their relationship as a couple, and with the child they desperately want, couples who are unsuccessful at conceiving a baby may be at increased risk of marital distress and divorce (Brodzinsky 1987; Snarey et al. 1987).

Of the four couples in our study who had wrestled with infertility before becoming pregnant, two were among the couples who were most satisfied with their marriages, but the other two were among the most unhappily married in the study. Perhaps the crisis of infertility, like so many other crises, presents a challenge that calls forth a successful effort to respond for some couples, but leads for others to deterioration under the strain. Seth and Karen and the other happily married couple had already successfully coped with a crisis or challenge to their relationship before being faced with the possibility of never conceiving. They gathered their strength to face this new obstacle and came out feeling that their relationship as a couple had grown stronger.

By contrast, the two couples whose satisfaction with marriage was low after their battle with infertility had been dealing for years with other issues they could neither discuss nor resolve. For them, the initial failure to conceive placed an added strain on an already overburdened emotional system. To draw more general conclusions about the effects of infertility, we will need systematic information about the state of couples' marriages before infertility becomes a problem, but we can conclude at this point that, regardless of whether they ever have a viable pregnancy, couples with fertility problems face a special emotional stress that can take a toll on their relationship.

THE ACCEPTANCE-OF-FATE COUPLES

One in seven, or 14 percent, of the expectant couples in our study were surprised by the news of their pregnancies but readily accepted the cards fate had dealt them.* In slightly more than half of these couples, both partners

---

*All the Acceptance-of-Fate couples, most of the Yes-No couples, and about half the Ambivalent couples had unplanned pregnancies—a total of about 35 percent of those participating in our study. So much for the increases in effective methods of birth control described in chapter 1.

definitely wanted to have children, but not yet. These couples generally took the news as a pleasant surprise.

Ariel and Harry had been living together for five years, married for three, when Ariel was in an automobile accident that left her seriously injured. Eighteen months later, still receiving medical treatments that included hormone therapy for a disrupted menstrual cycle, she discovered she was pregnant. They had not even begun to think about family plans:

> ARIEL: I didn't even have a sense of myself as being fertile—I was so shaken from the accident. And there it was. Part of me was saying, "Wait, we haven't really spent enough time together now that I know I'll live." But the more I thought about having this baby, the more excited I became.
>
> HARRY: I got this romantic picture of a pregnant woman, standing at the window, the sun shining in. Of course, I'm worried sometimes about having a child now, but sometimes you just have to trust that it will all work out.

Not all Acceptance-of-Fate couples sounded as glowing as Harry and Ariel. Some had an attitude of quiet welcome, neither joy nor despair. Bart and Sheila had not yet made a firm decision about parenthood, but neither was opposed to having a child: "When it was right it was going to happen. This pregnancy wouldn't have occurred unless we were at a point in our life where it was OK for a baby to come."

In the useful distinction made by Warren Miller (1978), the babies of the pleasantly surprised and quietly welcoming couples are not planned but, once conceived, are wanted by both partners. The reasons they give for their reaction to the pregnancy resemble those of the Planners: They expect a baby to enrich their lives, to enhance their sense of themselves, to bring them closer to their parents, or to add to the good feelings in their marriage. They do not anticipate that having a baby will interfere seriously with their work or their friendships.

Acceptance-of-Fate couples tend to have very strong and positive feelings about their relationships. Their satisfaction with the marriage may have led them to react quickly and resolutely to welcome their unplanned pregnancies, or their ability to cope well with the pregnancy may have led to feeling satisfied with their marriage. It seems plausible that the process works both ways. Furthermore, it is not unreasonable to wonder whether the Acceptance-of-Fate couples' positive involvement with each other may even have contributed to their reluctance to plan a family more deliberately. From what they recount, it seems clear that few, if any, of them became pregnant because of contraceptive failure. Rather, they seem to have been engaged in a partly unconscious or unspoken game of Russian roulette by being less vigilant about their use of contraception or, in several cases, by not using contraceptives at all. And yet, they expressed surprise when the pregnancy occurred.

Bart says: "We never really talked about it, never really discussed it. One day, even though we knew it wasn't a safe day, we were feeling very good about our relationship and life and we went ahead anyway." Sheila has a more fatalistic interpretation: "It just sort of happened. It seemed to be divinely directed."

Given how difficult it is to make a decision with such far-reaching consequences, some couples may need a little help from a higher being, or from their unconscious. This way they "win" whether she becomes pregnant or they remain "free" and "flexible."

THE AMBIVALENT COUPLES

The theme of ambivalence ran through our discussions with nearly all the couples. We placed a couple in the Ambivalent category when both partners expressed positive *and* negative feelings about parenthood, but one leaned more toward one side and the other more toward the other side. It was more common for men to be reluctant to go ahead, but a few women were not at all ready for parenthood. At the beginning of the study we found couples who fit this Ambivalent pattern among the childless group (44 percent) and among the parents-to-be (20 percent).

Rob and Joan, already quoted, live in a rented apartment near the courthouse where Rob works as a court reporter. They described their mixed feelings about what becoming a family could do *for* them and *to* them:

> JOAN: I thought I wanted a baby someday. But then I would think, "What will happen to me? Will I become a boring housewife, able to talk only about kids and diapers?" That would be a big change from my work at the bank.
>
> ROB: I can see two scenarios very clearly. In one I'm the kind of hero-daddy that I hope I'll be, but in the other I'm the wimp that I'm afraid I'll be.

In contrast to Shannon, who is eager to give up her job for now, and Evelyn, who is totally wrapped up in her work, Joan feels stuck at a difficult choice point in her life. She had to decide whether to apply for managerial training at the bank, but was also worried about being "one of those old moms, sort of decrepit when my kids were teenagers (*sighs*). So I sent in my application to the training program, really worked on it, and got pregnant three days before I was accepted!"

Rob and Joan provide a clear illustration of a couple who has discussed parenthood extensively before the baby "surprises" them. We have the strong impression that for a few women, like Joan, such an unexpected pregnancy can resolve, at least temporarily, an immobilizing dilemma about whether to step onto the family or the career path. While Joan did not consciously plan it this way, her accidental pregnancy provided a solution.

For Rob and Joan, and for many of the Ambivalent couples, a struggle has preceded the realization that both of them have mixed feelings. Seven months into the pregnancy, they report that their negotiations began with strong disagreements: One spouse was eager to have a baby, the other definitely opposed. Unlike the Yes-No couples, to be discussed next, Ambivalent partners were somehow able to tolerate their own and their partners' mixed feelings long enough to come to some joint resolution of the dilemma.

During our first interview with Steve and Yu-Mei, one of the Ambivalent couples who have not yet decided whether to have children, Steve says that he leans toward going ahead with it. Although he secretly shares his wife's fears that having a baby could change their life, he tries to convince her that her fears are unfounded.

But Yu-Mei doesn't want to hear Steve's fantasies about how things will be if they have a baby, even though she sometimes has similar daydreams: "Once Steve hears my positive feelings, he will say 'OK then, let's go ahead,' and I'm just not ready to do that."

Steve and Yu-Mei tell us in our interview that each feels partly ready to go ahead and partly fearful—but in talking with each other, Steve has mentioned only the "yes" and Yu-Mei only the "no." Thus their discussions feel polarized and antagonistic, and they cannot escape the common pattern for couples with important differences of opinion or experience: Instead of trying to resolve the conflict *within* each of them, they get into a struggle with each other. Each tries to reduce the inner turmoil by trying to convince the other to change. Not being aware of this pattern, both partners usually feel misunderstood and hurt. We believe that the marital polarization becomes more painful than it would be to resolve their inner turmoil, but they do not see this as an option. Some never get past the deadlock.

Those who do, including Steve and Yu-Mei, begin to let on that there are really two sides to both their stories. In the protected setting of our personal interview, Steve admits some of his reservations; Yu-Mei says she sometimes daydreams about the two of them with a baby. In the process of talking to each other and answering our questions, they realize that both of them understand and feel both sides of the dilemma; at the same time they each want and fear parenthood. They have shifted from a *decision* to a *discussion* mode in which expressing a feeling for or against having a child does not have to lead to immediate action. When both spouses can talk about both poles of their own inner struggle, it creates the possibility that they will feel they are on the same side and that, whatever the ultimate resolution, it will be based on both partners' needs.

Unfortunately, such an outcome was not achieved by most of the Ambivalent couples in our study. Both expectant and childless couples typically stopped at the polarized stage. It apparently felt less threatening for each partner to remain ambivalent, to back off and suffer in silence. Significantly, the Ambivalent couples tended to feel less positive about their marriages at the beginning of the study than did couples in any of the other groups.

THE YES-NO COUPLES

Ambivalence about having a child is one thing. Strong, unresolved conflict about becoming a family is another. As we mentioned earlier, nine of the original seventy-two couples who were expecting a baby when they entered our study were still in a Yes-No conflict about the wisdom of becoming parents in our initial interview with them in the sixth or seventh month of pregnancy.

A tenth Yes-No couple was one of the twenty-four couples not yet decided about having children. Tom and Valerie had been together for four years. Tom wanted to have a baby but Valerie was definitely not ready for this step. They had even separated over this issue once. In our first interview, Tom said he felt that Valerie had "welched" on their deal. For her part, Valerie made clear that she had always told him she wanted kids *someday,* but that for her someday was still a long way off.

Nine months later, when we called to set up our next interview, we found that Tom and Valerie were living separately again. Two years into the study (equivalent to the eighteen-months-after-birth follow-up of the couples who had had a baby), we reached Tom by telephone. He told us that Valerie had moved to another city to take a job and that they had filed for divorce.

Fourteen percent of the expectant couples and 5 percent of the childless couples fell into the Yes-No category. In two of the Yes-No couples who were expecting a baby, the husbands had been eager for the baby since the pregnancy was discovered but the wives' initial reaction had been negative. Both women came around, apparently without completely resolving their earlier misgivings. Although we could not have predicted from our first interviews which couples would wind up in the most marital difficulty, we know now that the marriage of one of these two couples has been in almost constant turmoil since their baby was born, and the other has been teetering between periods of amicable feeling and talk of divorce. Despite these painful early years as a family, both couples with the initially hesitant mothers were still together at the end of their first child's kindergarten year.

What happens when it is the man who says no, and when the partners' inability to resolve the conflict continues into the late stages of pregnancy? Recall thirty-four-year-old Alice and twenty-seven-year-old Andy from chapter 1. Alice became pregnant when they had been living together only four months. She was determined to have a child, regardless of whether Andy stayed in the picture. He did not feel ready to become a father, and was struggling to come to terms with Alice's pregnancy:

> ANDY: It was the hardest thing I ever had to deal with. I had this idea that I wasn't even going to have to think about being a father until I was over thirty, but here it was, and I had to decide now. I was concerned about my soul. I didn't want, under any circumstances, to compromise myself, but I knew it would be very hard on Alice if I took action that would result in her being a single parent. It would've meant that I'm the kind of person who turns his back on someone I care about, and that would destroy me as well as her.

It is important to understand that Alice and Andy were struggling with more than the dilemmas of impending parenthood. Individually and together, they have had to overcome serious adversities from their youth. Alice told us that she experiences her mother as emotionally aloof, critical, and rejecting. Her close relationship with her father—too close, according to Andy—was very important to her, but he died when Alice was in her early twenties. She had become disoriented for a time after he died, and seems not to have completed her mourning for him. She had been searching for that closeness elsewhere in her life ever since, and her relationship with Andy had made her hopeful of having found it. So, for Alice, having a baby with Andy dovetailed perfectly with where she had been heading on her journey through adulthood.

Andy, however, was working on a different aspect of his adult development. During his teen years, he suddenly realized that his parents were alcoholics. He would come home from school each night to his parents' unpredictable moods, which swung wildly from hilarity to violent anger. No wonder an unexpected pregnancy leaves him in turmoil. Longing for a true family, he is nevertheless troubled by Alice's pregnancy, although he loves her.

Both Alice and Andy are drawn to the tenderness and passion they find together, but Alice is also sometimes frightened by Andy's anger. As he explained: "When I have a few drinks, I tend to get nasty the way my father did. I was hoping to wait until I got that kind of thing under control before becoming a father myself."

Many of the men and women in our study had had unhappy or disturbing experiences while growing up, and these experiences play a part in how each of them envisions family making. Some who are choosing to become parents have been bolstered by the strong conviction that they can create more nurturing families than those they knew as children. A few feel that they are already dealing with all they can manage in the life they have constructed as a couple and cannot risk repeating a destructive pattern. Still others, like Alice and Andy, feel powerful but contradictory feelings about whether it is possible to break the chain of family dysfunction.

Alice longs to have a child now, in part to combat her feelings of insecurity and to make up for the loss of her truly accepting parent. But her need puts her in conflict with Andy, who needs to get himself and his relationship with Alice more comfortably settled before he takes on the care of yet another needy human being. Alice imagines that nurturing the baby that was conceived in a loving relationship will fill some of her longing for tenderness and love. Andy sounds as if he needs that kind of tenderness too, but he was counting on finding it in his new relationship with Alice. In addition to the turmoil within and between Andy and Alice, they must also untangle both the support and pressure from their close friends. According to Andy, his friends are urging him "to run." Alice's friends are very supportive of her having the baby, even if it means she has to be a single parent.

Here is our five-domain model in action. As they begin their journey to parenthood, Alice and Andy come face to face with the other four arenas of their lives: their sense of themselves, their relationships with their parents, and the stress and support provided by close friends. For obvious reasons, the pregnancy is having a dramatic effect on their relationship with each other.

It is difficult to convey the tone of Andy's and Alice's remarks on paper, but we were very moved by their emotion and warmth during our interviews with them. They talked about the pregnancy struggle with insight and understanding, and both sounded sympathetic to the other's point of view, even though the discussion got a bit abstract at times. They almost convinced us that the troubles between them were in the past. Swayed by their moving and articulate descriptions of their feelings, we missed some of the obvious danger signals.

In retrospect, we can see that many critical factors were working against Alice and Andy's relationship as a couple, exacerbating rather than helping to resolve their differences. The most obvious, of course, is that they had not lived together long enough to establish a firm intimate relationship before the pregnancy occurred. Second, each had a different picture of what life with a child would be like, a picture that reinforced their respective feelings about family life. Third, it was not so much the difference in their ages as in their different places in their developmental journeys at the time the pregnancy occurred that increased the intensity of Andy's negative feelings and Alice's determination to have the baby.

Finally, we learned later that there had been very little give-and-take in their discussions. Unlike Steve and Yu-Mei, neither Alice nor Andy experienced ambivalence about what he or she wanted. Their individual needs were so compelling that neither was able to recognize any feelings on the other side of the issue. As a result, their intense discussions remained polarized. Once Alice decided that she was going ahead with the pregnancy regardless of what Andy decided, Andy had a very difficult time coming to terms with his distress. Apparently, in contrast with the warm way they talked to each other in our presence, their private conversations were more like take-it-or-leave-it emotional showdowns, with Alice feeling pressure from both Andy's distress and her own gut feeling of need. She decided that to be true to herself and her needs, she had to have the baby. Andy decided finally that to preserve his self-respect and respond to his own need for intimacy, he had to stay with Alice and give in on the baby question.

We, and they, have learned a good deal since that initial interview in 1980. We can see more clearly now that major decisions with these conflicting, emotionally laden elements are probably destined to be short-run resolutions. For Alice and Andy, this one was to have painful long-term consequences, for both of them and for their daughter, Jessica. For several years, it looked as though there might be a hopeful resolution to their tumultuous family beginning. But, following a number of events over which he felt he had little control, Andy felt compelled to separate from Alice and Jessica when Jessica was three and a half. They tried to work out a life that would satisfy all of them, but one year later Alice and Andy reluctantly filed for divorce.

Decision Making, Problem-Solving Effectiveness, and Marital Satisfaction

We wanted to know more about the couple relationships of the partners in each of our four categories—how they fared in solving more general problems during pregnancy, and how their satisfaction with marriage changed over the next two years as they began to live with the results of their decision. First, we asked partners to choose a recent problem or disagreement and (on separate questionnaires) to explain how they tried to solve it, how they felt about that attempt, and whether they felt satisfied with the outcome. Among the examples they reported, one partner got upset with the other for not turning off the lights when leaving a room; one couple had a conflict about whether the wife should return to work; another argued repeatedly about who should take out the garbage; one spouse got irritated with the other for making an illegal U-turn; and another couple had a misunderstanding about whether one had given the other an unambiguous invitation to make love.

We constructed an overall measure of each partner's view of their problem-solving effectiveness by having our staff members independently rate the husband's and the wife's answers to each question.[1] Our premise was that partners who were able to maintain their individual points of view, understand their partners' points of view, and feel satisfied with the outcome of the discussion would feel more effective as problem solvers. We found that the Yes-No couples' problem-solving effectiveness, rated from both spouses' descriptions, was significantly lower than that of the Planners, Acceptance-of-Fate couples, and Ambivalent couples. These partners' inability to reconcile their views about having a baby appears to be part of a larger difficulty: They do not have a viable process for resolving major or minor problems between them.

Next, we examined changes over time in marital satisfaction (Locke and Wallace 1959). Scores below 100 on this scale are in a "danger zone," indicating that the couple is at risk for serious marital distress. The couples with these low scores are not necessarily heading for divorce, but their descriptions of their relationships are similar to those of couples who have sought therapy for a marriage that is disturbingly conflictful or cold and distant.

As you can see from the figure on the next page, both expectant parents and nonparents describe themselves on the happier end of the continuum at the beginning of the study.* Only the Ambivalent couples who are expecting a baby are significantly less happy than couples in the other groups. Their decision to go ahead with the pregnancy in spite of their ambivalence seems to place a burden on their relationship. To our surprise, the Yes-No couples whose decision-making effectiveness ratings were low in pregnancy began the study at about the same high level of marital satisfaction as the Planners.

---

*Because the trends are so similar, we have averaged the men's and women's marital satisfaction scores in the figure.

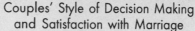

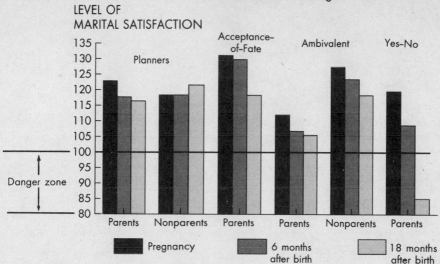

Couples' Style of Decision Making and Satisfaction with Marriage

This is consistent with our early experience with Alice and Andy. One of the reasons we were misled by their initial description of their situation is that their intense struggle, followed by Andy's agreement to go forward, had resulted in a temporarily rosy outlook on how they were doing as a couple.

The Planners, those who become parents and those who do not, show very little change in their feelings about their marriage over the two-year period. Although Acceptance-of-Fate couples show some decline in marital satisfaction, they start at such a high level that they are still satisfied when they are midway into the second year of parenthood. The Ambivalent couples who have become parents show enough of a decline in their satisfaction with marriage that their average scores are now close to the danger zone.

But it is among the Yes-No decision makers that we see the most dramatic changes. By the time they have been parents for six months, their descriptions of their marriages reveal a significant drop in satisfaction from their positive views in pregnancy. One year later, their scores plummet drastically, placing them as a group into the severely distressed range. Since this group is composed primarily of men who were very reluctant to have children, it is not surprising to find that the husbands' scores plunge even more steeply than do their wives'.

As we mentioned earlier, all seven of the couples in the kind of Yes-No deadlock that Alice and Andy described in late pregnancy had separated and then divorced by the time their first child entered elementary school. The sad irony is that when husbands give in reluctantly and resentfully to having a baby in order to preserve the marriage, the child and the marriage may ultimately be at risk.[2]

CHAPTER 3

The Pregnant Pause: Nine Long Months

When the doctor called with the news that I was pregnant, I was so excited I wanted to run out on the street and tell everybody I met.

One night she had a vivid dream about having a baby. She woke me up, turned to me, and I knew right away that she was pregnant. The whole thing felt like jumping off a cliff.

I felt confused—a mixture of up and down, stunned, in a daze, really.

When the test results came back positive, my reaction was, "Oh no, this can't happen now!"

These variations on a theme remind us that the enthusiastic Planners, the pleasantly surprised or acquiescent Acceptance-of-Fate partners, the dragging-their-feet Ambivalent couples, and the battling Yes-No spouses have traveled very different paths to the milestone of their first pregnancy. We first meet with couples in their sixth or seventh month of pregnancy, some time after their initial reactions of delight, surprise, resignation, or shock in finding out they are going to become parents have settled down. They typically have one of three pictures of pregnancy: They see it as a time of dreadful illness, as a period of refuge, or as a simple inconvenience.

Peggy, twenty-four, and Bill, twenty-seven, described themselves in the last chapter as ambivalent about their decision to have a family. As she talks about how the pregnancy has been going, Peggy's vivid pictures seem to be framed by her dark hair and vibrant eyes.

PEGGY: Well, I'm nauseous, weepy, irritable, and exhausted from making five middle-of-the-night trips to the bathroom. I limp through my day in a fog, and I seem to shift unpredictably from total optimism to buckets of tears without knowing why. I feel more and more dependent on Bill for support. Some of my old worries have come back to haunt me, and they are being joined by some new ones. Other than that, it's been terrific!

BILL: For a while it was scary. Lately the worst parts have tapered off a little, but I'm still worried.

Like medical doctors and some psychiatrists, Peggy and Bill focus on Peggy's debilitating physical and psychological symptoms.

Beth and Paul, the Planner couple with a very positive relationship whom we also introduced in chapter 2, are both thirty-four. They had timed it so that Beth would give birth in the summer, enabling her to return, part-time, to her job as a high school drama coach in the fall. Beth looks radiant when we first meet with her and Paul in their cozy living room. Her hand on her swelling belly, she sways to and fro in the rocker, the picture of health, serenity, and inner confidence.

BETH: There's really no way to describe it. I feel this awe at the magic of this child growing inside me.

PAUL: What about the times that you sit there and worry about what kind of mother you'll be?

BETH: Sometimes I do worry, but mostly I'm just wrapped up in a haze. Nothing else in the world seems important anymore, except you and me and this baby of ours.

In contrast with the medical view, some sociologists and a few psychoanalysts romanticize pregnancy as a protective cocoon in which a woman takes refuge for nine months until she emerges as a mother. Even though pregnancy may raise internal psychological issues and concerns, it is viewed as a time in which the mother, and sometimes the father, focus only on themselves, each other, and the baby.

Sonia and Eduardo are also Planners. From large Hispanic families, they both knew from the beginning that they wanted children. When we meet them, they appear to be taking everything in their stride. Sonia is twenty-four, an energetic woman who works in a small insurance firm. She has so much to accomplish in the next month, she can barely sit still for the interview. Eduardo, twenty-six, is very involved in his job as a technician in a medical laboratory.

SONIA: The pregnancy has been just great. It disrupted my work schedule
this week, but not much else. I'm having a lot of fun with it. We went
to Japan during my third month. I had to finish writing a report while
I was over there, but the only thing that bothered me was the smells.
And then, when I was six months pregnant, Eduardo and I went on a
two-week hike in the Sierras. That was hard. I wouldn't do it again. But
I haven't let the pregnancy stop me from doing anything I really want
to do.

EDUARDO: I wanted to plan a camping trip before it turns too cold, but the
doctor told us to forget it. I guess we'll just have to find some other
weekend adventure so that we can have some fun together before we
settle down with the baby.

In this "no big deal" view, pregnancy is normalized to the point of seeming
no more than a minor inconvenience for a woman or a couple who lead an
active and complex life.

We might be tempted to think of pregnancy as a medical condition when
we are talking with Peggy. The thought would hardly cross our minds when
talking to Beth and Sonia. The issue is not simply that some women are
relatively symptom-free, while others are physically debilitated. As we ask
couples entering the third trimester of pregnancy how it has been so far, we
are struck by a contradiction between what they report as the most challenging or affecting aspects of pregnancy and the issues to which doctors,
hospitals, and childbirth educators direct most of their attention. Expectant
parents talk primarily about the psychological and emotional changes they
are experiencing and about what is happening to their relationships with the
people who are important to them. Doctors and childbirth educators focus
primarily on the physical, physiological, and medical aspects of pregnancy
and delivery, paying attention to women's emotional reactions only when
they are unpredictable or disruptive.

In this chapter we discuss the journey to parenthood, beginning with the
physical changes in individual women, and men, during pregnancy and
showing that there is much room for disputing the assumption that pregnancy should be considered first and foremost a medical condition. Next, we
examine how women's and men's physical and psychological changes play
out in the couple's relationship. We then show how pregnancy creates new
issues in the relationships between the new parents and their own parents,
as well as in their alliances with co-workers and friends. In a final section we
summarize how all of these shifts lead to some uneasiness as couples prepare
for labor, delivery, and the reality of becoming parents.

Physical Changes in Women—And Men

The typical regime of prenatal care, including regular visits to the doctor and giving birth in a hospital rather than at home, is based on the beliefs that pregnant women need special care and may be at risk for becoming ill during pregnancy, and that preventive care and medical treatment by experts will result in better health for mothers and their babies. Should pregnant women be treated as potentially ill? All of them will undergo rapid changes in weight, size, shape, and hormone-endocrinological balance. One of the most familiar symptoms is nausea, or "morning sickness," which fortunately tends to decrease after the first three months. But backache, indigestion, tiredness, shortness of breath, painful intercourse, swollen ankles, and leg cramps tend to increase as the pregnancy progresses, especially in the last three months.

About half of the expectant mothers we interviewed in the last trimester of pregnancy said, like Beth and Sonia, that it was going very well. They reported few troubling symptoms, even in the first trimester. Data from a detailed British study by Eva Zajicek (1981) and a comprehensive American study by Doris Entwisle and Susan Doering (1981) reinforce the need to rethink pregnancy stereotypes. The women in Zajicek's study, in their seventh month of pregnancy, reported relatively mild symptoms: indigestion (43 percent), lack of energy (68 percent), breathlessness (46 percent), leg cramps (68 percent), backache (48 percent), tired legs (55 percent), and more urgent urination (66 percent). "Many other pregnancy symptoms were conspicuous by their infrequency, and even with the most common symptoms, it was clear that not all women were affected" (Zajicek 1981, p. 45).

A similar conclusion can be drawn from Entwisle and Doering's study of pregnant women in Maryland. Only about half of them experienced frequent nausea or vomiting in the first three months, allegedly a "certain" symptom of pregnancy. It seems clear that a substantial number of women do not fit the picture of pregnancy as a time of heightened physical distress. Those who do, though, suffer a range of severe, often unexpected symptoms.

PEGGY: Before I even knew for sure that I was pregnant, my breasts were sore as hell, I spent mornings for two weeks with my head in the toilet, and my joints hurt so much I couldn't walk downstairs. One day I woke up and said to myself, "Either I'm dying or I'm pregnant."

BILL: It felt like a little bit of both. I read that women are supposed to be sick in the first three months or so, but then they are supposed to get better. I guess Peggy hasn't been reading the same books. I'd say she's still feeling lousy at least part of every day, and she's in her seventh month.

Many self-help books on pregnancy imply that debilitating symptoms are almost universal. One unfortunate consequence of presenting pregnancy in this light is that women who feel well during their pregnancies may begin to worry that they are abnormal. Beth said that she kept phoning her obstetrician: "I wasn't getting any of those symptoms I was supposed to. I kept wondering whether maybe something had gone wrong inside."

In the traditional medical view of pregnancy, the woman goes for regular medical checkups while her partner, who is also expecting a baby and has concerns of his own, waits outside the door. Our study and others, however, reveal that men undergo physical changes in pregnancy too. A number of studies, primarily by English anthropologists, of what is called the *couvade* syndrome document the fact that in some non-Western, nonindustrialized cultures, fathers-to-be experience many of the same physical symptoms as their pregnant spouses do, sometimes to an even more extreme and incapacitating degree (Trethowan and Conlan 1965). While waiting for their babies to be born, these men retire to bed with unremitting nausea and incapacitating back problems, demand to be looked after, and otherwise raise an emotional fuss during the last months of their wives' pregnancies. Some American studies (Curtis 1955; Shereshefsky and Yarrow 1973) suggest that this phenomenon may be part of our culture as well, although there is no specific information on how many men may have such dramatic reactions to their wives' pregnancies.

In our study, men reported gaining weight, growing beards, losing weight, shaving beards, nursing obscure injuries, and other physical and behavioral changes. Some are unconscious of the parallels with their wives' symptoms, but others are quite aware of them. After Beth describes to us the changes that have taken place in her body over the last few months, Paul observes that he underwent "pregnant fathers' weight gain": "It's really funny. Now Beth's eating more than me, and I usually eat a lot. I guess I'm just trying to keep up."

As much as we pushed couples for detail, though, talk about physical symptoms usually ended quickly, while talk about psychological and relationship changes could have gone on long into the night. Perhaps the overshadowing of the physical aspects of pregnancy stemmed from the fact that our first meetings with couples took place after many of the physical surprises had already occurred. We do not think that this is the case, but more detailed psychological studies of pregnancy are needed to settle the matter. Based on our own interviews, and those of the other researchers we mentioned, we conclude that the physical changes associated with pregnancy function as a backdrop against which both spouses' feelings about themselves and each other are played out.

Psychological Changes

What is it about pregnancy that raises the risk of stormy weather for the couple? The men and women we spoke to talked about many issues, but there are five that topped their lists:

Changes in each partner's emotional life are not easy to talk about.

Changes in their sexual relationship leave them feeling vulnerable as a couple.

Partners tend not to share their expectations about the next steps of their journey; when they get to their destination, they are caught off guard by their different pictures of what they thought it would be like.

Both men and women anticipate a much more equal division of household chores and taking care of the baby than actually happens.

As the baby becomes more and more of a reality for both spouses, their balance of independence and interdependence as a couple begins to shift.

These issues become a problem for couples when they cannot find a nonaccusatory way of talking to each other about what they think is happening. Peggy and Bill, for example, cannot avoid blaming each other for their distress. She feels that his poor business decisions have forced him to work extra hours now, just when she could use his help getting the baby's room ready. If she were "the least bit encouraging" about his business, Bill claims, he wouldn't feel that he has to work so late every night.

Pregnancy heightens certain personal issues for men and women, some of which spill over into their relationship as a couple. Emotional changes can exact a particularly high toll. The stereotype of a pregnant woman's emotional state has her riding a rollercoaster that might veer out of control at any moment without warning. We can see from our brief portraits of Peggy, Beth, and Sonia that a more elaborate and differentiated set of metaphors is needed to cover a range of reactions, from virtually no change in women's emotional lives to dramatic mood swings during the course of a day.

WOMEN'S MOODS AND CONCERNS

Researchers attribute pregnant women's moods mostly to how they are feeling physically and psychologically as expectant mothers. But without similar studies of women at other stages of life, we do not know whether we might discover the same range of emotions, for example, in women who have just divorced, who have gone to back to work after many years at home, or whose children have just left the nest.

The common belief is that women's emotional states in pregnancy are a product of hormonal changes. Mary Brown Parlee (1973), in an early extensive review of studies that look for links between women's hormones and mood during the menstrual cycle, in fact failed to find a correspondence between individual differences in women's hormone levels and differences in their emotional states. In a similar vein, P. N. Nott and his colleagues (1976) found no systematic connections between women's pre- and postbirth hormone levels and their moods in early parenthood.

We feel that dismissing pregnant women's mood changes as attributable to "hormones" does them a disservice. Though not focused on pregnancy, findings in new studies by psychologists and endocrinologists suggest that we would do better in trying to understand pregnant women's emotional experiences by looking at the interaction between physiological and psychological reactions. For example, Jason Dura and Janice Kiecolt-Glazer (1991) have shown that during a stressful major life transition like divorce, hormone levels are altered and the immune system functions less effectively, with the result that divorcing and newly divorced women have an increased chance of becoming physically ill. Dura and Kiecolt-Glazer believe that these effects are circular: Psychological stress affects biological functioning, and biological disruptions increase psychological stress.

Most of the third-trimester women we spoke to (about three in five) said they had been worried about the viability of the fetus in the early stages of pregnancy. Understandably, these fears are especially strong in women who have had a miscarriage, who tend to resist becoming involved in the pregnancy until they are well beyond the time when miscarriage occurred in the earlier pregnancy.

By the second trimester, feeling the baby kick and move calms some of the fears, makes the baby seem more real, and leaves both parents feeling excited. During the third trimester, with the fetus's increased size and movement, women's focus shifts (or shifts back) to concerns about whether the baby will be healthy when it is born. Peggy worried about whether her baby would be normal and, if not, how she and Bill would deal with a retarded or deformed child. Some women are particularly haunted by movies and books featuring a child with a birth defect or a life-threatening illness; those images stay with them for a long time.

Another source of anxiety for pregnant women lies in worrying whether they will be good enough mothers. About one-third of the women in our study expressed such concerns. A few worried consciously or unconsciously about whether they would love their child as much as they feel parents ought to. One mother-to-be, Helen, said that her insecurity about being a parent came out while she was asleep: "I keep dreaming that I put the baby in a drawer and then forget about it."

In the late stages of pregnancy, most women report feeling less concern about the health implications of their weight gain (a big early worry) and less bothered by their lack of interest in sex. Their new concerns center on how they will cope with labor and delivery. Despite all the information from childbirth classes, it is not uncommon for a woman to become preoccupied briefly with the thought that she will not know what to do when the time comes: Will I know if my water breaks? What if I'm at work when I go into labor? How will I know when it's time to go to the hospital?

One of our most important discoveries was that couples who grapple with their concerns and the issues behind them seem to do better than those who ignore or deny their uneasy feelings. Whether the pregnancy is unexpected or money is a problem or there is general nervousness about the major change to come, some anxiety during pregnancy can be adaptive (Leifer

1980; Grossman et al. 1980). Husbands and wives who feel no trepidation about bringing a baby home may be in for quite a jolt.*

Beth, the quiet dreamer, and Sonia, who never let the pregnancy interfere with her active life, had some concerns about themselves, the baby, and their family. At the same time, like most expectant mothers (Feldman and Nash 1984; Leifer 1980; Grossman et al. 1980), they felt very positive about their lives and optimistic about the future. Even Peggy took care to set the record straight, emphasizing to us that despite her complaints she was sure it would be worth all the trouble.

MEN'S MOODS AND CONCERNS

About fifty years ago, psychoanalysts became interested in men's inner life during their wives' pregnancy. They focused on emotions at the extremes: depressive reactions, psychosis, mental illness (Zilboorg 1931; Towne and Afterman 1955; Wainwright 1966). As investigators became more systematic and turned to samples of men who were not patients, the picture of men's adaptation to pregnancy brightened (Benedek 1959, 1970; H. Osofsky 1982; Osofsky and Osofsky 1984; Parens 1975). But we still know little about men's emotional experience over the course of the pregnancy. Our impression from our interviews is that a majority of expectant fathers feel that they are doing very well. Some point to positive changes in themselves. Doug told us he seemed to have "mellowed out a little bit. I don't get quite as angry. I give up on my little annoyances a lot faster than I used to—and I think that Josie will vouch for me there." On the other hand, most men acknowledge worries about having the major responsibility of making enough money to support their families—especially during the period when their wives will not be bringing home a salary.

Al is twenty-nine and has been married for two years to Helen, twenty-three. Each of them had chosen to work part-time at a succession of jobs so that they would be free to pick up and travel at a moment's notice. This plan worked well for them until Helen became pregnant, which was an unexpected pleasure. After recounting with some nostalgia their footloose life before the pregnancy, Al becomes serious and determined as he explains: "I need to get my act together here. I've been goofing around with any old job, so that *I* can take time off when I want to and *we* can be spontaneous with

---

*Irving Janis (1958) conducted an intriguing study of patients who were about to undergo surgery in order to understand what people do with their concerns and fears when they are about to experience a stressful event. He found that men and women who "do the work of worrying" before they face the stress of hospitalization actually cope better and have smoother recoveries than people who experience no concerns before the event. This, of course, is one of the notions behind the couples group intervention in our study. By creating a setting in which we can encourage men and women to anticipate how they will handle some of the inevitable stress of having a newborn—at the same time trying to stay in touch as a couple—we hope to help them do some of the work of worrying before the inevitable 3:00 A.M. cries wake them to discover that they have totally different ideas about how to respond.

our travel plans. But now I've got to find something solid and steady. I hope it's not too late."

Like the women, some men worry about being adequate parents. Sometimes their fantasies extend their worries many years into the future:

AL: There's going to be this other person coming into my life. And things are going to have to change. At first I felt resentment about that. I took a while to sort it out. Today we met the doctor who will be our child's pediatrician, and we were filling out forms at her office. I felt a jolt when I had to fill in the line that said, "Father's name." I had all these visions about report cards and parental problems and permission forms and all these things—and *I'm* going to be the one signing where it says "Father"!

About 15 percent of the men in our study expressed deep concern during their wives' pregnancies. Paul stressed how vulnerable he and Beth felt. Once the pregnancy was under way, there was nothing more they could do: "It's all out of our control." Andy, discussed in chapter 2, had more specific anxieties:

ANDY: I went through about three months of heavy-duty worrying. I think about two issues: One is the responsibility issue, since Alice won't be working while the baby is young; the other is more of a selfish thing. Things are hitting me deeply. I keep thinking, "I'm a dying creature." Ideas about my own dying have really taken hold.

Recall that Andy and Alice had strong disagreements about whether to continue the pregnancy, which perhaps magnified his brooding about mortality and the darker side of life.

The men in our study were more worried than their wives about certain issues, especially about their wives' aches and pains. In our pregnancy interviews, few men broached their concern about the temptation to be unfaithful. We learned later that several had succumbed.* Both husbands and wives are concerned about the intactness and well-being of the baby during pregnancy, but wives are more concerned about the emotional climate of the family and their adequacy as mothers while husbands more often worry about the economic security of the family. The difference in their concerns is not usually what provokes tension for the couple during pregnancy; rather, it is

*In three of the seventy-two couples in our study who were having a baby, the husband had an extramarital affair. In one case, the wife discovered the other relationship early on, discussed it extensively with her husband, and the marriage continued. In the second case, the wife discovered in the first year of their baby's life that her husband had been having an extended affair. They separated and then divorced before the baby was two. A third couple reported that they had agreed to an "open relationship" in which both of them were free to have other sexual partners. This couple stayed together for some years, but were divorced by the time their child entered kindergarten.

the fact that husbands are much less willing than their wives to talk about what worries either of them.

Men are especially reluctant to raise a topic they think may lead to conflict or distress—their own, their wives', or both (Ball 1984; Gottman and Levenson 1989). Although men admitted having worries once they became comfortable talking to us, their wives said that their husbands rarely talked about these concerns to them spontaneously. When we asked Bill and Peggy what "pictures" they had of labor and delivery, for example, it went like this:

> BILL: I'll be there, of course, and it'll be fine. Well, actually, I'm concerned that when Peggy really gets into her pain, I'll find that it's worse than I can handle. And I have this big fear that I'm going to be grossed out by the physicalness of it. I wonder if men ever faint in the delivery room?
>
> PEGGY: Bill, you're so gung-ho in our Lamaze class, I had no idea that you were feeling that way. How come you didn't tell me?

Most of the men we talked to seemed to think there are "rules" for men in relationships with women. Especially when their partners are anxious, men feel that their task is to be calm, strong, and reassuring. Mentioning their own worries, they believe, will increase their wives' distress and reveal themselves as vulnerable at a time when their wives need them to be strong. Men's reluctance to talk about their worries and their motivation to stay calm at all costs create two problems: First, they deprive men of a chance to express their feelings and to learn from others that their fears are understandable and often experienced by others; and second, they prevent women from discovering that their worries are understood and shared by their mates.

Finally, when men keep their worries hidden, they stop talking to their wives about many of the things that matter to them. If one partner does raise a concern, and the other reacts immediately with a denial, a defense, or a more pressing concern of his own, many topics of conversation go undiscussed because they are not considered serious problems. The cost of protecting against upset can be silence or safe, but dull, conversations (Wile 1988). Occasionally, though, even the most vigilant attempts to keep things on an even keel give way to outbursts that are surprising in their intensity. Thus men's attempts to protect their wives—and themselves—from emotions that might stir things up can contribute instead to increased tension and distance, both within and between the partners:

> PEGGY: Bill and I got into a battle about having my mother come when the baby is born. I started to worry about where the baby would sleep when my mother and sister come, but I didn't want to raise it because I know how Bill feels about my mother. Then, one day, it was really on my mind so I mentioned it casually. Bill immediately began saying that it was silly to worry since the baby wasn't even born yet. Then he started suggesting that they should stay in a hotel in town. I got furious, more than

the situation warranted, I think. I was worried about the baby, but I didn't want my family to stay somewhere else. I assumed that I, or we, could eventually figure out an alternative. I just didn't want to bottle it up anymore. We both got really upset until I told him that I didn't want him to *solve* the problem, I just wanted him to let me *talk* to him about it.

BILL: I'm not very good at that. As soon as Peg gets upset, I go into action to try to make her feel better, and she always ends up shouting at me! She never gives me credit for the fact that I am only trying to help.

Not surprisingly, the couples who fare best during these emotional forays are those who can listen sympathetically to each other, without thinking they must talk the other out of his or her worry or come up with a solution immediately.

SEXUALITY

The physical and emotional changes that take place during pregnancy can have a direct effect on a couple's feelings of intimacy. The woman's (and, in minor ways, sometimes the man's) body is undergoing radical changes in size, shape, and maneuverability. "Leftovers" from the way couples decided about whether and when to have a baby inevitably color their perceptions and feelings about themselves and each other. And changes in a couple's sex life can become problematic when one or both partners feel that they cannot discuss them.

Expectant mothers, even those who suffer from physical symptoms, often describe a sense of awe and power in discovering what their bodies can do.

SONIA: I feel a little unattractive and lumpy right now. But, when I'm by myself, I find what's happening to my body fascinating.

BETH: I'm surprised to find what a miracle bodies are. I'm blown away about what's going on and about how it all works. I just can't get over it.

Approximately 25 percent of the pregnant women in our study said that they felt uneasy about their appearance: "awkward," "bloated," "like a blimp." The physical changes of pregnancy and their consequences for how women look and move may be the stuff of cartoons and comedies, but to women they are not amusing. A few, like Peggy, find their swelling bodies deeply disturbing:

PEGGY: I feel fat, ugly, and gross. My self-concept changes from mood to mood. I don't feel good about myself physically and I don't want anyone to look at me—even Bill most of the time. I am more introverted for physical reasons. I still want to talk to people and be part of things, but I really don't want to be seen.

Most of the husbands were supportive, and some were truly proud, of the changes in their wives' bodies as the pregnancy progressed. They were pleased by what they saw and by what their wives' full bodies signified. Eduardo watches his wife maneuver gracefully into a chair during our interview. "The great painters," he says, "tried to show the beauty of a pregnant woman, but when I look at Sonia, I feel they didn't do it justice." Occasionally, though, a husband made a sharp comment about his wife's weight gain. Since, especially in recent decades, women and men have been conditioned to regard thin women as pleasing and desirable, the lumbering expectant mother, and sometimes her partner, may find that her swelling body takes some getting used to. A critical father-to-be can make his pregnant wife very uneasy about her changing shape and size. This is one of those sensitive issues that couples don't talk much about, but their uncomfortable feelings can permeate the atmosphere between them and turn off one or both spouses sexually.

As they look back on it from the sixth or seventh month of pregnancy, couples tend to report a loss of sexual interest and activity during the first three months of pregnancy, an increase in interest in the middle three months, and another, greater loss of interest and activity as they enter the home stretch. They give several reasons for the slow down, or stopping altogether, of their sexual activity. The woman's general physical discomfort and fatigue are mentioned most often, followed by pain or feelings of physical awkwardness. Some men and women are fearful of hurting the baby or stimulating contractions. Men, more than women, feel some psychological inhibitions about physical intimacy with their pregnant wives; some say they "just don't feel like it" or that making love seems awkward "now that she's a mother."

Spouses' feelings about shifts in their relationship before and during pregnancy affect their sex life more often than changes in their sex life affect their relationship. We can hear in the tone of Peggy's and Bill's remarks that they are having a difficult time with the pregnancy and with each other. Their ambivalence about becoming pregnant may be contributing to their sexual difficulties now:

PEGGY: After a long time discussing it, going back and forth, we had been trying to get pregnant for about a year. We had a lot of false alarms. And every month we had to "re-choose." Were we still going to do it? Should we change our minds? It was hell.

BILL: So, the last time, we "unchose." We said no. And then it showed up. Peggy was pregnant, and it was very scary for me. I thought, "Oh my God, I don't know if this is exactly what I had in mind."

PEGGY: Now, the embarrassing part—I'm not sure I want to say this, but it's important. Terrible, but important. Sexuality simply dropped out. The first few months I was *so* nauseous and so tired that I couldn't be bothered. I was probably so nasty that Bill wasn't even interested. My breasts hurt. I was uncomfortable. Sleeping in the same bed with Bill was just horrible. And after that I was embarrassed—about how I looked and how I was shaped.

Now I'm not so embarrassed, but it's not the same. I've had this zillion-year legacy: Mom's aren't sexual, and now I'm a mom, so I'm not supposed to be interested in sex. I have fears that it's going to be like that forever. I'm never going to be a sexual being again, which is a little terrifying, I must say.

BILL: I'm embarrassed too, but I do want to talk about it. We've had a few nice times in bed in the last six or seven months, but only a few. I mean, it's so many things. First, we just couldn't do it after we found out she was pregnant. I think it was the unchoosing part, and the shock. Then I was withdrawn, out the door to work early every morning and staying late at the end of the day. My business has really been in a mess. In the last month or two, as we've gotten used to it, I really feel that there's nothing in the way. And yet, we don't do it. I'm walking around with the idea that many couples have a great sex life in pregnancy, but maybe I'm just making it up.

Very few of the couples spontaneously told us that they were having serious difficulties in their sexual relationships during pregnancy. Many others were probably experiencing sexual problems but did not want to mention it. Significantly, among the couples who did discuss lack of sex, the men were more unhappy about their work than were other men in the study, and the women had the most negative images of their bodies in late pregnancy.

It seems to us that it is often their perception of awkwardness rather than actual physical pain or discomfort that leads to much of the diminished lovemaking in the last months of pregnancy. We hear repeatedly how embarrassing it is for most partners to talk about what they long for, what they worry about, and what they experience in this intimate aspect of their relationship.

We have learned that most couples seem to have an either/or view of sex in pregnancy: Either they are making love as they did before the pregnancy began, or they are abstaining altogether. Many couples were having difficulty finding ways to touch, snuggle, or please each other without necessarily engaging in intercourse. Both men and women told us that they hesitated to make affectionate overtures if they were not sure they were ready to progress to intercourse. The reasoning goes something like this: "If he responds positively to my hug, and reads it as an invitation to make love, I'm afraid that I may not be ready to be aroused. He could see my pulling back as rejection, so it's probably safer for me not to begin in the first place." It is very common for partners to be out of sync in this way, but the problem is intensified because almost none of them feel they can talk about it.

And if they cannot talk about these ambivalent or uncomfortable feelings, they risk moving physically and psychologically farther apart at a time when mutual nurturance and support are especially needed. The couples who do find ways to stay in touch, physically and emotionally, seem much more relaxed about their relationship in the late months of pregnancy, but they are clearly in the minority.

UNSHARED EXPECTATIONS

Couples tell us that they spend a great deal of time before they become pregnant discussing their expectations about how life with a child will be, but a surprisingly large number seem to avoid the topic altogether as their due dates draw closer. Some, like Bill and Peggy, can give detailed fantasies about how they think labor and delivery will go, but when we ask if they have pictured the time when they will first bring the baby home, more than half of the couples look at us blankly.

After the birth of the baby, many partners are surprised to find that they differ on some of their basic ideas about the early phases of family life. Joan and Rob described in one of our couples groups the events around the birth of their son, Chuckie, as he lay quietly in a car seat in front of them:

JOAN: I had this picture. We would come home from the hospital, and my mom would be there and Dan and Ellen, our neighbors, and my sister Miriam. So, Chuckie's just been born and it's gone really well. I didn't have any anesthetic. I'm tired but wide awake. And Rob is going off to make some of the first phone calls. And I suggest that he invite everybody over. When I told him about what I had pictured that's when we had our first after-baby blowup.

ROB: It still gets me mad just to think of it. All I wanted was to get Joan out of the hospital with all the nurses and orderlies and noise, and bring Chuckie into our bedroom and quietly welcome him home—just our new little family together. And I find out that Joan wants the whole world to be there when we arrive!

It seems not to have occurred to Joan and Rob that they might have discussed their pictures of what would happen after the baby was born *before* Joan went into labor. By encouraging spouses in the couples groups to explore some of these before and after pictures, we wanted to help them anticipate some of the tricky issues that catch most new parents off guard: Should we invite our parents to visit right after the baby is born? Do you pick up a baby whenever she cries, or let her cry for a while if she is fed and dry? What happens if one of us changes our feelings about when the new mother will go back to work? How will we make time for our relationship after the baby is born? Even the most compatible spouses can turn out to have diametrically opposed inclinations on these issues. Since they will be particularly difficult to resolve over the wail of a fussy infant at the end of a busy day, a few tranquil conversations before the baby comes home would be invaluable.

One sign of the successful transition between before and after, we found, is in the connection between how a couple works together to manage the household and prepare for the baby and the level of intimacy they are able to establish in their relationship.

> PAUL: The pregnancy has been such a moving experience for me. I feel really committed to Beth and to being a parent with her.
>
> BETH: Certain things that have been issues between us, like sex, have somehow gotten tabled. But I feel a lot of closeness, especially since we started working on the baby's room. And some feelings—like, "Oh my God, if we don't work this out tonight it'll be the end of the world"— seem to be a thing of the past.
>
> PAUL: For me it doesn't feel like our issues are taking a back seat, it feels like they're in perspective. It also seems like we've had to make some heavy decisions. Say about things like money. When we first got married we had separate checking accounts. And separate friends. As we draw closer to having this baby, there is some merging going on. And she's been willing to say to me, "You know, money is not *your* problem. It's *our* problem." I feel like she made it really much easier for me.
>
> BETH: Household stuff, though, has always been pretty easy, but even that's going better. Paul is phenomenal about doing a lot around the house. I think it's been a little more balanced lately. He's been doing all the shopping, and some of the cooking, because I had zero energy, and if someone hadn't put food in front of me, I wouldn't have eaten.
>
> PAUL: And the two of us have spent days and days building shelves in the baby's room and getting all the things we need to have it ready.

Paul and Beth's pattern of doing more household tasks together as the pregnancy progresses may be common (Goldberg, Michaels, and Lamb 1985). As we will see in chapter 5, however, their more equal participation in the division of family labor does not tend to continue after the baby comes—and this, too, has implications for how the spouses feel about their overall relationship.

It may be easier to see the connection between intimacy and how household tasks are arranged and carried out by listening to a couple whose debate over who does what is heated. Sharon, whom we met while she was waiting for the results of her home pregnancy test, was worried about Daniel's willingness to do his part in preparing for the baby:

> SHARON: It's maddening. I asked him to paint the cupboards in the baby's room. He said he would do it, but weeks went by and nothing happened. I tried not to nag.
>
> DANIEL: Not successfully.
>
> SHARON: Well, I needed to know *if* you'd do it and *when* you'd do it. If you'd just been up front with me and said no, I'd have hired someone or done it myself.
>
> DANIEL: And been angry for a month.
>
> SHARON [*ignoring Daniel's last remark*]: So, one day I come home after

visiting my father, who's been sick, and Daniel's painted all the cup-
boards—purple! It doesn't go with anything in the room.

DANIEL: It's a bright color, one a baby would like. And I got it done two
months before the baby is due. I guess I just can't win with her.

This is not an unusual conversation between parents getting ready for the
baby's arrival. The sticking points arise not only around whether someone
will do something, but when and how it will get done. Each partner has a
different set of priorities, a different timetable, and a different picture of what
the end product should look like. The fact that both partners might also be
feeling some anxiety about becoming parents does not enter the discussion.
This means that it is unlikely that one spouse will think to say to the other,
"You know, I didn't mean to fly off the handle about that. I guess I'm actually
a little nervous about just what it will be like when the baby comes. I don't
want our life together to change totally." Sharon and Daniel might have been
able to avoid their fight if they had taken the time to discuss their explicit
expectations or pictures about painting the baby's room before Daniel
bought the paint. As reasonable as it seems, this kind of discussion is
apparently rare.

DEPENDENCE, INDEPENDENCE, AND INTERDEPENDENCE

In dealing with their emotions, their sexual relationships, their expectations,
and the nitty-gritty of who does the work of preparing for the baby, couples
are grappling with the issues of staying in touch with each other while
sometimes being pulled in different directions. Paul and Beth's description of
their increasing closeness during pregnancy is echoed by more than half of
our sample. As Al put it, "I no longer think of myself as just me, but as us."
Although many partners enjoy this increased sense of closeness, some are
worried about the accompanying feelings of greater dependency. Al's wife,
Helen, admits that "we depend on each other almost totally. I wonder if it's
good. Our friends don't do this." When she mentions the possibility of ever
losing Al, she begins to cry.

Although the partners may not recognize it, a pregnancy highlights a
challenge that is central to any couple relationship: how to balance both
partners' individuality or autonomy *and* enough mutuality or "coupleness"
to satisfy both of them. Most couples work on this balance throughout their
married lives, but pregnancy brings it into bold relief. Both partners are
about to add a major new role to their identities as adults, taking a step
forward in their individual lives and in their life as a couple. At the same time,
the arrival of the baby demands some collaborative work toward the mutual
goal of how to nurture a child and create a family.

Many expectant parents struggle with this conflict as though they had to
choose between individuality and coupleness. Because this struggle is mostly
unconscious, new parents rarely discuss the possibility that more interdependence—some dependence on each other and some independence for each

spouse—may make it possible for them to feel secure as individuals and as a couple during the family-making period.

Making, Changing, and Breaking Connections Across the Generations

Pregnancy galvanizes virtually every expectant parent to make connections with their own parents and their in-laws. Regardless of the quality of relationships between the generations, the couple's parents are usually the first to be told about the pregnancy. By the time the receivers are put down, the impending grandchild has begun to alter the relationships among the three families. The news is often received with delight and excitement, but their parents' reactions do not always match what the expectant couple had been hoping for. Joan told us that her mother was thrilled—she rushed right out that day and bought baby furniture. Joan and Rob wished she had consulted them about what kind of furniture they wanted, but they were touched by her reaction. James's mother reacted positively, too—at first: "But then she told Cindy she'd have to give up her work for fifteen years, followed by, 'You're messing up my son's life. Now he won't be able to continue his education.'"

The initial reactions of these expectant grandmothers have more to do with their own dreams than with their children's needs. In time, Joan would feel that she and Rob had to impress upon her mother their need to make the baby theirs. In this important phase, already-grown children must learn to differentiate from their parents once again. James's mother got past her negative reaction to the idea of her son becoming a father, and in fact made frequent visits to baby-sit for her new grandson, giving her son and daughter-in-law some time on their own.

Observing these generational dances as we ourselves approach this time of life has helped us to understand why becoming a grandparent can be a difficult adjustment. The timing is never under the grandparents' control, and it can catch them at a point where they are just beginning to experience a new freedom (Lowe 1991). Although many grandparents may be disequilibrated by the news, the initial shock is often followed by the pleasant realization that a new phase of their development is being ushered in (Tinsley and Parke 1988).

As the grandparent generation of the family begins to redefine their place in the extended family, the expectant parents often find that they are being treated differently by their parents and relatives:

JOAN: After we told my family, they suddenly began to include me in their discussions of the "family secrets." At Thanksgiving, we stayed at the "big table" after dinner, talking with my parents and aunts and uncles, while my sisters, who don't have children, went off with the little kids. I found out that Aunt Maude was married three times before she had a child with Uncle Harry, and all kinds of other things I had never known.

The pregnancy also stimulates the expectant parents' memories of their childhoods. They often relive both old joys and sorrows, resolving to recreate their early positive memories and to avoid a repetition of the painful experiences with their children.

It was the men in our study who talked most earnestly about doing things differently. The traditional families these couples grew up in seemed almost invariably to include a father who was away at work, and somewhat removed even when he was home. In interview after interview, almost every expectant father told us of his determination to have more of a presence with his sons and daughters than his father had with him. This is what men look forward to about having a baby, and it is what they worry about while they are waiting:

EDUARDO: My father left when I was twelve and I didn't see him for twenty-three years. That's not going to happen to my kid.

DOUG: My dad's always felt so distant. I still have trouble talking to him about anything that matters. My children are going to know me and be able to talk to me about whatever's on their minds. They're not going to have any doubt about how I feel about them.

Not all the fathers had been psychologically absent. Sometimes their positive presence figures influentially in their son's plans:

PAUL: My close relationship with my father is what saved my mental health growing up. Having a mother who was very ill meant that I had to really push myself to keep going some of the time. My dad's steady encouragement told me that I was an OK kid, even when I didn't feel that inside. I want to do that for my child.

While many expectant parents, in answer to our questions, can vividly describe their families' typical patterns, they continue to hope that their relationships with their parents and in-laws will change for the better. They seem to feel that having their baby will somehow set things right—they will feel closer as a couple, they will take on the care of their home and baby together, and their parents will be especially warm and nurturant—even if none of these things were so in their earlier years.

In our couples groups and our work with distressed couples, we try to capitalize on this tendency to dream of making things better, since it can lead to renewed attempts to connect the generations. While some couples are disappointed, especially if their initial overtures to their parents are not well received, those who do not give up often make some progress toward a better relationship.

Of course, renewing relationships with parents and in-laws does not always have positive consequences or leave room for optimism. We were moved by the intensity and sadness of Henry and Anna's experience. Henry is a Muslim from Jordan whose grandfather, on his deathbed, made Henry promise that he would never marry an "infidel." Henry moved to the United States, where he went to school, met Anna, an Italian-American woman, and married her. Henry's father, who also moved to the United States, was unhappy about Henry's marriage but did not sever contact with his son. After much urging on Henry's part, his father eventually agreed to meet Anna, with whom he maintained a distant but polite relationship.

Henry and his father had never gotten along well, even at the best of times, and the relationship continued to feel strained. Several years into the marriage, Henry told his father with some trepidation that he and Anna were expecting a child. Henry's father reacted by announcing that he would no longer see Anna. Henry felt that he had to make a choice between his father and his new family. Although there was no question that Anna and the baby came first, Henry's anguish at losing contact with his father is with him every day.

While Henry and Anna's experience with his family is extreme, it highlights a theme that is found among most new parents: Pregnancy tends to intensify already existing patterns in relationships with parents and extended family members. When the relationships are reasonably good, the pregnancy tends to bring the generations closer; when the relationships are troubled, old problems can resurface and feel more complex. If this is a family that busies itself with others' business, relatives may become involved in the pregnancy as if it were theirs. If one or both of the partners' families tend to keep their distance, the expectant parents may get little or no reaction to their news.

If the reaction is positive, the arrival of a grandchild does not magically mend the intergenerational rifts, but it often sets in motion new attempts at understanding and reconciliations across the generations. Naomi Lowinsky (1990, 1992) writes about daughters' efforts to connect with their mothers or grandmothers through the stories from their "motherline"—the generations of women who carry within them the history and biology of a family. If these attempts at reconnection are successful, the grandchildren can become the beneficiaries of strong generational ties. If not, as in the case of Henry and Anna, a legacy of sadness may leave its mark on the early family-making years.

Even successfully renewed relationships between the generations during pregnancy can pose new dilemmas for expectant couples. Already dealing with many new feelings within and between them, they may confront different issues in relating to their parents. One partner may want more closeness and contact with the parents while the other can't get far enough away. Cindy didn't want to go anywhere near James's mother after the remark about his education. When she invited them to dinner the next week, James felt they would hurt her feelings if they turned her down. They went, but Cindy wished James "had the guts to tell her off."

Partners' capacity to empathize with each other's generational dilemmas may become limited as they make the transition from couple to family. Efforts to reconnect or redefine their relationships with their parents and in-laws can create one more arena in which their differences trigger conflict or withdrawal.

Changing Relationships with the World Outside the Family

Pregnancy also has an impact on the relationships with important people and institutions outside the inner family circle. Well-meaning people who would not ordinarily approach a stranger on the street suddenly feel free to pat the protruding belly of a pregnant woman and tell their own stories or offer unsolicited advice about pregnancy and babies. This is a peculiar ritual that intrudes on the privacy of the expectant parents, at the same time drawing them into the larger world of families with children. Once they announce that they are going to be fathers, men also find that neighbors and co-workers they hardly know want to share stories about their experiences with babies and children.

Expectant parents begin to notice that they experience the world around them in new ways. In our interview, Sonia mentioned her new preoccupation with violence—"the random killings and so many missing children on posters and milk cartons."

Both men and women change their relationship to work in ways that are both expected and unexpected. We have already heard about Al's determination to get his work life on track. With similar reasoning, about 10 percent of the men we spoke to changed jobs over the nine months of their wives' pregnancies, and a number of others began planning for changes they would make as their babies grew into toddlers. The expectant fathers who were not changing direction seemed to be rededicating themselves to their work. Even though virtually all of them saw their job changes as a direct response to increased responsibility for providing for their wives and children, their wives tended to see their husbands' investment in work as a form of withdrawal from them and from the family. The gulf between their perceptions only widens as women begin to disengage from their work in the end stages of the pregnancy.

All of the women we interviewed were employed or going to school when they began the pregnancy, and a majority continued to work into the ninth month. But, unlike the men, every one of them planned to take some time off after the baby was born, for periods ranging from weeks to years. So, just as they are moving back into the family to do more of the hands-on care of the baby, their husbands are getting more involved in their work. Although many women formulate their plans voluntarily, early in the pregnancy, some become concerned as the pregnancy ends about what will happen to their jobs or careers:

> ANNA: I used to think that all I wanted in life was four kids and a good vacuum cleaner. But I take my career seriously. I'm an accountant in a busy practice, and I don't know whether my clients are going to wait for me while I get settled. I'm not sure how I'm going to look after my clients, my child, and me at the same time.

In addition to different changes in their work patterns, to the surprise of the couples in our study, their relationships with friends who are not pregnant begin to shift. Couples find themselves spending much more time with recent acquaintances who are expecting babies or who have young children than with old friends who are not parents or parents-to-be. Men, and especially women, described shifts in their engagement with and disengagement from people outside the family. As women withdraw from their jobs and co-workers, their opportunities for talking with adults who may be important sources of esteem and support are reduced. Theoretically, expectant mothers who have left work have more time to visit friends, but there is so much to do in late pregnancy that women are usually too tired. Staying close to home keeps them socially and emotionally isolated.

What we are seeing, then, is an accumulation of changes in the network of relationships that expectant parents have established with their families, their co-workers, and their friends. In essence, women who are expecting a baby come to rely on their husbands for much of their adult company and support. If husbands' social contacts are also reduced, then both partners may feel more dependent on each other for companionship and emotional nurturance. If, in addition, wives begin to feel deprived by their husbands' involvement in work and husbands begin to feel hemmed in by their wives' dependency, the last trimester of pregnancy can draw partners apart emotionally rather than pulling them together to meet the challenges of a new baby.

Pregnancy as an Opportunity for Development

As expectant parents begin to integrate Father or Mother into their identities as men and women, partners and lovers, workers and students, sons and daughters, and so on, they are faced with significant shifts in their relationships to their work, their parents, their friends, and each other. At the same time, both partners are becoming preoccupied with their emerging relationships with the baby. While all this is taking place internally and interpersonally, most expectant parents are also dealing with the medical establishment, which is focusing microscopically on physical changes in the woman's body. They are on their own in managing the psychological shifts that pregnancy stimulates in them as individuals and as a couple. Our recent work is teaching us that this presents quite a challenge, even to men and women in very well functioning relationships.

Despite the inherent difficulties, the kind of disequilibrium that often accompanies this major adult transition can serve as an opportunity for personal development for both men and women. Certainly, for some, expecting a baby can evoke painful memories of difficult or neglectful relationships with their parents when they were babies or young children. For others, the reawakening of conflicts from the past leads partners to begin to work on some of their unresolved conflicts, either on their own or with professional help. In our interviews with each couple over a seven-year period, we heard many examples of new fathers and mothers who felt a new sense of confidence and maturity, often from having successfully tackled the challenges of a very stressful period. Sonia told us she felt more confident about her artistic abilities since she'd become pregnant: "Two months ago I enrolled in an art class, and I'm preparing to have a show of my drawings after the baby comes—something I've always wanted but have been too timid to arrange. I may put some of my poetry in it too. It feels like there's been a transition in me, and somehow I'm beginning to feel like I know what I'm all about."

Her husband, Eduardo, explained that after many years of thinking about his father with bitterness (he deserted the family when Eduardo was a boy), he feels his attitude changing: "Something about the prospect of being a father myself is having this strange effect on me. I haven't forgiven him, exactly, because I don't think that what he did was forgivable. But I'm kind of letting it go now. I'm going to be different with my kid. Maybe I can get on with things without constantly comparing myself to what I remember of my father."

According to Erik Erikson's theory of development (1950, 1959), we experience shifts in our sense of ourselves as we move through life and bump up against each major transition. Even if the change is one we choose and prepare for, it can throw us off balance. We can find that our usual style of coping is not adequate to meet the demands of this new stage of life, and that we do not know how to change or add to our repertoire of coping skills.

Erikson's theory suggests that active grappling with the pain and self-doubt of personal crises is necessary if real development and growth are to occur. If we cannot acknowledge our feelings of uncertainty or anxiety or distress, we are in danger of becoming stalled or fixated at our present stage of development, or in some cases of slipping back to an earlier level of functioning.

Preparing for the Birth

We may need to be reminded about the source of all this excitement, anxiety, and upheaval: A baby is about to be born. Two sets of professionals are involved in helping couples get ready for the big day: Obstetricians and family doctors monitor women's pregnancies in regular checkups, and childbirth educators offer classes for both partners to help them become more active participants in the birth process. Based on what the couples in our study have been telling us, we are concerned that both doctors and childbirth educators are leaving important things out of the preparation package.

During the months of pregnancy, as we have seen, most expectant parents spend relatively little time focusing on physical symptoms and much more time dealing with psychological changes in themselves and in their relationships. Although there are some welcome exceptions, few obstetricians and family practitioners are attuned to these issues in the women they see. Virtually none of them provides opportunities for expectant fathers to discuss their concerns, or for couples to talk about marital issues raised in the course of the pregnancy.*

There is, then, a mismatch between the medical focus of the doctors and the central concerns of their patients. A number of British sociologists, Ann Oakley foremost among them (1980, 1986), have questioned why the medical profession has been allowed to exert so much control over pregnancy and childbirth since it tends to ignore the central psychological issues. This view has led some families to rely on midwives rather than doctors. We would be reluctant to give up all of the hard-won medical advances, especially in complicated pregnancies and deliveries. But we worry that current medical practice fosters the tendency to separate the concerns of women from the concerns of men, thereby contributing to men's and women's separation from each other, a separation that grows wider, as we will see, during the early child-rearing years.

In addition to doctors' visits, an increasingly large number of couples today take part in some kind of formal childbirth preparation.† Nevertheless, many feel surprised by their experience of the delivery. In one couples group, a mother practically shouted, "Why didn't they tell us how painful it would be? That woman we saw in the Lamaze film was *smiling* through it all!"

Time and again the women we spoke to explained that the instructors in their childbirth classes were so intent on convincing them that they could control their pain during labor and delivery that those who, during the event, accepted medication felt they had let down their classmates, their teacher, and themselves. In the excruciating pain of a long or difficult labor, their husbands and doctors may have urged them to ease their suffering, but many of them felt that in succumbing to it they had "failed" at childbirth. As Terrie said, "I keep feeling that if I had just been able to hang in there a little longer, I could have made it without any drugs. Carrie was so sleepy for the first day

---

*Of the obstetrical and clinical offices we worked with in the study, only one had a family-focused preventive orientation. The two obstetricians, the nurse practitioners, and the nutritionist offered a series of evening meetings for expectant couples and time to meet with fathers during regular office hours.

†Between 50 percent and 80 percent of pregnant women in the United States now attend childbirth preparation classes, a major historical shift that has taken place in just one generation (Duncan and Markman 1988).

or so—I can't help thinking that she might have been livelier and easier to nurse if I hadn't had any medication."

The intent of childbirth preparation classes is to demedicalize and humanize the process of giving birth, and it is a welcome and successful change. But as we talked with parents, it became clear that something is missing from these classes. In their efforts to be encouraging and reassuring, instructors tend to cut off discussion of the fears and concerns that every parent-to-be experiences. Women want to know that it will hurt—a lot!—and that drugs may be of great help. Men want to talk about the possibility of suddenly feeling unable to accompany their wives into the delivery room, or of feeling faint when the birth gets under way. Providing psychological support, including recommending that obviously troubled couples seek professional help, may be one of the most effective ways for an instructor to lower men's and women's anxiety and to reduce the incidence of medical complications during labor and delivery (Grossman et al. 1980; Markman and Kadushin 1986; Nuckolls, Cassell, and Kaplan 1972).

In addition, the heavy emphasis on natural childbirth obscures the fact that, for various and controversial reasons, more than 20 percent of deliveries will be performed by cesarean section (Alexander and Entwisle 1988). The almost exclusive focus in childbirth classes on vaginal delivery means that one in five couples will be ill prepared for the physical and emotional shock of undergoing major surgery to deliver their baby.

Despite all the confusion and increased choice—hospital delivery? midwife? home birth?—couples who successfully deliver a child experience a feeling unlike any other they have known. In the new tradition of fathers' participation in the birth of their babies, Jackson helped deliver his son and talked to us of how it made him feel:

JACKSON: I couldn't have imagined the incredibly powerful feelings that engulfed me when I saw Kevin slip out of Tanya. I was right there, and this was my son! All the next day whenever he began to cry or nurse, I was in tears. I'm still transfixed watching him. It's the most amazing experience I've ever had.

His wife, Tanya, adds her view:

TANYA: It was a shattering experience. I was huffing and puffing, crying and pushing, and suddenly his head emerged. Then, slowly, out came the rest of him in one long, unbearably painful, wonderful surge. After all of the wait and the worry and the wondering, our son had finally arrived. Later in my hospital room, I remember Kevin in my arms and Jackson holding me with one hand and Kevin with the other. It was magical. Our family!

Moments like these are the end of the nine long months of waiting. But in the journey to becoming a family, they are only the beginning.

PART II

Crossing the
Great Divide

CHAPTER 4

What's Happening to Me?

A S THEY BRING THEIR FIRST BABY home from the hospital, new mothers and fathers find themselves crossing the great divide. After months of anticipation, their transition from couple to family becomes a reality. Entering this new and unfamiliar family territory, men and women find themselves on different timetables and different trails of a journey they envisioned completing together. We set the stage for the changes they describe by recounting briefly how they see their lives when their babies are six months and eighteen months old. Then, in this and the next four chapters, we describe changes in each of the five domains in our model of family life.

We begin here with a focus on the view from the inside, as men and women experience the shifting sense of self that comes with first-time parenthood. Using a simple pie chart and a long list of adjectives to describe themselves during pregnancy, and again when their children are infants and toddlers, the couples in our study help us to understand both change and continuity as they settle into family territory. In the next chapter, we show how new mothers' and fathers' shifting sense of self plays out in the day-to-day realities of caring for a baby while trying to maintain their relationships as couples.

After many years of being parents ourselves, and more than fifteen years of working with couples becoming parents for the first time, we understand the impossibility of being fully prepared for parenthood—for the initial feelings of awe at having produced this fragile being, for the constant frantic state during the first months of never-ending feedings, for the maddening regularity of interrupted sleep. For most parents, both those whose labor and delivery went smoothly and those who faced the rigors of cesarean section delivery, the euphoria immediately after birth is followed by weeks of feeling dazed and operating on "automatic pilot." Men and women who were used to anticipating and mastering the complexities of demanding jobs and intimate relationships are overwhelmed by their unexpected and contradictory feelings.

Meeting with couples in their homes when their babies were six months and then eighteen months old, we tended to be treated as members of the family. We were immediately presented with either the latest baby pictures or, usually, with the baby, not yet quite awake from his or her nap or sleepily on the way to bed.

We are sitting in the garden of a small brown-shingle house, talking to Doug and Josie. Doug, thirty-seven, worked for the state for many years, but he has recently opened his own business consulting with corporations on environmental issues. Josie, thirty-six, is uninterested in going back to her former job, and moderately content to stay at home with their son, Zack. At the six-month mark, the shock of becoming a parent has usually subsided:

> JOSIE: It's a good thing you didn't come two months ago. We were just about at our wit's end. There was nothing that we could follow through on. Everything was disjointed.
>
> DOUG: Before the baby came, we used to take a walk every evening. We tried to do it about two weeks after Zack was born, but it felt like we were packing for a month-long trip so we gave it up.
>
> JOSIE: Things started to feel better when Zack really became more of a little human being, when he could laugh and babble and you could play games with him. Now it seems like he's a real person, not just an infant lying there and crying and that's all. I really enjoy him. I think he's done wonders for me. He's calmed me down considerably.

From being helpless, totally unpredictable newborns, babies at six months have usually settled into some routines. Most sleep through the night, although that description is misleading because the period of quiet typically lasts from some time after midnight to only 4:00 or 5:00 A.M. The babies are generally still nursing from breast or bottle, and many have begun to eat solid food. Having developed definite "personalities," they have very specific likes and dislikes. There are things that they simply cannot be forced or enticed to do, no matter how hard the parents try.

Some sociologists refer to the six-month-postpartum point as part of the honeymoon period in the life of a new family. This description certainly fits Victor and Natalie, whom we last heard discussing the problem of running shorts on the bathroom floor and Victor's fondness of taking his daughter bicycling in the rain. "After a major adjustment during the first three months, the last three months have been very, very nice. Kim's a delight."

Most parents feel powerfully drawn to their six-month-old babies and love the peaceful times with them. They are relieved at having survived all of the planning and worrying during the pregnancy, and are beginning to experience a new sense of excitement and competence at having learned how to provide for an infant whose needs are continuous but whose ability to communicate about them is limited. At the same time, many couples are showing signs that the *marital* honeymoon is drawing to an end. Sharon, whom you may remember from chapter 1, was initially ambivalent about having a child but got excited by the results of her home pregnancy test. She was also worried that, despite her husband's assurances, there would not be enough collaboration on the home front. Her fears, it seems, are being realized:

> SHARON: We aren't able to pay much attention to each other, because Amy needs so much. She's great, don't get me wrong. But Daniel comes home from work cranky, I'm cranky because I haven't talked to anyone who says anything back to me, Amy's cranky because she wants to eat *right now,* and we don't have time to find out how each other's day went. So I'm making dinner for three cranky people. And as a consequence, we have not been as close as before she came. We're going through a transition and I'm sure it's going to work itself out. We've almost got it down, I think.

Mothers of six-month-olds sound as if they are emerging from a period of total immersion in their infants. In our sample, about 55 percent of the women are back at work, more of them part-time (36 percent) than full-time (19 percent). Fathers talk about their increased feelings of responsibility for their families, mostly in relation to being good providers. It is rare for the men to be centrally involved in the day-to-day tasks of caring for their infants. Many describe themselves as "baby-sitting" for their children while their wives prepare dinner or go out for an occasional evening or weekend morning. Some husbands refer to "helping" their wives by taking their turn getting up with the baby in the middle of the night. New mothers have mixed feelings, not knowing whether to feel grateful or resentful about their husbands' "help."

Men and women clearly have different experiences of being new parents. Especially for partners who managed their lives pretty equally before they became parents and expected that life after baby would retain this quality, the shift in the family balance can be surprising and unsettling.

When we pay our call a year later, when the children are eighteen months old, the scene has changed. A number of the couples have moved to different homes, usually for space, sometimes to live in neighborhoods more congenial to rearing young children. Toys and books are scattered about, mostly on top of parents' unread magazines, mail, and newspapers. Six-month-olds who had stayed put are now explorers on the move—toward light sockets, delicate vases, pets, toilet bowls, open doors, and, of course, our tape recorder. And most of them are talking! Parents who had been mystified because they didn't know what their infants' cries meant now hear incessant commands of "Want 'dat" with every attractive new object or "No!" in reaction to limits.

Our two strongest impressions at this stage are that the parents want us to see how their children have grown, and that some have difficulty putting them to bed. The bedtime routine seems particularly difficult for parents who are away at work for much of the children's waking time. Because their children must adhere to the parents' schedules all day, they try to avoid more conflict in the evening.

Besides, many couples are finding that they have different ideas about what toddlers need in order to feel that life is predictable and secure. Their discussions about how to get their toddler undressed or into bed are sometimes strained. For parents who have been working since the early morning hours, dealing with these differences can be the last straw, stretching the limits of their patience at the end of a wearing day. Some couples react by sweeping their differences under the carpet.

In response to our questions about their experiences of family life, parents sound as though they have climbed up one side of a huge mountain. Our interviews catch many of them at a plateau from which they try to take stock of how far they have come:

> JOSIE: The older Zack gets, the better it is, in terms of me feeling more like a person instead of just his mom. I'm nowhere near as selfish as I used to be. He's really taught me that it's possible to look after someone's needs first, and to feel OK about that. At moments when he's upset, I don't say, "Oh God, what have I done wrong?" I just say to myself, "OK, here we go again." I must have become more easygoing or something.

For parents like Josie, the view from the mountain is fairly peaceful and gratifying. For others whose ascent has been more strenuous, it sounds as if an avalanche could descend at any moment:

> SHARON: I went through this whole stage of feeling very trapped. It seemed like all my waking hours were spent on caring for Amy, caring for Daniel and thinking about him, caring for the house and thinking about the house. There was no time for myself, absolutely none. And I was just really feeling boxed in.

When their children are eighteen months old, 57 percent of the mothers are working outside the home, about the same proportion as a year ago. Now, the employed women are almost evenly divided between part-time (30 percent) and full-time (27 percent), the latter logging up to forty hours a week away from home. Fathers, all employed, work from thirty-two to eighty hours a week. They are not as involved in the daily chores at home as they and their wives expected them to be, but they have become more involved in the care of their children and more psychologically involved in the family than they had been a year before:

> DANIEL: Last year, when I came home from work, Sharon would just shove Amy at me so that she could get the dinner done. And that was hard. But now, Amy asks about me when I'm gone, and when I get in the door she runs to me and wants me to read her stories. We play together at night before she goes to bed, while Sharon is cleaning up.

The living environments and routines have altered drastically in one year. Parents now talk about who they are, who they are becoming, and the kind of partners and parents they are striving to be. Josie says her son's arrival has calmed her down and made her less selfish. Her husband, Doug, like many of the new fathers in our study, reports equally positive changes in his sense of himself:

> DOUG: Well, it's not that I look in the mirror every morning wondering who's looking back. It's still me. But I'm different since Zack was born. I'm more aggressive in recruiting new business for my consulting firm. I'm more organized at work and at home. But I'm also loosening up a little socially; I even enjoy a party every now and then—I hated them before. I'm enjoying being a father. I'd recommend it to anybody.

Josie and Doug seem delighted with some of the psychological shifts they are experiencing. Other new parents tell us that having a baby has brought them up against some less desirable parts of themselves. Recall Alice and Andy, who were having a difficult struggle deciding whether they could stay together after Alice became pregnant. Their daughter, Jessica, is now eighteen months old:

> ALICE: Some days I feel that my brain turned to mush on the day Jessica was born. I can't seem to keep to a decision. I get confused easily. I have a much harder time talking with people than I did before. I guess I'm not much fun to be with. Except with Jessica. When she's nursing, I'm transported to a different place. I feel so different now that I'm a mother.
>
> ANDY: I used to be real spontaneous. I could take unexpected things in my stride. Since I've become a father I don't feel as flexible or resilient as I was or as I want to be.

As they talked to us about both changes and continuities in their characteristic ways of dealing with the world, both men and women reported positive, negative, or mixed feelings about themselves as they moved closer to or farther from their ideal pictures.

Identity Changes: Parent, Worker/Student, Partner

In order to understand how parents integrate Mother or Father as a central component of their identity, we asked them to think about the various aspects of their lives (worker, friend, daughter, father, and so on), and to mark them off on a pie chart[1] based on how large each portion feels, not on how much time they spend "being it." During pregnancy, and again when their children were six months and eighteen months old, we also asked them to fill out a second pie indicating how they would like it to be divided among these important parts of themselves. The size of each pie piece, we thought, would reflect their psychological involvement or investment in that aspect of themselves. Their reactions to this graphic representation took some of the new parents by surprise.

Looking at the chart she had filled in before the baby was born, Joan said: "I see I drew this immense piece and labeled it Mom. I didn't realize that so much of me was already invested in being this pregnant woman about to be a mother. I hardly had enough space left for the other important parts." Indeed, about one-third of her pie was taken up with motherhood. Her husband, Rob, on the other hand, had not even included the role of father in his pie at that time. Were Rob and Joan to remain so out of sync after they had their baby, their ability to communicate effectively would be severely hampered.

People include a variety of aspects of themselves but almost all show pieces that represent parent, worker or student, and partner or lover. The most vivid identity changes during the transition to parenthood take place between pregnancy and six months postpartum. Neither men's nor women's drawings show much change between the time their children are six months and eighteen months old.[2] The part of the self that women call Mother takes up an average of 10 percent of their pictures of themselves in late pregnancy. It then leaps to 34 percent at six months after birth, and stays there through the second year of parenthood.

For some women, the psychological investment in motherhood is much greater than the average. At the six-month follow-up, for example, Peggy drew a wedge that filled almost three-quarters of her pie and called it "mother/child-care person." You may recall that Peggy had a difficult pregnancy, with uncomfortable physical symptoms all the way along. She felt badly about her body and about the high level of conflict with her husband, Bill. With her six-month-old daughter, Mindy, in her arms, Peggy's spirits now soar:

PEGGY: I can't believe how wonderful this is—how wonderful *she* is. I'm so glad I didn't plan on going back to work. I couldn't pull myself away. Even during the day when she's asleep, I keep coming into her room just to look at her. I feel like a whole different person. I'm not sick anymore. The breastfeeding is going well. If Bill and I could just get it together, things would be perfect.

Bill looks away in some embarrassment and distress. Then, almost as if he's talking to himself:

> BILL: You guys are sure close, all right. Sometimes I wonder if it's too close.
> PEGGY: Too close for what? Sometimes I wonder if you have any idea what being a parent is all about.

Although Bill's critical tone was unusual, he was typical of the husbands we interviewed, most of whom took on the identity of parent more slowly than their wives did. During pregnancy, Father takes half as much of men's pies as their wives' Mother sections do, and when their children are eighteen months old, husbands' identity as parent is still less than one-third as large as their wives'.

Investment in the identity of parent has different meanings for men and women. For example, midway through the child's first year, men with larger pieces of the pie allocated to parent had higher self-esteem as we measured it on the Adjective Check List (Gough and Heilbrun 1980). But women with larger investment in their parent identity tended to have lower self-esteem. What's going on here?

New mothers like Peggy with a great deal of investment in their parent self have very little room for anything else in their inner lives. They may have become highly involved in parenthood as a way of feeling better about themselves. The men with the largest parent pieces are not much more involved in that aspect of themselves than the average woman. It looks like new fathers who feel good about themselves are able to devote more energy to their parent identity without giving up other central aspects of their psychological lives. And what they get back from this relationship helps them to keep their self-esteem on a positive track.

Peggy and Bill are a couple with highly discrepant levels of psychological investment in parenthood. Their interaction suggests that this discrepancy is taking a toll on their relationship as a couple. When we examine the pies of all the couples this way, we find that the larger the difference between husbands and wives in the size of their parent piece of the pie when their babies are six months old, the less satisfied both spouses are with the quality of their marriage, and the more their satisfaction with marriage declines by the time their babies are eighteen months old.[3]

Once they have had a baby, men's and women's sense of themselves as parents is certainly expected to increase. What comes as a surprise is that other central aspects of the self are getting short shrift as their parent piece of the pie expands. In their sixth or seventh month of pregnancy, most women are still in school or working, although some report a declining interest in their jobs. On the average, women show that Worker or Student takes up 18 percent of who they are, probably lower than before they became pregnant. For expectant fathers, Worker claims an average of 28 percent of the pie at our first interview.

By the time their children are eighteen months old, the Mother aspect of women's identity is twice as large as the Worker/Student part. Even when women work full-time, their sense of self as Mother is more than 50 percent greater than their psychological investment in their identity as Worker. This sits in bold contrast to their husbands' experience. Despite men's increasing psychological investment as fathers, their Worker or Student aspect of self remains virtually unchanged. Even at its height, the Father aspect of men's sense of self is smaller than the Worker/Student part.

The greatest surprise for us and for the couples in the study is what gets squeezed as new parents' identities shift. Women apportion 34 percent to the Partner or Lover aspect of themselves in pregnancy, 22 percent at six months after birth, and 21 percent when their children are eighteen months old. Men's sense of themselves as Partner or Lover also shows a decline—from 35 percent to 30 percent to 25 percent over the two-year transition period.

The size of the Partner piece of the pie is connected with how new parents feel about themselves: A larger psychological investment in their relationship seems to be good for both of them. Six months after the birth of their first child, both men and women with larger Partner or Lover pieces have higher self-esteem and lower parenting stress. This could mean that when new parents resist the tendency to ignore their relationship as a couple, they feel better about themselves—or that when they feel better about themselves, they are more likely to stay at least moderately involved in their marriage.

At our eighteen-month follow-up, Stephanie and Art talk about the consequences for their marriage of trying to balance—within them and between them—the pulls among the Parent, Worker, and Partner aspects of themselves:

> STEPHANIE: We're managing Linda really well. But with Art's promotion from teacher to principal, and my going back to work and feeling guilty about being away from Linda, we don't get much time for us. I try to make time for the two of us at home but there's no point in making time to be with somebody if he doesn't want to be with you. Sometimes when we finally get everything done and Linda is asleep, I want to sit down and talk, but Art says this is a perfect opportunity to get some preparation done for one of his teachers' meetings. Or he starts to fix one of Linda's toys—things that apparently are more important to him than spending time with me.
>
> ART: That does happen. But Stephanie's wrong when she says that those things are more important to me than she is. The end of the day is just not my best time to start a deep conversation. I keep asking her to get a sitter so that we can go out for a quiet dinner, but she always finds a reason not to. It's like being turned down for a date week after week.
>
> STEPHANIE: Art, you know I'd love to go out with you. I just don't think we can leave Linda so often.

Stephanie and Art are looking at the problem from their separate vantage points. Art is very devoted to fatherhood, but is more psychologically invested in his relationship with Stephanie than with Linda. In his struggle to hold on to his sense of himself as Partner, he makes the reasonable request that he and Stephanie spend some time alone so that they can nurture their relationship as a couple. Stephanie struggles with other parts of her shifting sense of self. Although Art knows that Stephanie spends a great deal of time with Linda when she gets home from work, he does not understand that juggling her increasing involvement as Mother while trying to maintain her investment as Worker is creating a great deal of internal pressure for her. The Partner/Lover part of Stephanie is getting squeezed not only by time demands but also by the psychological reshuffling that is taking place inside her. Art knows only that Stephanie is not responding to his needs, and to him her behavior seems unreasonable, insensitive, and rejecting.

Stephanie knows that Art's view of himself has changed as he has become a parent, but she is unaware of the fact that it has not changed in the same way or to the same degree as hers. In fact, typical of the men in our study, Art's psychological investment in their relationship as a couple has declined slightly since Linda was born but his Worker identity has not changed much. He is proud and pleased to be a father, but these feelings are not crowding out his feelings about himself as a partner and lover. All Stephanie knows is that Art is repeatedly asking her to go out to dinner, and ignoring her inner turmoil. To her, his behavior toward her seems unreasonable, insensitive, and rejecting.

Connections Between Identity and Well-being

These internal changes in each of the new parents begin to have an impact on their relationship as a couple. Art adds Father to his identity but preserves the other central parts of himself. Stephanie adds Mother, a new and even larger part of her sense of self, but loses and then regains her sense of self as a Worker, which absorbs most of her psychological energy so that she has little available for the part of her that is a wife and partner to Art. These discrepancies between his and her shifting sense of self during this major adult transition create a climate in which their transition as a couple is moving through potentially hostile territory.

To put these changes in new parents in perspective, we can compare them with what happened to the childless couples in our study. Among those who were still childless and who stayed together (20 percent became parents; 16 percent divorced), the women showed a decline in their psychological involvement as a Partner, though it is 10 percent higher than that of mothers. There was, however, a large increase in their identity as Worker or Student. The men's identity as Partner and as Worker remained virtually the same over time, creating an even more equal balance between childless partners.

It might have been tempting to conclude that it is natural for psychological involvement in one's identity as a partner and lover to wane over time, had we not had the patterns of the childless men to refute such an assumption. The childless couples also helped us contrast the balance between spouses in these two groups of couples. The husband and wife who do not have a baby experience similar shifts as individuals, and their satisfaction with their relationship as a couple remains stable. In the couples who become parents, he and she begin diverging in terms of their individual changes and, as we will see more graphically in the next chapter, in terms of both their mutual roles and the intimate aspects of their marriage. The costs of making such different shifts appear to borne in the relationship between the spouses.

Let us be clear that remaining childless does not guarantee marital bliss. As we have seen, 16 percent of the couples not having a baby have become unhappy or discouraged enough to separate or file for divorce two years into the study. The couples who stayed together and did not have a baby during the same period appear to have had the option of expanding some of the existing parts of their identities and roles without having to cope with the stress of any major additions to their sense of self. Perhaps the most salient difference between the two groups of women is that the childless women seem to have room, if they choose, to expand their work and career identities while keeping a substantial portion of their psychological energy for their marriages. This is in contrast to what we have seen in the new parents; when women add Mother to their identity, *both* Worker and Partner or Lover get squeezed.

Although parents hope that they will have energy for the old aspects of their identity as they add the new one of Parent, their pie charts reflect the reality that as some parts get larger, there is less "room" for others. The challenge, then, is how to allow Parent a central place in one's identity without abandoning or neglecting Partner. The couples who manage to do this feel better about themselves and their lives.

Changes in Self-esteem

Filling in a pie chart lets men and women give us a global picture of how they are changing as they become parents. A more specific way they can communicate how they think and feel about themselves during this transition is by choosing from an Adjective Check List (Gough and Heilbrun 1980) those words they feel accurately describe them.* Selecting from three hundred adjectives, each man and woman filled out three checklists at each phase of

*Examples from the Adjective Check List: active, affectionate, aggressive, dependent, emotional, feminine, intelligent, logical, masculine, mature, nervous, preoccupied, sexy, shy, sociable, stubborn, trusting, zany.

It is reasonable to be skeptical about whether self-descriptions can provide accurate information about real-life behavior, but Gough and Heilbrun have found that the Adjective Check List scales correlate well with other personality tests and with direct observations of people's behavior in both laboratory and naturalistic settings.

the study: one describing "me as I am," a second for "me as I'd like to be," and a third describing "my partner."

Harrison Gough and Alfred Heilbrun constructed these personality scales to assess an individual's tendency to be dominant, aggressive, nurturant, self-confident, masculine, feminine, well-adjusted, and so on. Personality traits remained very stable over time for all of the men and women in our study. We used the discrepancy between each person's description of "me as I am" and "me as I'd like to be" to measure their self-esteem. We assumed, as have Gough and his colleagues (Gough, Fioravanti, and Lazzari 1982), that people who describe themselves very differently from their ideal picture of themselves tend to have low self-esteem: They describe themselves in negative terms, they have little self-confidence, and they have difficulty being active rather than passive in the face of threat and challenge.

We found that one's age seems to make a difference to self-esteem during the transition to parenthood. Remember that the women and men in our study ranged from twenty-one to forty-nine when they entered the study, with the average age of the expectant parents being twenty-nine for the women and thirty for the men. We find different patterns in what happens to men and women who are twenty-nine or younger and those who are thirty or older when they have a first baby. Younger men and women (temporarily) appear to be more at risk for declining self-esteem than those who are at least thirty when they become parents. Younger mothers' self-esteem drops significantly between pregnancy and six months after giving birth. By the time their babies are in their second year, though, these younger mothers bounce back to their earlier level of satisfaction with themselves. Younger fathers' self-esteem declines later than their wives'—between six and eighteen months after they have become fathers. So, just as the wives are on the way up, their husbands are on their way down in terms of how satisfied they feel about themselves.

Mothers in their thirties maintain their satisfaction with themselves throughout the two years from pregnancy to eighteen months after their child is born. In contrast to the younger men whose self-esteem is dropping between six and eighteen months after childbirth, fathers in their thirties and forties describe themselves in even more positive ways during their second year of parenthood.

Even with these age differences in self-esteem, we cannot conclude that later is better than sooner until we consider what happens to the marriages of the younger and older parents. Although the older couples maintain their satisfaction with themselves as individuals during the transition to parenthood, they experience a significantly larger decline in marital satisfaction than the younger couples.

Why would this be so? The older parents have had a longer time to establish themselves, to build up a greater number of accomplishments, and to develop alternative resources for bolstering their self-esteem. At the same time, since they tend to have been married longer before becoming parents, integrating a baby into their lives may present a greater challenge to their established routines, flexibility, and spontaneity as a couple. This is supported by our finding that the older couples felt the reduction in intimacy most keenly, and reported more decline in satisfaction with their relationships as couples than the younger couples did.

The younger couples, on the other hand, seem to be more vulnerable to feeling less competent and less pleased with themselves as individuals once they become parents. Even if they have been working since they were young, as many of them have, taking on the care of a needy infant while maintaining contact as a couple and managing their work outside the family presents a hefty challenge for adults under thirty. Even so, they have not had time to build up as many expectations and to set patterns as a couple to be disrupted by the baby. Their relationships seem more resilient than those of the older parents in the sense that the partners show less dissatisfaction with them over time.

Tanya, twenty-six, and Jackson, twenty-seven, described their sense of themselves from the time their son, Kevin, was six months old to a year later:

TANYA: I was feeling trapped because Jackson was still going out, not only to work but with friends. And there I was, at home taking care of Kevin. Being with Kevin was marvelous, up to a point, but I felt cut off from everything else. Even when Jackson was there, he sometimes created more mess than he cleaned up. But I wasn't feeling nearly as bad about him as I was about me.

JACKSON: The irony was that Tanya was resenting the fact that I was going off to work every day, and I *hated* it. I would've quit two years ago. My job at the post office was not what I wanted to do for the rest of my life. But when Kevin came, I had to dig in and make a go of it. I'd go into work every day and grit my teeth. My boss was critical. Inside, I knew he was right. I was a fraud. I just wasn't the person I wanted to be.

TANYA: About two or three months ago, I got tired of feeling like a victim and realized that it wasn't making sense. Sometimes you just have to tell Jackson gently what needs to be done and he will do it. He just had to snap out of his own funk and realize that there were other people in the family who needed him to get on the stick.

During the months when Tanya and Jackson were having a difficult time, feeling badly about themselves, their connection with each other and their sense of humor helped pull them through. So did Tanya's ability to make some explicit demands for Jackson's involvement in the family. He accepted her complaints as reasonable and became more involved with Kevin, which began to rebalance Tanya's and Jackson's roles in the family. Although we could not tell from our conversation with them, the questionnaire data confirmed that Jackson's self-esteem had not returned to the level it had been during Tanya's pregnancy, but he was more satisfied with his marriage when Kevin was eighteen months old than he had been a year earlier. Having

Tanya's help in drawing him in to the family may have enhanced Jackson's evaluation of his relationship with her.

Marian and Bruce were older when they had their first baby. She is thirty-seven and he is thirty-nine when we visit on a rainy Sunday for our eighteen-month-postpartum follow-up. Bruce is very involved in his small but newly successful window design company. Marian, a lawyer in a large law firm, is working hard to make partner while becoming a parent. Given her complex schedule, we have had difficulty arranging this interview. Their daughter, Gayle, is closer to two years than eighteen months when we finally pin them down. When we ask them about the changes in their sense of themselves they have undergone in the past two years, Marian's initial answer is reminiscent of the responses of many mothers in our study, especially the women in their thirties: She talks more about the baby than about herself.

We get the sense that how Marian feels about herself depends in part on how each day goes with her daughter. But as we talk further, we come to appreciate her overall sense of ease and her ability to put things in perspective. The previous week Gayle had been sick and Marian had to bring her to work with her since they couldn't leave her with the usual day care. One of the senior partners in the firm came into her office and, not noticing Gayle's crayons on the floor, slid right into Marian's desk. "I started to laugh," Marian says, "but Paul was not amused and walked out in a huff. For a minute I thought, There goes *his* vote, but then I thought, Screw it! If I don't make partner because my sick kid is coloring in my office, then I'm working for the wrong firm. What's happened to my sense of myself? I guess I'm feeling pretty good about me. I wish I could say the same about *us.*"

Bruce describes changes in his sense of himself. "If you can believe it, I've gotten nicer," he says, while Marian makes a face of mock disapproval, which he ignores. "My business has really taken off. I feel terrific about Gayle. I'm not home much but when I am, we just hang out together in the park or down in my work room. I've been waiting for my life to come together like this for a long time."

Asked about any changes in their sexual relationship after having a baby, they both laugh and ask, "What sexual relationship?" Bruce explains that Marian is hardly home long enough for them to get together. And when she is home, she's poring over her files, spread out all over the dining room table. This is a common phenomenon, the new mother working at the dining room table because her home office has become the baby's room. They continue to discuss the changes:

BRUCE: We used to have all the time in the world, you know. Reading the Sunday papers. Going out in the middle of the week. I still remember it, and I miss it.

MARIAN: Bruce, you sound like you're totally available and I'm not. It seems to me that you're down in your work room about as much as I'm at the table. But the fact that we haven't made love in months does worry me.

BRUCE: I guess I take the long view. We did have our time. And we'll have

> our time again. But right now, we choose to do other things. By the time
> we turn around again, Gayle will be grown up. We'll just pick up where
> we left off.
> MARIAN: I'm just hoping we're not too old, and that we'll have something
> left to pick up.

Like other couples in their thirties, Marian and Bruce are feeling pretty good
about themselves, but at least from her point of view, their relationship with
each other is showing signs of strain. Postponing parenthood until partners
are in their thirties may provide a foundation for the development of a
stronger sense of self, one that tends to be maintained or even enhanced after
having a baby. Yet maintaining their growth as individuals, especially with
regard to furthering their careers, may be possible only at some cost to their
marital intimacy and satisfaction.

Continuity Despite Change

It is important to tell the other side of the story, which establishes that for
most men and women who become parents there is not only change but
continuity in their personalities and in their way of being in the world. Even
though the new identity of parent may crowd out some of the other central
aspects of men's and women's sense of themselves, and despite a possible
increase or decline in their self-esteem, there is a core of stability, predictability, and continuity in personality style as people make the transition to
parenthood. Many men and women *feel* that they have changed since becoming parents, but we found no systematic change in their self-described
personality traits from pregnancy through eighteen months after birth according to the Adjective Check Lists.[4] So, despite Doug's feeling that he has
become more aggressive in his business dealings and more comfortable at
social gatherings than he was before becoming a father, overall men and
women show little real personality change in any consistent direction. (Toni
Antonucci and Karen Mikus [1988] reviewed the results of the studies that
followed men and women from pregnancy into parenthood. They found no
evidence of personality change in a systematic direction. This is also consistent with psychoanalytic ideas that "new" conflicts during the transition to
parenthood are usually reawakened conflicts from the past [Benedek 1970;
Osofsky and Osofsky 1984; Wenner et al. 1969]).

In addition to this stability of personality traits, in every family domain,
especially in their views of themselves, we found remarkable predictability
across the transition to parenthood. That is, when we know something about
men's and women's perceptions, opinions, feelings, and behavior before they
became parents, we can predict with some degree of accuracy how they will
see themselves, feel, and behave when their children are six months and
eighteen months old.

Although the size of the Parent piece of the pie in pregnancy does not predict psychological involvement two years later, the Partner, Worker, and Leisure pieces measured in pregnancy are all significant predictors of those aspects of men's and women's identities six months and eighteen months after becoming parents.[5] In the same way, despite the change in their average scores on our measures of well-being or distress, parents who are very satisfied with themselves during pregnancy tend to have higher self-esteem eighteen months after the birth of their first child. Conversely, men and women who are feeling distressed about themselves before the baby comes tend to have lower self-esteem when their children are toddlers. A number of other research teams have found similar continuities in new parents' lives, leading them to conclude that parents' adaptation measured in pregnancy is the best predictor of how well they will function during the first year or two of parenthood (Belsky, Lang, and Rovine 1985; Grossman et al. 1980; Heinicke et al. 1986; Shereshefsky and Yarrow 1973). As we describe in chapter 8, we can predict the reactions of the parents in our study as far ahead as the children's kindergarten year.

The notion of continuity during a time of transition is important for three reasons. First, it adds something essential to our understanding of the impact of becoming a parent on men, women, and marriage. Having a baby does not turn men and women into different people. It does not plunge parents from the heights to the depths of feeling about themselves or their marriage, nor does it rescue a troubled parent or bridge the gap between spouses who were already miles apart. The most important piece of information to forecast how men and women will fare as parents is how they are doing before they begin their journey to parenthood.

Second, the fact that there is continuity during the transition to parenthood makes it possible to identify individuals, couples, and children who are at risk for distress during the early years of family life—essential information if we are ever to develop preventive services for families. In her dissertation based on the Becoming a Family Project data, Trudie Heming (1985, 1987) finds it possible to make fairly good predictions of who will report most depression on our depression symptom checklist (Radloff 1977) when their babies are eighteen months old, based on men's and women's descriptions of themselves during the pregnancy. If couples most likely to be in distress after their baby arrives can be helped earlier on, we may be able to prevent predictable family problems from escalating to a point beyond repair.

Finally, if it is possible to predict who is at risk for later distress, it is also possible for couples themselves to become informed about what might lie ahead in their journey to parenthood. Our information, after all, comes from what men and women have been telling us as we follow them on their journey from couple to family. We can alert expectant couples, and health professionals who are concerned with early family life, that long-term, enduring negative feelings that husband and wives hold about themselves, their partners, or their relationships before they have babies are not likely to disappear after the first flush of excitement of bringing the baby home. At the same time, expectant couples who are worried about what life with a baby will bring can be reassured to know that if they are coping well with the challenges of their lives, they can probably afford to be optimistic about how the becoming a family journey will turn out.

CHAPTER 5

What's Happening to Us?

SHARON: I really thought we'd discussed it before Amy was born—that Daniel was going to be more help around the house. But he just wasn't. I stewed for a long time and felt angry when I could have just said something. He'd never been around anyone who'd had a C-section or any major surgery. He didn't know that he wasn't supposed to let me cart tubs of wet diapers down the hall for the first month. I was feeling so shaky, and before I knew it our whole relationship was on shaky ground.

I finally said something to Daniel when Amy was about four months old. But I've had to *keep* doing it. I'm not very good about saying, "Things are not going well here." I usually give out a couple of hints, and then wait until I get really irritated. I'll sit on it for a couple of months before I come to Daniel and say something like, "Who died and left me in charge of the laundry?"

Sharon and Daniel are describing to us what has happened to their relationship in the six months since Amy was born. Daniel is used to Sharon's humorous but cutting complaints; he says something conciliatory but has some complaints of his own:

DANIEL: Looking back, I can see now that I wasn't as sensitive as I could have been. But what Sharon is leaving out is that I did all the shopping and errands during that time—and some of the housecleaning and all of the dishes and stuff and, of course, I worked all day too. I never got credit for that. All she talked about was how stressed out she was and how things were going wrong.

A combination of the stress of recovering from major surgery and caring for a new baby, along with Sharon and Daniel's holding-it-back-and-then-blurting-it-out style of expressing their feelings, are taking a toll on their relationship. Daniel had apparently not understood what Sharon needed after her surgery. Sharon did not know how to tell him what her needs were until she felt so upset that she angrily accused him of not offering any help. Feeling unacknowledged for what he *has* done, Daniel is unwilling to tell her that he is sorry he missed the cues.

In the last chapter we described changes in new parents' internal sense of themselves. Here we explore how some of the internal shifts in new fathers' and mothers' identity play out in their marriage. We focus on two related issues. First, we take a detailed look at the shifts in couples' division of the daily work of managing a household and family, especially how they share the work of caring for their child. We find that "who does what?" issues are central, not only in how husbands and wives feel about themselves but in how they feel about their marriage. Second, we describe alterations in the emotional fabric of the couple's relationship, showing that how caring and intimacy get expressed and how couples manage their conflict and disagreement have a direct effect on their marital satisfaction.

We find that husbands and wives, different to begin with, become even more separate and distant in the years after their first child is born. The increasing specialization of family roles and the emotional distance between partners who have become parents combine to affect their satisfaction with the overall quality of their relationship. Jessie Bernard (1972) observed that "in every marriage there are two marriages—his and hers." We find that in every transition to parenthood there are three transitions—his, hers, and theirs (Cowan et al. 1985).

Who Does What?

Gustav Geijer, a Swedish historian, said that "the position of women in a society provides an exact measure of the development of that society." If he was right, we are in deep trouble. His observation implies that in more highly developed societies, women's position would not differ from men's. Since the new wave of the women's movement in the 1960s, feminist literature and features in popular news media have made us more conscious of the unequal roles of men and women within the family and in the outside world. These news features have been stimulated in part by the fact that mothers a generation ago felt hemmed in by their constricted family roles (see Friedan

1963) and that today's mothers are entering the work force in increasing numbers. The implication seems to be that as women have become more equally involved in the world of work, men have increased their share of the work at home. But the men and women who have been talking to us over the last fifteen years have made it clear that behind the ideology of the egalitarian couple lies a much more traditional reality.

Scholars in a number of fields have been studying couples' role arrangements for managing the work of the house, bringing home the bacon, and rearing the children (Chodorow 1978; Hoffman and Nye 1974). The results of research over the past fifteen years tell a pretty consistent story about what sociologists call the instrumental tasks of family life (Parsons and Bales 1955): Although more than half the mothers with children under five have entered the labor force and contemporary fathers have been taking a small but significantly greater role in cooking, cleaning, and looking after their children than fathers used to do, women continue to carry the overwhelming responsibility for managing the household and caring for the children (Pleck 1985; Strelitz in Rapoport, Rapoport, and Strelitz 1977; Robinson 1977). Furthermore, studies of many different samples of couples leave no doubt that most women have the primary responsibility for family work even when both partners are employed full-time outside the home (Barnett and Baruch 1988; Hochschild 1989; Stafford, Backman, and Dibona 1977) and even in countries whose official policies dictate an equal division of labor (Szinovacz 1977).

As we discussed earlier, couples whose division of household and family tasks was not equitable when they began our study tended to predict that it would be after the baby was born—not that they expected to split the baby care 50-50, but that they would work as a team in rearing their children. Once their babies are born, however, the women do more of the housework than before they became mothers, and the men do much less of the care of the baby than they or their wives predicted they would.

Like many of the over-thirty parents in our study, Doug and Josie were feeling good about themselves but their marriage was a little strained. Doug tells us about their arrangements to care for six-month-old Zack, explaining how the burden came to fall almost entirely on Josie. When she was breast-feeding, it seemed impossible to have it any other way. He estimates that 95 percent of the labor in taking care of Zack has been done by Josie, then adds: "But I thoroughly enjoy him and don't feel deprived."

Josie, on the other hand, is outraged. All the talk about men and women sharing the responsibility and equal parenting, she says, "is just bullshit! Someone is going off and putting in eight or nine hours every day and the other parent is staying home doing not just the feeding but the constant changing of diapers, the laundry, the meal planning, the housecleaning— everything that keeps this family going! That's where the inequality starts, and it just goes on from there."

Doug describes their changes in theoretical terms, almost as if he were a sociologist explaining how historical trends and societal norms affect what happens in families. Josie, still disconcerted by her realization that she is in charge of most of Zack's daily care and everything else at home, stays focused on what is happening to their family. While Doug appears to be listening to his wife during this interview, he does not know how to respond supportively to her distress: "I would have gone along with the hypothesis of equal parenting right at first, though I admit that I didn't think about it much. But the way it works out, it falls on the mother."

This last sentence of Doug's is a succinct illustration of how couples explain that their egalitarian ideology is not easily put into practice. They talk about their arrangements of work inside and outside the family as if they have happened to them instead of as if they have worked them out. If one partner tries to get the other to look at the difference between their initial expectations and where they have ended up, as Josie does here, the quandary seems too big for the couple to solve alone:

JOSIE: Last week we had our hundredth talk about my going back to work. But, as Doug says, there's no way I can possibly earn anything close to his salary so that he could consider cutting back on his time.

DOUG: I'd say our discussion was academic. If Josie could go out and make sufficient money to support our lifestyle, I'd be perfectly willing to discuss taking a year off or six months off and staying home with Zack once he's weaned. Perhaps it's just as well that she doesn't, though. I wouldn't want to trade jobs with Josie. On my worst day I wouldn't want to trade jobs with her.

In recent years, the division of labor in the family when partners become parents has tended to be treated as a woman's issue, because the consequences of an unequal division of labor usually fall on mothers. Our findings suggest that who does what becomes an issue for fathers too when children appear because it is then that a couple's role arrangements—and how both the husband and the wife feel about them—become linked with their well-being as individuals and as couples.

Contemporary jokes, cartoons, and situation comedies frequently parody couples' heated disputes about who watches the children or takes out the garbage, reflecting the friction caused by the division of family labor in most couples' lives. Far from being amused by it, new parents are disillusioned and at the same time worried about being petty in complaining about who is folding the laundry, cooking the dinners, taking out the garbage, or getting up with the baby in the middle of the night. These have become hot issues not only for feminists but for all couples trying to raise healthy children, do serious work, and keep up with the soaring costs of housing, food, and medical bills.

Most studies of couples' role arrangements focus on who actually performs the roles, but this ignores how they *feel* about their arrangements and misses the connection between partners' feelings about their family and work arrangements and their satisfaction with their marriage. Arlie Hochschild began to unearth this link in *The Second Shift* (1989). In this chapter we will show how these parts of life become connected as partners become parents.

We expected the California couples who participated in our study, starting the families of the 1980s and 1990s, to be more egalitarian than the couples of the 1960s and 1970s. We were impressed with their pioneer spirit. Hopeful of becoming leaders at the frontier of modern family life, many felt ready to break new ground.

Natalie and Victor were hoping to right the wrongs in their families of origin, and expected to do their family making as a team:

> NATALIE: This family of ours is already different than the one I grew up in. Victor and I work much more closely as a couple than our parents did and we are determined to keep it that way. I'm not going to make our kids my whole existence the way my mother did.
>
> VICTOR: And I'm going to be there for my kids, the way my father *wasn't*.
>
> NATALIE: My mother's sacrifice in staying home to look after us full-time didn't really help. Although she was doing what she thought good mothers were supposed to, she was depressed a lot of the time and we ended up feeling like we had to take care of her. I'm determined that that's not going to happen in this family.

Each time we met with them, couples indicated on our Who Does What? questionnaire (Cowan and Cowan 1990b) how they actually divide the responsibilities for household tasks, family decisions, and the care of their baby, and how satisfied they felt with those arrangements. Couples who were not expecting a baby answered the same questions over the same period of time. A closer look at their responses will help us understand how the division of labor becomes entwined with a couple's intimacy when they try to put the rhetoric of equality to the test.

HOUSEHOLD AND FAMILY TASKS

The first twelve items on the questionnaire ask each spouse to use a 9-point scale to rate their division of responsibility for household and family tasks, in reality and according to their ideal. We assume that the greater the distance between how it is and how they would like it to be, the less satisfied they are with the current arrangements. A rating of 1 indicates that *she* takes all of the responsibility for that task. A rating of 5 means that they divide the task about equally, and a 9 shows that *he* is responsible for managing all of that task. The final question asks outright how satisfied they are with the way they divide these household and family tasks (very satisfied; pretty satisfied; neutral; somewhat dissatisfied; or very dissatisfied).

Simply adding up and taking the average of men's and women's ratings for all twelve household and family tasks at our first visit indicates that, in both expectant and childless couples, spouses are dividing the *overall* burden of family tasks fairly equitably. (The husbands' average rating was 4.8 and the wives' 4.5.) There is little change overall in couples' division of these twelve household and family tasks during the transition to parenthood. But simply averaging the scores for all of these items conceals important realities of life with young babies. In our first interview, almost all the couples agreed that men had more responsibility than women for repairs around the home, taking out the garbage, and looking after the car (6.9, 6.5, and 7.0, respectively, combining his and her ratings). In the last trimester of pregnancy, expectant fathers are also providing more of the family income than their wives are (6.2). Over the next two years, there is virtually no change in the arrangements of these tasks among the couples who remain childless, whereas the new parents begin to divide these tasks in more gender-stereotyped ways.

Six months after the birth, with 45 percent of the women at home full-time, men are providing even more of the family income than they were at the end of the pregnancy (from 6.2 to 7.3). They are doing a smaller proportion of the mounting loads of laundry than they were doing before the children were born, but they show significant increases in preparing meals, cleaning the house, and shopping for food. The average rating of the three household tasks in which men increase their participation never goes higher than 3.9, however, which means that even with men taking on more of the burden women are still doing more of the work. On the new parents' ratings of the other seven tasks, the division remains stable; wives continue to take more of the responsibility than their husbands throughout the transition to parenthood.

Eighteen months after the birth, men have cut back on meal preparation (average scores go from 3.6 to 3.2) and taking out the garbage (6.7 to 6.3), but they are beginning to shop (3.5 to 4.0) and take care of the yard or garden (5.0 to 5.3) more, presumably tasks they can do on the way to and from work or on the weekends.

How do couples react to these shifts? One subtle change is that instead of both partners performing some of each task, a common pattern for childless couples, now he tends to take on a few specific household responsibilities and she tends to do most of the others. So his and her overall responsibility for maintaining the household may not shift significantly after having a baby, but it feels more traditional because each has become more specialized. This leaves some husbands and wives feeling more separate. Given their shifting internal identities and their vows to be different from their parents, this separation can feel disappointing, a little frightening, and somewhat lonely:

VICTOR: Sometimes I think that our lives are working out great. We have this great kid, and this great marriage, and this great family. It's just that Natalie and I hardly see each other. It seems that while I'm looking after one thing, she's always looking after something else.

NATALIE: I know. I'm so preoccupied with the baby during the day. And I miss our time together as a couple. It takes some getting used to that by the time each day is over, we just give each other a peck on the cheek and fall into bed like an old married couple.

FAMILY DECISIONS

On a second page of the questionnaire, we asked how family decisions are made on twelve common issues, both actual and ideal arrangements, so that we could calculate the discrepancy between them, and determine how each partner feels about their decision-making pattern overall.

Family decision making was the one arena in our study that came close to the egalitarian idea of equal influence or responsibility. According to both spouses' ratings, men have a little more influence than their wives do on decisions about financial planning, work outside the family, and initiating lovemaking (an average rating of about 6). Women, on the other hand, tend to have a little more influence on decisions about the couple's social arrangements and about participation in community activities and religious organizations (an average rating of about 4). On most of the other issues, such as major expenses, how to spend time at home, and how people should behave in the family, both new parents and childless spouses reported about the same amount of influence and responsibility for deciding.

This pattern of family decision making does not change much from late pregnancy until the children are almost two. Men's and women's satisfaction with their balance of decision making also stays stable for both parents and childless couples.

TAKING CARE OF THE BABY

A third set of items for couples to rate described some of the major tasks involved in caring for a baby.[1] One unique feature of having expectant parents complete this list is that in addition to asking about their current role arrangements, we could ask how they expected to do things after the baby arrived.

Men's and women's ratings in the last trimester of pregnancy show that they predict that the mothers will be responsible for more of the baby-care tasks than will the fathers. Their ratings range from a low of 2.0 (mothers will do most of the feeding) to a high of 3.8 (mothers will do more of the choosing of toys for the baby). Clearly, expectant parents are predicting less than a 50-50 division of the daily care of their babies. Approximately nine months later, when the babies are six months old, a majority describe their arrangements for taking care of the baby as even more Mother's and less Father's responsibility than either parent had predicted. This is the basis of our contention that the ideology of the new egalitarian couple is way ahead of the reality. The fallout from their unmet expectations seems to convert both spouses' surprise and disappointment into tension between them.

Jackson and Tanya talked a lot in one of our couples groups about their commitment to raising Kevin together. Three months later, when the baby was six months old, Tanya explained that Jackson had begun to do more housework than ever before but he wasn't available for Kevin nearly as much as she would have liked:

> TANYA: He wasn't being a chauvinist or anything, expecting me to do everything and him to do nothing. He just didn't *volunteer* to do things that obviously needed doing, so I had to put down some ground rules. Like if I'm in a bad mood, I may just yell: "I work eight hours, just like you. This is half your house and half your child, too. You've got to do your share!" Jackson never changed the kitty litter box once in four years, but he changes it now, so we've made great progress. I just didn't expect it to take so much work. We planned this child together, and we went through Lamaze together, and Jackson stayed home for the first two weeks. But then—wham!—the partnership was over!

Tanya underscores a theme we heard over and over: The tension between new parents about the father's involvement in the family threatens the equilibrium between them.

Among parents of six-month-old babies, mothers are shouldering more of the baby care than either parent predicted on eight of the twelve items of the questionnaire: deciding about meals, managing mealtime, diapering, bathing, taking the baby out, playing with the baby, arranging for baby-sitters, and dealing with the pediatrician. On four items, women and men predicted that mothers would do more and their expectations proved to be on the mark: responding to the baby's cries, getting up in the middle of the night, doing the child's laundry, and choosing the baby's toys.

The fact that mothers are doing most of the primary child care in the first months of parenthood is hardly news. What we are demonstrating is that couples' arrangements for taking care of their infants are less equitable *than they expected* them to be. Shannon, one of the new mothers, said that she and her husband, John, were astounded. They had always shared the chores around the house pretty evenly, but since she has been home with the baby she has assumed almost all of the household and child-care work. John is amazed that they became so traditional so fast.

It's not just that couples are startled by how the division of labor falls along gender lines, but they describe the change as if it were a mysterious virus they picked up when they were in the hospital having their baby; they don't seem to view their arrangements as *choices* they have made. This is why both mothers and fathers of infants show significantly greater discrepancies than do childless couples between "how it is now" and "how I'd like it to be." Since the greater burden of care has fallen to mothers, this is also why, at each follow-up interview during the transition to parenthood, mothers express much less satisfaction than fathers with the sharing of the baby care. The fathers are dissatisfied too—they say they would like to be more involved in the care of their babies, but they cannot figure out how to arrange it.

During the year between their babies' six- and eighteen-month birthdays, men do begin to take on a little more of their care. This increase is evident on eight of the twelve tasks we ask about, including bathing the baby, getting up during the night, and taking the baby out. On the remaining four tasks—playing with the baby, doing the baby's laundry, and arranging for baby-sitters and doctor's visits—fathers' involvement stays fairly constant from the year before. Tanya has noticed this shift in Jackson's involvement with Kevin by the next time we visit, when Kevin is about nineteen months old. Kevin's age makes it much easier for his father to take him out, sometimes for a whole day. But then she explains that by the time she gets Kevin up, feeds him, dresses him, makes him lunch, and so on, she is often too tired to enjoy the peace and quiet.

Despite fathers' increased involvement with their babies during this second year of parenthood, even the item that gets the highest ratings for fathers' participation—playing with the baby—receives average ratings of only 4.1 on our scale, still something mothers do more than fathers. Like the couple's specialization of household and family tasks, the care of their children becomes more specialized; they are less likely to make joint contributions to it. The modest increase in fathers' involvement in the care of their children between six and eighteen months after birth is not, therefore, accompanied by an increase in men's or women's satisfaction with the division of child care.

HIS AND HER VIEWS

Husbands' and wives' descriptions of their division of labor are quite similar,[2] but they do shade things differently: Each claims to be doing more than the other gives him or her credit for.* The feeling of not being appreciated for the endless amount of work each partner actually does undoubtedly increases the tension between them.

In our couples groups, we use the participants' responses to the Who Does What? questionnaire to talk about some of these issues. We soon learn that some couples treat the ratings quite seriously, which can lead to a heated exchange:

JACKSON: What do you *mean,* you take out the garbage more than I do? What score did you give it? Every day when I come home the bag in the kitchen is full, and I take it out to the incinerator.

TANYA: Jackson, how can you say that? Maybe once or twice during the week you do, but I have to ask you to throw out the baby's disposable diapers almost every day. I gave it a 3.

JACKSON: Amazing! I thought it was *really* about 4.5, but I put down 4 because I know you do it when I'm not home.

*Partners tend to agree most about who takes out the garbage, pays the bills, responds to the baby's cries, buys the toys, and plays with the baby. They agree least about how they divide the shopping, the preparation of meals, looking after the car, and taking the child out or arranging baby-sitting and doctor's appointments.

With this last remark, Jackson looked at the rest of us and shrugged as if to say, "Can you believe that couples argue about this petty stuff?" We believe it.

For the childless couples, *overall satisfaction* with role arrangements (household tasks plus decision making) remained stable over the first two years of the study. By contrast, new parents' overall satisfaction with their role arrangements (household tasks plus decision making plus child care) declined significantly—most dramatically between pregnancy and six months after the baby's birth (C. Cowan and P. Cowan 1988). We will discuss in chapter 9 the fact that trends were different for men and women who had been in one of our couples groups than for couples who did not take part in our intervention. When we compared the satisfaction of parents who had been in one of our couples groups and those who had had no intervention, the former *maintained* their satisfaction with the division of household and family tasks. This trend is particularly true for women. Since the actual role arrangements in the group and nongroup participants were very similar, we can see that men's and women's satisfaction with who does what is, at least in part, a matter of perspective.

Fathers' Involvement in Family Tasks

Group trends clearly show that fathers of babies and young children do much less work in the family than mothers do, right from the day they bring the baby home. Given the fact that most new mothers take more time off work than their husbands do, this may be inevitable in the first months. But the inequities continue into the second year of life, long past the time when many women return to work. Arlie Hochschild (1989) has also documented that mothers who work full-time are coming home to a "second shift" in which they do about two-thirds of the family work. Hochschild calls this current state of affairs a "stalled revolution," in reference to the unfulfilled promise of the prevailing egalitarian ideology. In detailed case studies, she demonstrates how the subterranean struggles involved in managing inequitable arrangements are subtly eroding the quality of men's and women's relationships as couples.

Although our data document these imbalances in the division of labor in a majority of families, there is a small cadre of men who *are* taking a significantly more active role in running their households and rearing their children. If we listen carefully to what those men and their wives are telling us, we can see that these men tend to feel better about themselves and about their family relationships than men who are less involved in family work. What's more, their wives feel significantly better too.

THE RANGE OF ARRANGEMENTS

In the 1980s, the popular press delighted in running stories of men who "gave up" their careers to take on the primary care of their children. Who are these unusual men, what leads to their decisions to care for their children, and how do they fare? Researchers have talked with such men in California, Connecticut, Michigan, Sweden, Israel, and Australia (Ehrensaft 1987; Pruett 1986; Radin 1988; Russell 1983). Of course, many men who are widowed (Schwebel, Fine, and Moreland 1988), divorced (Hanson 1988; Loewen 1988), or gay (Bozett 1988) can be primary parents, but here we are focusing on men who take on a major share of the care of very young children when their families are beginning. On the whole these studies show that men who choose to be the primary caretakers of their young children are involved and nurturant parents, although they tend not to continue in this role over the long haul. Only about 20 percent of them are still in the primary parent role two years after they take it on (Radin 1988; Russell 1983).

In our study, two of the seventy-two families having a baby described a reversal of parents' traditional roles during the preschool years: The husband was the primary caretaker of the baby and the wife was the primary wage earner. One of the couples made an active choice to arrange their lives this way. In the other, the father had been laid off for six months and then assigned to the night shift; the couple decided that the mother would keep her daytime job and the father would look after their son during the day until he was two years old. In another six couples, both parents worked full-time and shared the care of the house and children almost equally. In the remaining 88 percent of the families, the arrangements have a more traditional split: She is the primary caretaker and his involvement ranges from very little of the child's care to somewhere less than 50-50 on most of the child-care tasks on our list.

We discussed in the previous chapter our finding that there are advantages for men's and women's self-esteem when men feel more psychologically involved in being a parent. Are there benefits as well when men have more actual involvement in their children's day-to-day care? To answer this question, we correlated his and her ratings of his actual care of the baby, and their satisfaction with their arrangement of family roles, with measures of their well-being as individuals, as a couple, in the parent-child relationship, and with regard to stress outside the family.[3]

In late pregnancy, the wives who predicted that their husbands would be more involved in caring for the baby were more satisfied with their marriage and described their life together as warmer, more expressive, and less conflictful (a more cohesive family) than did other women. Husbands who predicted that they would be more involved in caring for their babies also perceived their family life during pregnancy as more cohesive.[4]

Six months after the birth of their child, when these fathers are actually taking care of their children more, they have higher self-esteem and so do their wives. Both partners describe their marriages as more satisfying, their families as more cohesive, and their parenting stress as lower. They also feel that they have more social support and fewer stressful events in their lives.*

When their children are eighteen months old, fathers' involvement in

---

*These findings are very similar to the links between men's greater psychological involvement in fatherhood (a larger Parent piece of the pie) and both men's and women's well-being.

caring for their children is no longer related to how they describe their satisfaction with themselves or their marriage, their view of the family atmosphere, or their level of life stress and support. Nevertheless, more involved fathers continue to have lower parenting stress and report fewer symptoms of depression. Men's involvement with the children still makes a difference to their wives' feelings about the quality of marriage and family life. Women whose husbands took more of a role in the care of their child were more maritally satisfied and described their family as having greater cohesion than mothers whose mates were less involved with the children. Parents' satisfaction with the division of the child-care tasks was even more highly correlated with their own and their spouses' well-being than was the fathers' actual amount of involvement (C. Cowan and P. Cowan 1988).

Tanya describes how Jackson's active involvement with Kevin affects her: "When I see Jackson making an extra effort with Kevin, I feel that he's telling me that he loves me. Rationally, I know that he and Kevin have their own thing going, but it makes me feel so good about him. And when we were fighting because Jackson wasn't really doing anything with Kevin, that just felt like a slap in my face."

Victor and Natalie, who share Kim's care and are less stressed than many of the other parents of eighteen-month-olds, also benefit from sharing the load—and seem to realize that their contentment is not typical. Victor told us: "I know that we're supposed to be stressed out now, but frankly we're having a fine time." And Natalie added: "I know things are fine. He's stopped leaving his shorts in the bathroom! But, seriously, when I see how involved Victor is with Kim and then I hear my friends complaining about how their husbands are out to lunch, I'm really thankful."

We cannot really tell which comes first—fathers' involvement in the family or both parents' feelings of well-being. It could be that when partners are feeling good about themselves and their relationship, men are more motivated to get involved with their children. Evidence supporting this view comes from our ability to *predict* which fathers will be more involved with their children's care, using a combination of their self-esteem and satisfaction-with-marriage ratings before their babies are born (Cowan and Cowan 1987a). It is also possible that fathers' involvement has a positive payoff in terms of the quality of the relationship they develop not only with their children but also with their wives; that, in turn, may keep active fathers feeling good about themselves. This view is supported by analyses showing that when fathers are involved in caring for their six-month-old infants, their own satisfaction with marriage, and especially their wives' satisfaction with marriage, tends to go up in the two-year period between pregnancy and eighteen months after their babies are born.[5]

On the distressing side of this equation, the less involved a father becomes with the baby's care, the more likely it is that he and his wife will become disenchanted with their relationship as a couple over the next year. If, in addition, both spouses are dissatisfied with their arrangements for looking after their baby, they and the marriage will suffer. Clearly, the higher fathers' involvement with their children is, the happier they and their wives are. What prevents a large majority of couples from living out this arrangement?

THE OBSTACLES

There are powerful barriers to creating egalitarian family arrangements. Discussions of who does what in the family usually assume that men will do as little child care as they can get away with. Most of the men in our study, however, wanted desperately to have a central role in their child's life. Despite some support for the notion of the new, involved father, powerful obstacles inside and outside the family prevent men from becoming equal participants in the business of raising a family (see also Russell 1983). When couples want to move in the direction of a shared division of family labor, just saying yes is not enough.

1. *It is hard to shake the idea that child rearing is women's work.* Most of today's parents were raised primarily by their mothers. The men have no models of male nurturers, and the women have internalized prohibitions against abdicating their role as primary caretakers of their babies. Even for couples who want to expand the traditional parental roles, these early models and constraints conspire to make it very difficult to create new kinds of family relationships (see Chodorow 1978).

2. *Men clearly expect their wives to be competent with babies right from the start.* We were surprised at how little time fathers allowed themselves for uncertainty, and at how quickly mothers would step in the moment their partner or the baby looked uneasy. Given the frequent male discomfort with feeling incompetent, it takes a minimum of implicit criticism or "help" for them to hand the baby back to "the expert," as many fathers dub their wives. And once men step out, it becomes hard for them to get back in.

3. *The "marital dance" tends to discourage men's active involvement in child care.* No matter how much they want their husbands to establish a wonderful relationship with the child, women who become full-time mothers can feel threatened if their husbands become too active or skilled. As Shannon put it: "I love seeing the closeness between John and John Junior, especially because I didn't have that with my father. But if John does well at his work *and* his relationship with the baby, what's my special contribution?"

The marital dance can be seen clearly in couples' discussions about feeding the baby. Many nurses and doctors emphasize breastfeeding almost exclusively. They may not mention or may actively frown upon the use of supplemental bottles in the early postpartum period. Doug, the "sociological observer," comments sardonically: "Josie has the kid on her breast about every two hours. And then, for ten minutes, I get to clean up the poop and diaper him and put him back to sleep. What's the point? I might as well be out bringing in some more money."

Because holding a squalling infant before feeding, or changing a soggy diaper, do not feel like significant contributions to child rearing, many fathers feel unnecessary or pushed out of a central role with their newborns.

They back away and turn to their work, where they know they can make a visible contribution to their family's welfare. The merits of breastfeeding are not at issue here; but its benefits may have unintended side effects, and couples may want to consider supplemental bottles as a way of encouraging fathers' early involvement.

4. *The more men attempt to take an active role in the care of their children, the more mixed or negative feedback they report from their own parents.* Victor said that every time he told his father about some wonderful thing that Kim had just done, his father asked him a question about work. And when his parents visit, they always ask Natalie about the baby, even though Victor knows as much or more about Kim than she does.

Many grandparents find their children's attempts to establish egalitarian family roles a threat or implied criticism of the "old way" of family making. This intergenerational tension creates a subtle but imposing obstacle to fathers becoming as involved with their children as they had hoped to be.

5. *The economics of the workplace and the lack of quality child care encourage fathers to work and mothers to stay home while children are young.* Maternity leave is available, but often without pay. Paternity leave, if offered at all, is usually short, only teasing both parents with a taste of what it could be like to share the care of their child. When both partners work outside the home, the lack of high-quality, affordable child care drains parents' natural excitement about parenthood and creates anxiety about leaving their children in someone else's care.

For those parents in our study who did overcome social pressures and tried to arrange it so that both could be home more, the marked differences between men's and women's wages often placed an additional financial burden on the new family. These practical realities can be the last straw, forcing partners to assume more traditional parenting arrangements than they had intended (Coysh 1983).

Because of these social realities, many fathers in our study did not accept the prevailing definitions of a father's "involvement" in the family:

RAY: Most of my responsibility for the family is providing the bread. You know, Daddy is at work, Mommy is at home. Daddy makes the money, Mommy makes the house and takes care of Faith. I get really pissed off at Celie's friends. They're always asking her, "How come Ray doesn't look after Faith more?" Man, I'm looking after Faith six days a week, ten hours a day, busting my ass at the plant.

Despite all the obstacles, some of the men in our study made great efforts to be actively involved in the care of their children, enabling a few couples to make arrangements that approached their ideal. Unfortunately, they are swimming upstream, fighting off a formidable array of forces as they try to make their way forward.

What's Happened to the Marriage?

Ironically, many partners expend enormous energy on deciding and preparing to bring a child into their lives, only to feel that their marriage is shaky once they have become a family. Couples in our study who felt upbeat, the way Victor and Natalie and even Tanya and Jackson did in their first years as a family, were decidedly a minority.

Indeed, almost every study of the transition to parenthood has found that most new parents feel some disenchantment in their marriage. It is tempting to blame this on two related facts reported by every couple. First, after having a baby *time* becomes their most precious commodity (LaRossa and LaRossa 1981). Couples say that there are simply not enough hours in the day to look after the baby, keep the household running, go to work, talk with a co-worker or friend, and have any time left to nurture their relationship.

Second, even if a couple can eke out a little time together, the effort seems to require a major mobilization of forces on the part of both spouses: sitters need to be recruited; bottles must be prepared; instructions need to be left. New parents say that by the time they get out the door, they feel none of the spontaneity that had kept their relationship alive when they were only a twosome.

As we have seen, new parents' sense of themselves is shifting in unexpected directions. He is feeling the responsibility of supporting a family. She is wondering what to do about her job or career. Dissatisfaction with the family division of labor is increasing, and support from parents, friends, and co-workers seems hard to come by. Because most of these changes are unexpected, and because some have different implications for men's and women's lives, partners end up feeling that the balance between them is shifting too. These mounting strains and pressures begin to affect the more intimate aspects of the relationship between them—their caring, closeness, and sexual relationship; the amount of conflict and disagreement; and their feelings about the overall marriage.

EMOTIONAL INTIMACY AND SEX

We asked husbands and wives to describe in an open-ended way what they do to show their partners that they care and what their partners do to show their caring. It soon became clear that different things feel caring to different people—some romantic, others mundane: bringing flowers or special surprises; being a good listener; touching in certain ways; picking up the cleaning without being asked.

Also, husbands and wives often interpret caring differently. Bill says that when Peggy is sick, he tries to stay close by and bring her things. But Peggy says she likes to be left alone when she's not feeling well. She gets irritable when he hovers and fusses over her. Bill is doing "for Peggy" what *he* would find caring if *he* were ill. In many similar examples, the wife intends what she does to be caring, but her husband misses the point. It is as if partners follow the golden rule about caring—Do unto others as you would have them do unto you—only to have it backfire. Understandably, they may then feel hurt, misunderstood, or unappreciated.

New parents describe fewer examples of caring after having a baby compared to before, but as we keep finding in each domain of family life, men's and women's changes occur at different times. Six months after the birth of their babies, new mothers say that they are doing the same number of caring things for their husbands as they did in pregnancy, but their husbands report doing significantly fewer caring things for them. Perhaps not coincidentally, this is the period when wives' overall satisfaction with marriage declines most. This subtle shift in intimacy between the partners may be coloring women's perception of the whole relationship.

Between the babies' six- and eighteen-month birthdays, wives and husbands report that the women are doing fewer caring things for their husbands than the year before. This is the year in which the *men's* overall satisfaction with marriage takes its greatest plunge. We don't know whether the decline in caring contributes to the feeling that the marriage is less satisfying, or whether one partner's increasingly negative view of the marriage leads to less caring behavior. What we do know is that in the parents' natural preoccupation with caring for the baby, they seem less able to care for each other.

Both husbands and wives also report a negative change in their sexual relationship after having a baby. The frequency of lovemaking declines for almost all couples in the early months of parenthood, after having declined for about half of them during the last stages of the pregnancy. Sharon speaks for all new mothers: "It's all I can do to keep my eyes open until nine o'clock. As soon as the baby is down I race for the bed, and I'm asleep most nights before my head hits the pillow."

Couples are about evenly divided between those who report that sex is very good when they do get around to it and those who describe a decline in the quality of their sexual relationship as well. Sharon's husband, Daniel, said that as new parents, neither of them seemed very interested in sex. And when one of them was, the other was usually too busy or tired.

There are both physical and psychological deterrents to pleasurable sex for new parents. Some women have slow-healing scars from an episiotomy, which can make intercourse very painful. Others have temporary breast infections, or are embarrassed by the flow of breast milk when they become aroused. Even without any of these impediments to spontaneity or sensuality, almost all mothers are exhausted during the early weeks and months of what feels like twenty-four-hour-a-day on-call baby care, particularly if they are recovering from the major surgery of cesarean section delivery. A more subtle psychological deterrent, not often discussed but mentioned in chapter 3 with regard to sexual tendencies in late pregnancy, has to do with both partners' shifts in identity and roles. Joan told us that on the few nights when she is wide awake and even thinking about making love with Rob, "I have this little voice that begins to nag at me, saying, 'Parents don't have sex.'" Rob has the same feelings: "You're my wife but you're also a mother now, and it's not OK to turn on to a mother."

Probably the greatest interference with what happens in the bedroom comes from what happens between the partners outside the bedroom. Martin and Sandi, for example, tell us that making love has become problematic since Ellen's birth. To give an example of a recent disappointment, Martin explains that he had had an extremely stressful day at work. Sandi greeted him with a "tirade" about Ellen's fussy day, the plumber failing to come, and the baby-sitter's latest illness. Sandi picks up the story at the point when she asked Martin to take care of Ellen while she finished preparing dinner, which he did without enthusiasm or comment. Dinnertime was tense, and they spent the rest of the evening in different rooms. When they got into bed they watched television for a few minutes, and then Martin reached out to touch Sandi. She pulled away, feeling guilty that she was not ready to make love.

Like so many couples, Sandi and Martin were disregarding the tensions that had been building up over the previous hours. They had never had a chance to talk in anything like a collaborative or intimate way. This is the first step of the common scenario for one or both partners to feel "not in the mood."

Although men and women tend to give similar descriptions of the negative changes in their sexual relationship after becoming parents, they often see the positive changes differently. New fathers report fewer positive changes in their sexual relationship, whereas new mothers describe about the same number of positive changes at each point in the study. This difference in perception is reminiscent of the couple in Woody Allen's film *Annie Hall.* The partners, played by Woody Allen and Diane Keaton, are shown, after a difficult period in their relationship, on a split screen, having separate conversations with their therapists. The woman's therapist asks her how often they are having sex, and she answers, "Oh, constantly. At least three times a week." The man's therapist asks him the same question, to which he replies, "Uh, hardly at all. Only three times a week."

CONFLICT, DISSATISFACTION, AND DIVORCE

We have seen that the changes couples report in their division of labor and in the caring and intimacy of their marriages appear to be affecting how they feel about their relationships as couples. Here we focus directly on the difficulties new parents describe in their relationships: their conflict and disagreement, their dissatisfaction, and, for a small, unhappy group, their discouragement about being able to stay together as a couple.

Ninety-two percent of the men and women in our study who became parents described more conflict and disagreement after having their baby than they had described before they became parents. Using a questionnaire (adapted from one by Sheldon Starr, no date), we asked them to rate the amount of conflict and disagreement (a great deal, a moderate amount, a little, or none) they have as a couple in ten common aspects of family life and to indicate which three issues of the ten are most likely to lead to conflict for them: the division of the workload in the family; the amount of time spent together as a couple; willingness to talk about their sexual relationship; management of family money; the need for time alone; the quality of time spent together as a couple; relationships with in-laws; ideas about how to raise children; willingness to work for improvement in the relationship; or the way they communicate with each other.

From the reports of men and women in both one-job and two-job families, the division of the workload in the family wins, hands down, as the issue most likely to cause conflict in the first two years of family making.[6] This makes it graphically clear that there is a link between shifts in the day-to-day quality of a parent's family life and his or her feelings about the quality of the couple relationship. Art told us that a lot of things that hadn't been important before he and Stephanie became parents suddenly began to cause trouble. They had never kept tabs on who cleaned up after dinner; whoever had the time would take care of it. Now, Stephanie explained, "I know that Art is tired from working all day, but I need to have him get rid of the dishes after we eat. If things aren't in order, I can't start to relax. If he doesn't help me with that, we're likely to start getting cross with one another almost before we realize what's happening."

Most of the couples we spoke to did not, of course, go from a state of shared bliss to one of shouting and carrying on once they became parents. But regardless of their level of disagreement and conflict before they had babies, between pregnancy and eighteen months after becoming parents they described an average increase in conflict of 1 point on a 7-point scale for each item on the list[7]—a small average increase, but one that is reported by almost every new parent in our study.

Given this pervasive increase in marital conflict, our next area of investigation centered on establishing what happens to the marital satisfaction of the couples in our study. We used both partners' descriptions of their marriage from pregnancy to eighteen months after the baby is born on our marital satisfaction questionnaire (Locke and Wallace 1959).[8] Of course, some spouses feel differently about their relationship, but in our study most husbands' and wives' ratings were quite similar.[9]

Let us begin with how the parents who did *not* take part in our couples group intervention described their marriages over time, since they are comparable to most couples having babies with no special help during their transition to parenthood. The typical scores on the questionnaire range from about 40, which would indicate a marriage in serious distress, through 100, which is about average, to 140, which suggests a very satisfying couple relationship. During late pregnancy, the average level of marital satisfaction is quite high in a majority of the expectant parents with no intervention (129 for women, 126 for men), although 9 percent of the women and 14 percent of the men are already in the distressed range.

From late pregnancy to six months after giving birth, the mothers' average marital satisfaction scores decline by eight points, and then drop another seven points between six and eighteen months postpartum—both statistically significant changes. New fathers' marital satisfaction scores drop five points from pregnancy to six months after the birth, then plunge twelve points during the following year.[10] Here we see the now-familiar pattern in which women feel the impact of the transition more strongly during the first six months after birth, and their husbands feel it more strongly in the following year.

The average scores suggest a small downward slide in new parents' satisfaction with their marriages, but still quite positive views. By the time their babies are eighteen months old, however, almost one-quarter—24 percent of new mothers and 22 percent of new fathers—are indicating that their marriage is in some distress. Keep in mind that these figures do *not* include those husbands and wives who separated or divorced during these two years. Among the forty-eight expectant couples who did not participate in our couples groups, 12.5 percent were announcing separations or divorces before their children were eighteen months old and another 3.5 percent divorced by the time their child was three years old. A cumulative total of 20 percent divorced by the end of their first child's kindergarten year.

Although our sample was relatively small, our divorce figures appear to be in line with national trends (Bumpass and Rindfuss 1979). If so, the 12.5 percent divorce rate among parents whose first child is less than eighteen months old suggests that one-quarter (12.5 percent divided by 50 percent) of divorces will have taken place before a child is old enough to remember living with both biological parents. Approximately 40 percent (twenty out of fifty) have taken place by the end of the child's kindergarten year.

Two comparisons help us to place these divorce figures in a broader perspective. First, we compared the divorce rate of the new parents in our study with that of couples who had participated in one of our intervention groups during their transition to parenthood. During the same two-year period, all of the couples in the group intervention were still in intact marriages. (We will see in chapter 9 that this impressive effect did not last forever.) By the time the children were three and a half, only one couple from the intervention sample (4 percent) had divorced. This comparison suggests that some of the marital disruption that occurs very early in the life of a child can be prevented or at least delayed.

A second comparison sample is most enlightening. What happens over the same period of time to the marriages of couples who do not have a baby? Six years after the study began, the divorce rate of the new parents was 20 percent, but the divorce rate of the couples who remained childless throughout that period approached the national average of 50 percent. It seems that having a child decreases, or at least delays, a couple's likelihood of divorce.

At first, these comparisons between parents and nonparents may seem contradictory: How could having a baby be associated with an increase in marital dissatisfaction and a decrease in the rate of divorce in the early family-making years? We are talking about two different aspects of marriage: how partners feel their marriage is working, or marital quality, and whether they stay together, or marital stability. Couples who are satisfied with their relationships will be more likely to stay together, but some will stay married even when one or both partners are unhappy with the marriage (Lewis and Spanier 1979). The marital stability of couples who have preschool children is "protected" (Cherlin 1977). Although new parents may be experiencing increased tension or dissatisfaction as couples, their joint involvement with managing the baby's and the family's needs may lead them to put off, or possibly to work harder on, the problems in their marriage—at least while the children are young.

Where are the bright spots in this somber picture of marital distress? There are a significant number of couples, though they are clearly in the minority, whose relationships feel qualitatively better in the first eighteen months after having a child. In Jay Belsky's study (Belsky and Rovine 1990), about 20 to 35 percent of couples showed "modest positive change" according to different measures, without any intervention or therapy. In our study, about 18 percent of the parents who did not take part in one of our couples groups and about 38 percent of the group participants showed increased satisfaction with their relationships as couples during the transition to parenthood.

Paul and Beth enthusiastically described their life as they tried to find the right balance. Their life with Willie could get "really crazy," they said, but they approached each difficulty as a challenge, and put their heads together to come up with a plan. It helped that Paul was very involved in the day-to-day child care. Beth said, "I appreciate his strength even more than I used to. But I was afraid that he was giving up his own work too much." "Well, I did, some," Paul responded. "But I kept thinking, 'It's hard now, but it won't last forever.'"

Paul and Beth did so well because, when things got difficult or chaotic, they were able to avoid blaming each other for the strain. Somehow they managed to keep working as a team, "on the same side" (Ball 1984), helping each other maintain the perspective that the hard stretches would not last forever. Given many spouses' tendency to blame the other in times of stress, this seems like a heroic achievement for overextended new parents.

WHY DOES SATISFACTION WITH MARRIAGE GO DOWN?

The question we are asked most often by parents, writers, and people from the media is why there is such a consistent finding of disenchantment with marriage among new parents. It begins, we think, with the issue of men's and women's roles, the topic with which we opened this chapter. The new ideology of egalitarian relationships between men and women has made some inroads on the work front, in the sense that mothers are more likely to be employed than they used to be. Most couples, however, are not prepared for the strain of creating more egalitarian relationships at home, and it is this strain that seems to lead men and women to feel more negatively about their partners and the state of their marriage. But why?

The more we thought about this question, the more complicated and elusive it became. Even with sophisticated research and analytic strategies, there is very little systematic information to help us understand the processes or mechanisms that drive marital satisfaction down during the sensitive family-making period. Part of the increase in conflict and the decline in sexual and marital satisfaction after having a baby is self-explanatory. Major life changes, even positive ones, are stressful, and negative ones can exact a high toll on one's sense of well-being (Holmes and Rahe 1967; Lazarus and Folkman 1984). Given the consistent pattern of shifts in a negative direction during the transition to parenthood, we might *expect* to see a decline in satisfaction with marriage; and the more negative the changes, the greater the decline in marital satisfaction should be. But our results do not support this hypothesis. In fact, we found very little correlation between declining marital satisfaction and any single negative change reported by new parents—the loss of the lover aspect of self, the more traditional division of family work, declines in role satisfaction, changes in ideas about parenting, declining social support, or shifting work patterns. Although each of these aspects of life is related to how partners feel about their marriage *at a given time,* when things become increasingly problematic from one period to the next there is not a corresponding decline in satisfaction with marriage. How, then, can we explain the drop in satisfaction with marriage for a majority of the couples who have had a baby?

First, as we described in chapter 2, couples enter the transition to parenthood with very different attitudes and decision-making processes. We saw that those different decision-making patterns led to different patterns in the parents' feelings about their relationships as couples from pregnancy to almost two years after having their babies. The Planners and the Acceptance-of-Fate couples continued to feel quite happy with how their relationships as couples were feeling once they became parents. The Ambivalent and Yes-No couples, on the other hand, described feeling less enthusiastic—or very distressed—about their marriages in the first years of parenthood. Some of the decline in marital satisfaction, then, must be attributed to the couples who did not embark on their journey to parenthood wholeheartedly in the first place.

We also noted that childbirth preparation classes seem to set the stage for couples to think about parenthood as a joint venture. The increased visibility of prepared childbirth classes, most of which include mothers and fathers, says to men, in effect: Preparing for the baby's arrival is for fathers, too. What we are hearing is that men's increasing involvement in the preparation for the *day* of their baby's birth leads both spouses to expect that he will be involved in what follows—the ongoing daily care and rearing of the children. How ironic that the recent widespread participation of fathers in the births of their babies has become a source of new parents' disappointment when the men do not stay involved in their babies' early care. We know now that both parents' disappointment about his involvement can have consequences for the marriage. In our study, when there was a larger discrepancy between the wives' expectations of their husbands' involvement in looking after the baby and the husbands' *actual* involvement, the wives showed a greater decline in marital satisfaction between late pregnancy and eighteen months after giving birth (Garrett 1983). (Belsky and colleagues [Belsky, Ward, and Rovine 1986] report a similar finding.)

Third, as we have described with a number of critical aspects of couples' lives, a husband and a wife have different experiences of becoming parents. In our interviews and couples group discussions, husbands and wives kept emphasizing different things: She's the one carrying the baby; he's the one who has to go to work early every morning; he thinks they should let the baby cry; she can't stand to hear the baby crying. Almost all of these differences were being recounted as stimulators of friction between the parents. It seemed clear that the differences between husbands' and wives' experience of the transition were leading to their feeling distant, which stimulated conflict, which, in turn, affected both partners' satisfaction with their overall relationship.

In several important respects, men and women are changing in different directions while becoming parents: in the division of household tasks and child care, in social support outside the marriage, in work life, and so on. Furthermore, those differences grow larger along the journey to parenthood. In some couples, the increased difference between the partners is modest, but in others the growing differences become marked. The more different he and she become from each other in their descriptions of themselves, their role arrangements, their sexual relationship, their ideas about parenting, and the families they grew up in, the more they report increases in conflict between them.

As we suspected, couples with the greatest increases in both differences and conflict from pregnancy to six months after they have a baby showed the greatest decline in marital satisfaction over the two-year period from pregnancy to eighteen months after the birth.[11] Clearly it is difference *and* conflict, rather than conflict alone, that explains most about the partners' declines in satisfaction with marriage once they have become parents.

Recall Peggy and Bill, whose difficulty began with their ambivalence about having a child, extended through Peggy's very difficult pregnancy, and continued after their daughter, Mindy, was born. Eighteen months after the birth, this is how they described their relationship:

BILL: I thought we were doing OK. I was pitching in at home. We'd started to make love again, after all that difficulty when Peggy was pregnant. But mostly she's just mad before I go to work in the morning and mad as soon as I get back at night.

PEGGY: Well, I know we're making love more often, but it still hurts about half the time, from that terrible episiotomy. And we've got very different ideas about your "pitching in." I don't consider changing a diaper once a month and feeding Mindy when you've got nothing else to do much of a "pitch." What's really getting to me, though, is that we hardly ever agree about how to handle her. I think you're too rough and you think I'm spoiling her, and neither of us wants to change. I know your business problems are bugging you, but that's no excuse to take out your frustrations on Mindy and me.

Peggy and Bill have different perceptions of the "same" events. They have different sets of physical and emotional stresses both within and between them. They have different ideas about what to do with Mindy. They perceive that they are moving ever farther apart. It is not difficult to see how this has begun to take its toll in greater dissatisfaction with each other and with their relationship.

Of course, we cannot be sure that these differences *caused* the conflict in Peggy and Bill or in the sample as a whole. But experience and research data suggest that marital tensions are more likely to erupt when fathers and mothers become polarized (cf. Block, Block, and Morrison 1981). Because our culture still promotes gender-stereotyped family and work arrangements, the transition to parenthood heightens the differences between men and women, and these differences threaten the equilibrium of their marriage.

Perhaps Ray best captured, in his typically humorous style, both the complexity and the dramatic simplicity of what happens to marriage when partners become parents. His and Celie's daughter, Faith, was three and a half years old when we asked him what had been the *hardest* part of becoming a family. His answer: "The changes in our relationship as a couple." And the *best* part of becoming a family? He grinned. "The changes in our relationship as a couple!"

CHAPTER 6

Beyond the Doorstep:
New Problems, New Solutions

WOMEN MAKE MANY DIFFERENT KINDS OF CHOICES about whether, when, and under what conditions they will return to work after having a baby. We found a substantial number who were relatively happy with their choice to stay home while their babies were young, and others who felt sure that they and their children were benefiting from their decision to return to work. Whatever their ultimate work/family arrangements, *every* woman we talked with continued to think about the possibility that perhaps she made the wrong choice. "In my mom's day they said, 'To be a full-fledged woman, you've got to be a mother and not a career woman,' and now it's switched. I'm expected to have a career and *not* be a mother. Or be a mother, but keep my career on track. So I'm at home looking after little John, but I keep wondering whether I ought to be at work. Meanwhile, my friend Abby is back at work feeling desperate because she feels she ought to be home!"

We are talking to Shannon and John when their baby is six months old. One of the most up-beat women in our study, Shannon is in a couple who were Planners (chapter 2) and had a fairly serene pregnancy (chapter 3). Despite their surprise at how "traditional" their arrangements of who does what have become, John and Shannon are still feeling quite positive about their relationship as a couple (chapter 5). Compared to other couples in our study they are feeling less strain, yet Shannon's deliberations about staying home or going back to work were echoed in some form by every woman in our study.

Balancing family and work life after the baby comes is one of the major tasks that couples face when they come up for air and turn their attention to the outside world. A second task to be accomplished, whether or not women return to their jobs, is finding acceptable, affordable caregivers when neither parent is available to look after the child. These tasks are part of an ongoing challenge for new parents. Following families over the past fifteen years, we have discovered that it is typical for couples to make not one but several major shifts in their lives during this period of family formation. Some are undertaken voluntarily, others are out of their control. But almost all of them increase a couple's strain. A couple might move to larger or more congenial quarters, which usually means higher expenses and being farther away from the people they count on for support. A partner loses or gives up a job. A grandparent or one of the new parents themselves becomes seriously ill. During the course of our longitudinal study, at least six of the new parents suffered serious illnesses—postpartum depression, a severe back injury, lupus, multiple sclerosis, rheumatoid arthritis—while countless others grieved for a parent who had become ill and died.

When life changes and the stresses they bring loom large, as they inevitably do during the transition to parenthood, couples must look to their personal resources and their network of support, people they can turn to for advice, financial backing, empathy, or emotional sustenance. The theory is that social support can buffer or reduce the impact of life stress (Crnic et al. 1983; Crockenberg 1981). In this chapter we follow couples as they turn from adapting to the unexpected shifts in themselves and their marriage to coping with changes in their worlds outside the family.

In chapter 4 we listened to Art and Stephanie's struggle about whether she would agree to get a baby-sitter so that they could spend some time together as a couple. It seemed like a typical inside-the-family issue. As we listen more closely, however, we hear how pressures from outside the family are contributing to the strain in Stephanie and Art's relationship as a couple.

A few months before our eighteen-months-after-birth conversation, Stephanie had returned to her job in the dental office four days a week and Art had been promoted from teacher to principal of an experimental elementary school. In addition to these major shifts, they had also moved to a new community in order to be closer to his school. Stephanie said it had taken six months of phone calls, letters, and meetings to convince the dentist she worked for that she could do the job on a four-day-a-week schedule: "It is too good a job to give up, but I was ready to tell him to stuff it until he finally gave in. He's a good guy, but he just doesn't understand. He's got a wife at home full-time, and his kids have grown up. He gets everything at home taken care of by her, and at the office by me, and he just assumes that that's what women do."

It doesn't help, she tells Art, that his work is so demanding that she and Linda hardly see him during the week. Art knew that working long hours made him miss some of the most important times in Linda's life: "But I don't know how to manage it all with this new job. I obviously couldn't turn down the promotion, and I just can't do it on a nine-to-five schedule. It's for you and Linda, too. I wish you'd back off a little."

Although couples themselves can take a long time to recognize that pressures from the outside world spill over into their relationship, we see here how difficult it can be for them to juggle the demands of the job and the needs of the baby and still have energy and time for each other. As if this task were not difficult enough, Stephanie goes on to other serious concerns. She doesn't know where the local child-care facilities in her new neighborhood are. She has not met any neighbors yet, and their new home is too far away from their old one to see much of their former next-door neighbors, who had become close friends.

Three of the most common outside-the-family challenges are how to find a balance between work and family life; how to find adequate child care; and how to find stable sources of support in a world that seems to be dominated by change. Each unresolved challenge becomes a source of increased stress, each challenge successfully met, a source of added support. Despite all the talk about stress, struggle, and obstacles, these negative-sounding conditions do not necessarily lead to unhappy outcomes. In fact, if parents are to keep changing and growing as their children develop, some challenge may be necessary. An important case in point, as we will see, is that when women with young children do juggle work and family roles successfully, they tend to feel better about themselves and their marriages, even if they are breathless at times.

Work

Although every one of our interview questions is addressed to both members of the couple, when we ask about returning to work after the baby is born, it is the women who tend to answer. Men do not think that this question is meant for them. There is a little variation in *when* new fathers plan to go back to work: Some arrange to stay home for several days after their babies are born; a few might take more than a week off. But the basic assumption is so automatic that it is never stated directly: Fathers do not quit or cut back on their jobs once the baby comes home. It is mothers who must decide whether or when to return to their work outside the family.

Despite the cultural shift in ideology toward a more egalitarian stance, gender-stereotyped attitudes have crept into the framing of most researchers' questions about mothers' work. Early studies focused on identifying the potentially harmful consequences of mothers' work outside the family, especially for young children. We can hear that parents have been affected by knowing about journalists' and researchers' writing about this issue. Does working increase a woman's stress or depression? Does it create problems in her marriage? Does a mother's working deprive her husband and children of nurturance and support? (Here we are reminded of the man in Gail Sheehy's *Passages* [1976] who said that ever since his wife went back to work, their family had had no butter and no desserts!) No one thinks to ask a father what his wife and baby might miss when *he* goes back to work.

There are advantages *and* drawbacks to both parents working when children are young. When all of the findings are toted up, the balance appears to be generally positive, especially for mothers and daughters (Greenberger and Goldberg 1989; Moorehouse in press). Perhaps even more important, our results suggest that when fathers and mothers manage to balance family and work to their satisfaction, there is positive spillover for the wife's satisfaction with herself, for the quality of the relationships both parents develop with their children, and for *both* spouses' satisfaction with their marriage.

PARENTS' WORK/FAMILY ARRANGEMENTS AND SATISFACTION

The majority of mothers with children under three are working outside the home, and this will soon be true of mothers of one-year-olds. Given these rapid historical shifts and the powerful competing ideologies about how men and women should balance work and family life, we expected to find a variety of work/family arrangements in the couples in our study. The patterns in our sample seem to match the national demographics fairly closely. When their infants were six months old, 55 percent of the mothers were back at work, 36 percent part-time (less than twenty hours a week) and 19 percent working between twenty and forty hours a week. One year later, when the children were one and a half, 57 percent of the mothers were employed, 30 percent part-time and 27 percent full-time.

These apparently stable averages over time hide an important fact. About one-third of the women are making shifts in their work arrangements over the year between their babies' six- and eighteen-month birthdays—some entering the labor force, some leaving it, others increasing their work hours from part-time to full-time, and others cutting back from full-time to part time. Even within two-worker families, "full-time" work can mean different things for mothers and fathers. The mothers working full-time in our study were employed between thirty-two and forty hours a week during their children's toddler years, but some of the fathers were away from home as many as fifty to eighty hours a week. Any way we look at these figures, they spell potential strain for a couple with very young children. A discussion of four common work/family arrangements will help show that each alternative involves trade-offs.

Mom is home, but anguished. When we meet them in late pregnancy, Gail and Michael describe themselves as happily married.* As a couple, they are

---

*An extended case study of this couple can be found in a chapter by Bradburn and Kaplan (in press).

feeling closer together than ever before, but both worry about what will happen when they try to balance work and parenthood after their child is born. Gail has decided to stay home for a while but is concerned about how they are going to manage: "How guilty am I going to feel not working? How guilty am I going to feel working? How are we going to arrange child care and all that?" Michael's job demands intense involvement. His worries center on how much his work will take away time he could be spending with the baby: "I've made the resolution that I want the child to be uppermost."

When we visit Gail and Michael six months after their daughter, Sarah, is born, we find that, just as they had feared, juggling family and work is creating a good deal of stress for both of them. Michael's job as a medical researcher does offer flexible hours, so he takes care of some of the morning and evening routines with Sarah. But recently work has become hectic and he has had to put in about sixty-five hours a week:

MICHAEL: I'm used to working in the evenings, but now, either I don't get to do it at all or I finish and I'm exhausted. I'm in a bind. I miss watching every detail of Sarah's development. But if I really want to build my career and get off on a solid footing, now's the time to do it.

GAIL: I'm in a bind, too. I feel restless being at home all the time. I've been thinking that a part-time job would be good for me, doing something practical, something other than being a mother. But at the same time I feel guilty at the thought of leaving Sarah with strangers. I firmly believe that children should stay at home with one parent.

MICHAEL: I really disagree with Gail about child care. I think it would be good for her to work, and good for Sarah, too. Others find good part-time day care, and I know we can, too.

GAIL: We could sure use the extra money, but it seems that what it costs for decent child care would take everything I can earn.

As we follow Gail and Michael over the next five years, there is little resolution of this issue. When their second child, Jason, comes along, Gail continues to feel ambivalent about working or arranging any regular day care for the children. Michael's work becomes even more demanding, the typical pattern for men in the family-making period. Gail says that she is longing for a career direction but pursues it "halfheartedly" because of her conflict about leaving the children with someone else. She eventually finds part-time work that she can do at home.

As they struggle with these conflicts between family and work—within and between them—Michael and Gail describe more conflict and distance in their relationship as a couple. When Sarah is about three years old, they seek couples therapy to see whether they can recapture their earlier closeness. Although most couples do not look for professional help for their marital strain, this is a typical example of how outside-the-family pressures begin to play out in the marriage.

There are many reasons for Michael and Gail's work choices and their subsequent distress about them, but several stand out. Gail has been truly confused about how to get on with her own career and still be with the children during the period when they need her regular care and attention. Since she has not been able to understand what is fueling her confusion, she feels unsure about her competence as a mother and a professional, especially when she looks at Michael's rising career. Husbands' support for their wives' work is important, but Michael's "support" for Gail finding a job has not been helpful because it fails to recognize the underlying emotional dilemmas that pull her to stay home. To complicate matters further, the combination of Michael's increasingly demanding work schedule and his direct involvement with the children leaves him little time and energy for his relationship with Gail, so the marriage feels a little shaky to both of them.

Finally, like most of the couples in our study, Michael and Gail use what to us is a curious approach to calculating the financial "costs and benefits" of a mother's going back to work. For some reason, the common assumption is that the cost of child care should be subtracted from the *wife's* salary. This line of reasoning ignores the fact that if parents must work, *someone* must look after the children. If the husband works outside the home and the wife looks after the children, part of his salary could be thought of as subsidizing that choice. By the same logic, if both the husband and wife work outside the home, part of each of their salaries could be earmarked for the care of the children. Locked into a traditional view of a mother's role, however, most parents assume that if the wife chooses to work, *she* should pay for someone to look after *their* child. So even if both parents acknowledge that the wife's work is important to her, she can become discouraged from resuming her job if she cannot earn more than the cost of their children's care. It is important to reexamine the price of this kind of logic—in actual dollars and in emotional toll—on the wife, the husband, the marriage, and the children.

Mom planned to continue working, but changed her mind. Sharon is one of the mothers who decided not to go back to work as early as she had planned. This is how she explained it to us six months after Amy was born:

> SHARON: It was understood that I would take six months off work. I took one month off before she was born, so that left five. Then, as the end of the fifth month approached, I realized that I didn't want to go back to work. Boy, we went through a lot at that point. Can we survive on just one salary? I really didn't want to leave Amy with anybody. I had no idea I would be so possessive. It was about that time that I heard on the news that a child-care center had caught fire, and that somebody had kidnapped somebody else's baby, and I'm saying, "I'm not sending my child anywhere!"
>
> So I asked for an extension to my leave, and I figured I'd get Amy a little more self-reliant because she was still strictly a breast-fed baby. At the same time, Daniel went through a job change and got a large bonus. So he told me that I didn't have to go back to work for a while.

Regardless of how well-thought-out their plans are, few couples can predict how the women will feel about going back to work after the baby is born. Many women tell us that their feelings about being with their babies and about the importance of their work alter dramatically once they become mothers. Some say that work simply doesn't feel as important as it used to, and others say that they are so much more drawn to their babies than they had anticipated. Thus, decisions that seemed firm before they became mothers become "unmade." This pattern is consistent with the results of a recent study of new mothers by Karen Harber (1991), who found that 75 percent of the mothers felt significant conflict between wanting to work and wanting to be with their babies in the first months of motherhood.

Women's uncertainty does not disappear as their babies grow older. When we talk with Sharon and Daniel again a year later, her plans about returning to full-time work have changed again. Like Gail, Sharon has been reluctant to leave her daughter and argues that the wages and commuting costs—taken, of course, out of *her* salary—will not result in much more money for the family. Still, because she is determined to use her working skills before she loses them, Sharon has taken a job with a cosmetics firm where she can set her own hours: "I don't work *for* anyone. It's the first time having a job has been fun. Amy goes to the baby-sitter twenty hours a week. If I'm not out doing a demonstration or a facial, I have time for catching up around the house. And then she comes home and has a nap, and then her father comes home. It works out well as long as I get back early. If Daniel and I come home at the same time—watch out!"

Women like Sharon are going to great lengths to make adjustments in their work outside the family so that their family lives will feel more nurturant and less frantic. By contrast, when fathers make shifts in their jobs, it is to keep them moving up the career ladder. These moves feel especially important, the men say, now that they are supporting a family.

Mom is a student, but is always frazzled. Cindy and James have been fighting a lot lately. He is working as a chemist in a paint company between his undergraduate and graduate training in chemistry so that Cindy can complete her studies in economics and business. They are frustrated with juggling so many hours of work, rushing to complete their education, and trying to spend "quality time" with their son, Eddie. Their stress is aggravated by Cindy's one-hour commute to and from school each day. She must get Eddie to a sitter near her college at 7:30 A.M. and pick him up at 4:30 P.M.:

CINDY: I feel like I don't have a moment's peace. In the morning I have to rush Eddie, rush James, get everybody moving, get ready, drive like mad, take the time to get Eddie settled at day care, and get to classes. When I sit down in the quiet of the library to begin my assignments, I find myself thinking about Eddie and what he's doing. Or thinking about the last fight that James and I had, and what we're going to do about it. Trying to get my reading and assignments done before I leave to pick Eddie up at the end of the day is like being in a Charlie Chaplin movie. By the end of the day, I'm really uptight. And then in the late afternoon, we replay the whole scene in reverse. By the time everything stops moving and Eddie's in bed, my head is already into what I have to face at school tomorrow.

Cindy and James's pace is more frenetic than that of the typical new family, but we see variations on this theme in every family with two parents who work or have full-time school schedules. It is not surprising that, when the days begin and end with parents and children feeling rushed and frazzled, thoughtful and tender moments between the parents are rare.

Mom is at work and pleased about her situation, sort of. Natalie and Victor, you may recall, have been doing well as a couple. Their daughter, Kim, is eighteen months old, and Victor's and Natalie's sense of humor and flexibility seem to be pulling them through the early challenges of parenthood.

Reflecting on the fact that her mother's sacrifice in staying home did not make her a satisfied woman, Natalie has been determined since the beginning of her pregnancy to return to her job, which she loves. This she does, although, like Stephanie, she finds herself engaged in complex negotiations with her company to reduce her schedule to four days a week. Victor, wanting to be available to his child in a way that his father was not for him, is taking a very active role in Kim's daily routines. Although he was working for his father when we first met him, he has recently taken an interim job in which he can set his own hours and earn a decent salary while he sorts out "what I really want to be when I grow up." When his and Natalie's work hours overlap, Kim's two sets of grandparents, who live nearby, take turns looking after her. It seems as if Natalie and Victor have the kinds of support that couples need to manage the stress of the early family years.

But these "solutions" leave Natalie feeling uneasy a lot of the time. Although she realizes that she and Victor share work and family time more equally than most other couples, and have the extra benefit of grandparents who love to care for Kim, she has mixed feelings about her work/family balance: "On one hand, I'm feeling more and more independent, able to take business trips without feeling guilty. Feeling good that I can put a limit on my work time. But I'm still uneasy about leaving Kim, even though she's with Victor or our parents. I want to be with her *and* be at work. The dilemma does not feel totally resolvable right now." Natalie is not alone: Even when they are reasonably contented with how their lives are shaping up, *not one* of the employed mothers in our study was entirely satisfied that she was devoting enough energy to her work outside the family or that she had chosen the best way to be with the baby.

The compelling ideology of the egalitarian family has saddled new mothers with two major decisions: *whether* to work while their children are young, and *how* to arrange their work so that their children will feel loved and secure. The pressure of making arrangements so that men and women will have more equal roles at work and at home affects the emotional atmosphere in the family much more than it affects couples' behavior. And work/family arrangements clearly exact a greater toll on women's progress in their jobs and careers than on men's. Many women say that this state of affairs would probably be acceptable if it lasted just for the first family-making year. But most are concerned that any substantial impediment to increasing their earning power could put them and their children at risk if anything were to happen to their husbands or their marriages. Their fears are not assuaged by reading the shocking statistics about how women's and children's standard of living plummets when families are torn apart by death or divorce (Wallerstein and Blakeslee 1989; Weitzman 1985).

PARENTS' WORK PATTERNS

Just as we found that the impact of a new baby on parents depends on how they were doing before the baby came along, so we learned that couples' decisions about how to balance work inside and outside the family after having a baby stem from attitudes in the workplace and from the partners' work and family histories, especially those of the wife.

Women's Work History and Well-being During Pregnancy   A woman's decision about working after her baby is born is influenced by how invested she was in her job or career before. We noted that Gail has been ambivalent about going out to work since her children were born. If we go farther back in her preparenthood history, we find that she was torn about "who she was going to be" even before she became a mother. Gail says that her sense of a work or career direction has been cloudy since she completed her schooling. Even when she had the luxury of time, her search for work was not very serious. Not surprisingly, it remained so after Sarah came along.

Working outside the home appears to play a role in women's well-being. The mothers in our study who had returned to work by the time their children were eighteen months old reported slightly but significantly fewer symptoms of depression. Was this because new mothers who are less depressed are more likely to be motivated to return to their work outside the family, or because the time spent working and the feelings of self-worth that jobs can promote lower the probability that mothers will feel depressed? If we go back to what the women told us about themselves during pregnancy, we know that both self-esteem and marital satisfaction in late pregnancy predicted women's level of depression when their children were eighteen months old (Heming 1985, 1987), although they did not predict whether women went back to work. Nevertheless, women who had returned to work part- or full-time by the time their child was a year and a half reported fewer symptoms of depression, whereas those who remained at home full-time reported more depression than their well-being during pregnancy had led us to expect.

It does not seem to be the case that feeling less depressed makes it more likely that mothers return to work. It looks as if going back to work helps to protect them against feeling depressed.[1]

These results make more sense of Gail's symptoms of depression. Not only was she discouraged about her career direction before she became a mother but she had not had the advantage some mothers have of finding their sense of competence in a job they are invested in. Some of her husband's encouragement is based on his knowledge of Gail's skills and his belief that work will help her feel better about herself, but she has not felt ready to take this step.

Attitudes and Practices in the Workplace   How new parents make and manage their work choices is influenced partly by their work histories and attitudes, and partly by their general level of distress or well-being before they become parents. Clearly, attitudes and practices in the working world play a significant role too. Only the United States and South Africa, of all the world's industrialized countries, lack a national policy for maternity leave (Steinberg and Belsky 1991).

Most of the women in our study know all about the maternity leave or family policies where they work. At most, women are allowed up to six months' leave, usually without pay, if they are employed in a business that has at least twenty workers. Self-employed women—writers, therapists, and freelance workers, for example—are on their own in figuring out whether they can afford to take time off to recuperate from giving birth and to spend the first weeks or months with their infants. Marian, a thirty-seven-year-old attorney, tells us about the double messages she feels from her colleagues: "I did take the six-month maternity leave my firm offers. But I'm feeling that behind their smiles, the partners think that any woman who would actually take time off from the practice of law is not 'partner material.'"

We hear stories like Marian's from men, too, although they are less likely to be familiar with, or to take advantage of, their employers' paternity or family-leave policies. Tom, who describes himself as a troubleshooter for a firm that makes computers, is astonished at his boss's attitude when he returns to work immediately after his daughter's birth: "My buddies at work were full of congratulations when I came back in on a Friday to announce that Kristin had just been born. Then my boss, Alec, pops into my office, offers me a cigar, and says, 'Congratulations, Tom! I hear it's a girl. By the way, I'll need that report of yours on my desk on Monday morning.' That's it—and he's out the door!"

Juggling Work and Family   Researchers have worried that the strain of juggling work and family life may contribute to family stress, particularly for women. Yet systematic studies of women's work and home lives find that women who manage multiple roles actually feel better about themselves and their lives (Baruch, Barnett, and Rivers 1983).

A critical question about the impact of both partners having jobs, as we discussed in chapter 5, is what happens to the division of work at home (Hochschild 1989). Our study and others (Pleck 1985) indicate that husbands whose wives are employed do a little more housework and caring for the children than husbands whose wives do not work outside the home.[2] In our study, the more fathers were involved in the day-to-day tasks of running the family, the more satisfied both parents were with themselves and their marriage. When mothers are employed, then, the impact of their work on the family depends not only on what they do outside the family but on what their husbands do inside.

For many modern couples, coordinating a number of work and family roles that they consider important represents a challenge and an opportunity to show their competence. Managing it all can be hectic for both parents, but when they feel that they are part of a team that is managing it all successfully, there seem to be benefits for how they both end up feeling about themselves and their marriage. Part of the excitement of the journey for pioneers is mastering the hardships they encounter.

Some couples tell us that life runs more calmly and smoothly in the early family-making period when one parent stays home to care for the baby while the other functions as the breadwinner—of course, the stay-at-home parent is almost always the mother. In theory, the parent at home should have more time to be responsive to the baby's unpredictable fluctuations in schedule and mood, to get through the laundry, cleaning, and cooking on a more relaxed schedule, and to greet the breadwinner on his or her return. Indeed, for a small number of couples, like Shannon and John, this is exactly what they describe: a relatively satisfying traditional division of labor both inside and outside the family.

But both practical and psychological considerations seem to get in the way of homemaker/breadwinner arrangements being satisfying for most of the single-earner families we saw. As the at-home parent described it, the traditional way of doing things demands a considerable balancing act, too. To begin with, in order for one partner to stay home with the children, both must feel that they can manage on one income. For the couples in our study, considerations other than finances play an even more salient role in such decisions. Parents' notions about what a baby needs to feel secure and cared for are central in their decisions about "mother or other care." But ideas about what babies need are colliding with the new ideology about what men and women *ought* to be doing inside and outside the family. Particularly in a culture that values accomplishments that are rewarded with a paycheck, the stay-at-home parent must feel very strongly about the baby's and family's needs to feel satisfied with the more traditional arrangements of the previous generation.

What Is the Impact on Children?   The women in our study worried about the potentially negative impact of their working on their children. There is little we can say yet, positive or negative, about the direct links between mothers' work and how their children are developing (see Bronfenbrenner and Crouter 1982; Hoffman 1989; Moorehouse in press). We will have a more realistic picture of what works best for parents and children when we can assess how fathers' and mothers' work and family relationships play out in the parents' feelings about themselves, their marriage, and their relationships with their children.

There is at least one consistent finding in the research on the effects of mothers' employment on children: Whereas preschool-age sons of working mothers are sometimes found to be more distressed than sons of mothers at home full-time, daughters of working mothers appear to benefit in both their cognitive and social development compared to girls whose mothers stay home. What could account for this gender difference?

Studies of the way parents socialize their sons and daughters show that parents tend to encourage boys' independence and girls' dependence (Block 1984; see also chapter 8). Perhaps when mothers are at home full-time, they have a tendency to help and protect their daughters more than working mothers do, which may leave these daughters less room than daughters of working mothers to develop self-reliance, independence, and competence. Mothers who must manage a household and a job outside the family may expect their children to do more for themselves, which could encourage more self-reliance as well as providing a model of both competence and achievement for their children to emulate, a model that might be especially important for their daughters.

What gets set in motion when a couple decides whether the mother will return to work? One intriguing finding from our study suggests that spouses' disagreements about this issue may reverberate throughout the family (Schulz 1991). Husbands and wives who disagree about who should be bringing in the family income[3] are more likely to be angry and competitive with each other while they are working and playing with their children in our playroom. Such parents are less warm, responsive, structured, and limit setting with their three-and-a-half-year-old preschoolers. Finally, the preschoolers whose parents disagreed about their work/family arrangements were rated two years later by their kindergarten teachers as more shy and withdrawn. What we are seeing here is that the parents' feelings about their work/family arrangements play out in their relationship as a couple. This finding is quite consistent with Arlie Hochschild's (1989) study, in which she finds negative effects on the couple's relationship of women doing the second shift at home after working outside the family. What our data add is that when husbands and wives disagree about their arrangements of family and work, the effects of their differences are felt in their marriage, in their relationships with the child, *and* in the child's social development.

Child Care

More than half of the preschool children in the United States spend a substantial part of the work week being cared for by someone other than their parents. Recent estimates show that even though 35 million American children under fourteen years of age have mothers who work, there are only 5 million places available for them in before- and afterschool care centers

(Quindlen 1991). The psychologist Sandra Scarr has made a thorough investigation of the child-care shortage and concluded that it is a "national scandal" (1984, p. 224).

Scarr's judgment is based on the premise that child-care resources are a necessity. During the late 1970s and early 1980s, influential reviews of the research on the impact of child care on young children's development (Belsky and Steinberg 1978; Belsky, Steinberg, and Walker 1982) were generally reassuring to working mothers. Not only were researchers finding no negative effects of day care on children's intellectual development; their results were suggesting that children might actually reap advantages in their social development by being in a reasonably good child-care setting while their parents were at work. In a startling reversal, Jay Belsky and his colleagues (Belsky 1986, 1988; Belsky and Rovine 1988), citing their own and others' research, recently expressed concern that infants who are in "nonmaternal care" for more than twenty hours a week before they are one year old might be at risk of developing insecure attachments to their parents: Having been separated and then reunited with Mother or Father, such children might be more likely to avoid the parent or to respond angrily, and less likely to use the parent as a "secure base" when they are anxious or distressed.

We cannot reassure parents who avail themselves of day care in this situation that Belsky's view is mistaken, although some important and thoughtful reviews by other researchers raise serious questions about his conclusions (Clarke-Stewart 1989; Phillips et al. 1987). We can point out, though, that simple comparisons of young children who are or are not in child care can give a distorted picture of a very complex issue. First, we must not lump all child-care arrangements together when evaluating their impact on children: Obviously, they are not all alike, and within each type are wide variations in the quality of care (Phillips and Howes 1987). Second, as we have seen in our discussion of women's work, we cannot simply evaluate the impact of outside-the-family care without considering the influence of family processes on the parents' choice of whether to seek child care and what kind of care they seek. Belsky himself, in an excellent review and rethinking of this issue (1990), agrees that we must include information about family processes in any study of the effects of day care.

DO WE CHOOSE CHILD CARE?

At the six-months-after-birth follow-up, 6 percent of the babies are being cared for primarily by both parents and approximately 45 percent primarily by their mothers. The families are divided almost equally into those who do and those who do not place the child in the care of a nonfamily member for more than five hours per week. By the time the children are one and a half, the proportion of babies being cared for primarily by one or both parents has declined to 32 percent, and by the time they are three and a half, only 17 percent of the parents are doing the primary care.

Obviously, considerations about both parents' wanting or needing to work top the list of whether and when to use child care. Second, questions of child-care costs and availability affect couples' decisions. In talking about whether they use child care regularly, couples in our study mention three additional considerations that affect their decisions: their beliefs and feelings about whether it is helpful or harmful for young children to spend time in the care of someone else; their experience of how easy or difficult it is to be separated from their child; and the legacies of attitudes from their parents that can make outside child care feel like a positive or a negative option.

It does not take much historical or anthropological research to realize that what is regarded as normal—in this case, children reared primarily by their parents—has not been common throughout the course of human history. In other times and cultures, and in much of the world today, extended family members, nonrelated adults, and older children in the community take care of the young. But modern couples have grown up with a powerful message that mother care is optimal and any other care is a poor substitute.

This opinion has been reinforced by a number of influential psychoanalytic theorists (A. Freud 1965; Mahler, Pine, and Bergman 1975) and child-rearing experts. Until very recently, the most widely quoted pediatricians and developmententalists in North America and England stated clearly that babies need their mothers to be with them to assure their optimal development. Benjamin Spock and Berry Brazelton held this view early on but have revised it in recent years. Burton White and Penelope Leach still advise mothers to stay at home with their young children. Beyond these views of the "experts," a number of the parents we spoke to were being swayed by their own experience of having felt abandoned as children when their parents were away at work. This leaves parents in a serious bind if they want or need to work.

Laurie Leventhal-Belfer (1990) asked the parents in our study to write down their thoughts and feelings about the child-care choices they made. One mother responded:

> I don't enjoy staying at home all day long with our child, but I don't think I could allow myself to use any other child-care arrangement. It also is not economically feasible for us to do something different, because good child-care alternatives are so expensive. So I've just stayed home. I've even taken care of other people's children five days a week from 8:30 to 6:00 to earn a little extra money because of my husband's reduced salary. It's hard to believe, isn't it?

This mother's painfully honest response gives us pause. Her beliefs about who should bring up children, in combination with her economic circumstances, have led her to create a twenty-four-hour-a-day role in which she is clearly not invested. We feel concern for her well-being, her child's and that of the other children who spend their day with her. Clearly, we cannot assume that a parent will always provide better care than a child-care provider, especially if the parent wants to be somewhere else.

At the other end of the spectrum are those women who find it difficult to spend any time away from their children. While some fathers talk about how much they miss their child during the day, and about occasionally wanting to come home early to see them from an evening out or a weekend away, such feelings are expressed most powerfully by mothers.

Gail describes this feeling vividly when she mentions her confusion about going to work. She feels guilty about the thought of leaving Sarah and Jason "with strangers," but her feelings seem to be based on deeper concerns. She has strong ties to both of her children, so strong that she identifies with what she imagines are *their* feelings based on her own early distressing experiences. "I think I'm Sarah. I think I'm Jason. And I think they're me. I think Sarah's exactly like I am, with all my anxieties, and I think I deal with her based on that. It's like I turned into her, and she turned into how I was as a kid."

Gail conveys the notion that placing their children in someone else's care will be a personal loss to *her*. Indeed, the more hours babies spend in alternative care when they are six months and eighteen months old, the more likely the mothers in our study were to draw smaller Mother pieces on their pie charts.[4] It may be that for women like Gail, who have not settled on who else they are besides Mother, the prospect of giving the children over to someone else's care is too threatening. For other women whose psychological and actual involvement as Mother is less than average, there seem to be positive trade-offs in that their identity as Partner or Lover can expand. We have seen that this is one of the "pieces" that Gail and Michael are trying to put back into their lives.

Although most discussions about work and child care focus on what children need, parents' needs are an important part of the equation. As Nancy Chodorow argues eloquently in *The Reproduction of Mothering* (1978), women are much more susceptible than men to powerful feelings of connectedness, especially in relation to their roles as mothers. Their feeling that women must do the mothering is certainly reinforced by attitudes and arrangements in our society that make it almost impossible for men and women to make equal and independent choices about balancing work and family life.

It is also reinforced by the example of new parents' parents. From the information we gathered about the relationships of the parents we studied with *their* parents, we learned that Gail's mother had also felt guilty about leaving Gail when she was young. This also goes some way toward explaining Gail's unrelenting ambivalence about work and motherhood. The tendency to repeat generational patterns, especially those that have to do with a parent's anxiety or anger, seems to have Gail in its grip. We discuss this in more detail in the next chapter.

We have been moved in following Gail in her struggle to keep from replaying the painful part of her own and her mother's history. Several years after becoming a mother, Gail begins to discover that this part of the pattern from her childhood has not served her well. Something about her own growing up has left her feeling stalled in her development as an adult, and it is also beginning to get in the way of her being able to allow her children to have their own experiences, separate from hers. These revelations lead Gail to seek professional help in an effort to understand and modify this pattern in her relationship with her children.

Becoming a mother has led to a personal crisis for Gail, although it took some years for her to articulate it that way. The support of getting her relationship with Michael back on track gives her the strength to begin facing the conflict she has been feeling about her life. And, as Victor uses the support of his wife, Natalie, to shift his troubling work situation, Gail uses Michael's encouragement to begin some part-time work that will help her to spend some time separate from the children. At the same time, she and Michael work on reestablishing the intimacy of their relationship as a couple.

By the time Sarah is in kindergarten, Gail has begun to talk with her mother about why she was reluctant to leave Gail in someone else's care. This seems to be helping Gail put her own anxiety about this into a broader perspective. As Naomi Lowinsky (1990, 1992) suggests, when women make opportunities to hear the stories from their own "motherline," the women in their extended families, they can often begin to come to grips with a fuller sense of themselves as mothers, daughters, wives, and fully conscious women. We are confident that Gail's explorations into the source of her confusion will eventually shed more light on what has kept her in conflict about finding her career direction, being a mother, and maintaining an intimate relationship with Michael.

In Gail's example we see the twin meanings of crisis: danger and opportunity. When she experienced danger, she was frightened for a time and different parts of her life felt shaky. But she has been able to use the occasion of her children's growth to move on with her own development by confronting some of the unresolved fears and problems from her past (P. Cowan 1988a). While it is too soon to be sure about how her story will end, Sarah is now in the fifth grade and doing well, Jason is in second grade, and both parents feel that they are getting back on track as individuals, as a couple, and as a family.

WHAT KIND OF CHILD CARE?

Some couples begin their search for child care with an image of a smiling middle-aged woman who takes a few children into her comfortable old house. Others believe that only pert and energetic young women in clean and tidy child-care centers will take adequate care of their child. Some parents want a child-care person who will be actively involved in stimulating their child's intellectual development, while others are equally or more concerned about fostering their children's social relationships and giving them room to play in a relaxed setting.

Even after extensive searching, parents rarely find a day-care arrangement that completely fits their initial hopes. As one mother wrote: "It's difficult to accept that no child-care arrangement is as perfect as I fantasized before we confronted the real world." Only a few couples feel they were lucky enough to have found the "perfect situation." Beth and Paul are thrilled with Margo, who provides just the kind of loving care for Willie that they want. Paul refers to her as "part of our family team." Most are more like Tanya and Jackson. In addition to assuming most of the responsibility for the household and looking after Kevin, Tanya has also taken the major role in finding someone to care for Kevin when she returns to work. She is clearly distressed:

> TANYA: I found this one place that looks great. It's close to my work and I could easily drop Kevin off, but it's $20 a day. That might not sound unreasonable, but it's $5,000 a year that we don't have—it didn't cost me $5,000 a year to go to college! There's this other place that's great and it's cheaper, but it's all the way across town. A third place is cheap, but I wouldn't leave any kid there for a minute.
>
> JACKSON: As I see it, the most important thing we have to figure out is what will be best for Kevin.
>
> TANYA: But you *don't* see it, Jackson. You haven't visited *one* of these places. And I'm the one who's going to take Kevin every day and pick him up. The other possibility is a day-care center that's a little big, but the staff seems great, the equipment is brand-new, and it costs only a little more than I think we can afford. I'd really hoped to have Kevin in a small place, with a loving, motherly person, but I just don't think that's going to work.

With a few notable exceptions, it was the mothers in our study who gathered all the information about child-care resources, made most of the visits, and spent hours worrying about alternatives. Then, usually in consultation with their husbands, they would make the final decision. Even though most of the women seem to assume that this is their job, many resent the responsibility, particularly because the choices are so difficult and seem to have such far-reaching consequences.

Although the task of figuring it out is considered "women's work," men's feelings about their child-care decisions and arrangements make a difference to both parents. A few fathers have serious reservations about using any major outside child care during their baby's first year. In light of modern notions about male-female equality, some of the fathers are almost apologetic in suggesting that they really prefer their wives to stay home with their child.

One intriguing finding (Leventhal-Belfer 1990; Leventhal-Belfer, Cowan, and Cowan in press) is that the family's actual day-care arrangements—mother care or other care—are not related to either parent's well-being or distress (their marital satisfaction, self-esteem, depression, or parenting stress), but that *wives'* well-being or distress is related to their *husbands'* satisfaction with the child-care decision. If the fathers are satisfied with the child-care arrangements, the mothers report less parenting stress and fewer symptoms of depression. Furthermore, mothers' satisfaction with their arrangements for the children's care is related to their perceptions of their husbands' support for their role in them.

Husbands' involvement is important not only in the major decisions about child care but also in the occasional baby-sitting arrangements. Again, wives are stuck with most of the work in finding baby-sitters, even when husbands are insistent that the couple needs to go out. Remember Stephanie and Art's arguments about this issue? They told us that their discussions eventually led them to decide to go out together at least once every two weeks. This has given them more time alone together but has not solved the problem entirely:

> STEPHANIE: Art thinks that somehow sitters just magically appear when you need them. Last week I made fifteen calls and then at the last minute I got a sitter I didn't know, and I really didn't like her very much. I keep wondering why he can't do some of the calling.
>
> ART: I know I should. And I've tried. But every time I phone one of those girls' houses, a voice asks suspiciously exactly who I am and what I want. And then I talk to the girl, and she doesn't know whether she can come or not. It's like asking for a date. I find it humiliating and embarrassing.

From the large dilemmas of child care to the small ones, men and women must deal with a set of complex issues. They arrive at different conclusions through very different processes. Some of them feel good about their choices, and others are in mild or severe distress over them. Their problems are intensified by the frustrating ambivalence on the part of politicians and business people who make, or neglect to make, policies that affect the families of workers. The reluctance to take a stand that would support parents with young children puts families in a classic double bind. On one hand, the economy continues to depend on women workers; on the other, government and business policies support neither dual-worker families nor child-care facilities, especially for parents of preschool children. Parents are caught in this squeeze and they and their children feel the effects of the strain. The unresolved threads of these important work/family issues are weaving their way into the fabric of family life.

Social Support

It is not always possible to reduce or eliminate the stress involved in coping with life inside and outside the family. One way that new parents can feel better about themselves and make their lives more manageable is to find additional sources of support. People or situations that provide new parents with satisfaction, challenge, understanding, or direct advice and services can help them solve specific problems, stop worrying so much about their family responsibilities, relax and have some fun, and feel emotionally connected with others.

Where do new parents find support? Although we have emphasized the strain of trying to balance work and family and find the best care for their children, these can be sources of support and satisfaction as well. The stimulation of a meaningful job and co-workers can bolster a parent's confidence. Similarly, a caring child-care person can provide essential support for parents: instrumentally, by facilitating their ability to earn more income for the family; emotionally, by relieving anxiety about their child's care. Most of the parents in our study longed for or actively sought support from four other sources as they made their journey to parenthood: friends, members of their extended families, organized support groups, and health professionals.

FRIENDS

We asked about each partner's support from others with a questionnaire about the key people who provide it (Curtis-Boles 1979). Partners were asked to name four people who are important in their lives and to tell how far away they live, what kind of support they provide, and how satisfying their support feels.[5] One finding from the parents' responses on this questionnaire surprised us, but perhaps we could have expected it. About 20 percent of the expectant and new fathers told us that they did not have four people they could list. This seems to reflect the fact that in our society, men are much less likely than women to be part of a network of relationships with people in whom they can confide.

Most of the couples in our study live far from their parents and the communities in which they grew up. In contrast with their parents' generation, they have not come of age at a time when young people routinely marry and start families in lock step in their early twenties. The friends they spent time with before becoming pregnant often have no children themselves. As a consequence, when couples start having babies and facing some of the changes we have been describing, they can feel out of step with their close friends and may find themselves rushing to make new friendships, or strengthening old ones, with other parents. Shannon said that from the day she told people she was pregnant, their friends who had children began to call more often, offering advice as well as baby clothes and furniture. She and John received it all gratefully, but "could have lived without some of the war stories—things about rough times with each of their kids." They spent more and more of their free time with friends who were parents, and by the time little John was born their relationships with single or childless friends began to feel strained.

We heard similar stories over and over. In part, of course, new parents simply have less time to socialize than they used to. A few nonparent friends may make an active effort to take on the mantle of a favorite uncle or aunt to the new baby and to keep up their interest in the new parents, but more often such friendships, especially with friends who are single, begin to go through a period of disengagement. New parents often feel hurt or insulted when their childless friends suggest a spontaneous get-together, neglect to invite the baby, and "forget" that the parents can't respond without making complex arrangements for their baby.

As the babies grow, most of the couples are surprised to find how much of their social life they are spending with couples who are parents. These are the people they can talk to about things that hold little interest for their childless friends but are essential to them: cloth versus disposable diapers, the safest car seats and strollers, pediatricians, baby foods, nursery schools. If these friends are new, they can provide important information and support but cannot replace the shared history that makes old friends so comforting to be with, leaving parents to feel the loss of those more intimate relationships.

EXTENDED FAMILY

There seems to be a great nostalgia for earlier times when couples lived close to their extended families and could get help from them in times of joy, sorrow, and strain. The truth of the matter is that then was probably not so different from now (Skolnick 1991). For some couples, having extended families close by while they are becoming parents is truly a blessing. Family gatherings feel warm and welcoming to both the new parents and the baby. For others, the advice and visits of relatives and parents can be a burden.

Beth mentions that she felt close to her mother when she was young. A period of strain between them began in her late teens and extended through her college years. As a new mother, she is trying to reconnect: "We still have some tense times, but it's been good to visit her and talk about what it was like when I was growing up. I'm learning more about *her* struggles as a mother and wife. And I've gotten closer to my brothers and sisters too."

Bill and Peggy have a harder time with family togetherness:

BILL: Each Sunday and holiday, there's a "command performance." We have to show up at Peggy's folks' and Mindy has to "perform." Last year, I said to Peggy, "Hey, it's Father's Day at our house, too. What do you say we celebrate it at home?" She said her father would be crushed if we didn't go, so we went.

PEGGY: I sympathize with Bill, but I can't seem to get out of it. I think it would be OK if it was fun when we got there. Being with my parents and my sister and her family. My sister's mission in life seems to be to make me feel stupid. Her kids are teenagers now, and she thinks that makes her the expert. All I hear when we are there is what I'm doing wrong with Mindy, and what I could do different. By the time we leave, I'm ready to scream.

MOTHERS' AND FATHERS' SUPPORT GROUPS

About one in eight of the mothers in our study attend a mothers' group regularly. Some are led by a trained leader, while others are informal meetings for mutual support and conversation. At some, there are provisions for the children to play while the mothers talk. At first, almost all of the women find the groups invaluable. As Shannon said, "I don't think I could have survived without it. Every time I went, I would have a concern or worry that I thought was silly, and every week I would find that I wasn't the only one. It was so reassuring to know that my worries weren't way out of line." But after a while, some women say, several kinds of issues begin to pose problems that make the groups feel less productive. Sometimes a child's uncontrollable behavior creates tension. Mothers who work may feel indirect criticism about having decided to return to their jobs, while mothers at home may feel challenged by the women who are back at work. The topic of husbands comes up often, and, though most women find solace in expressing irritation with their husbands, the group leaders are rarely able to help the mothers make headway on what is troubling them because the men are not there in the group.

We were both puzzled and saddened by what we heard about groups for fathers. In contrast with mothers' groups, which meet regularly over an extended period of time, sometimes for several years, groups for fathers tend to be offered once or at most twice on successive weekends, with rare exceptions (Bittman and Zalk 1978; Levant 1988). It is difficult to know whether this is what group leaders believe men need, or whether it is all they think men will be willing to attend.

HEALTH PROFESSIONALS

Parents tell us that when their babies are ill or upset, pediatricians and pediatric nurses are very responsive and reassuring. But it is the rare medical practitioner who routinely asks new mothers or fathers about how they are managing. It is even rarer, apparently, to find obstetricians or pediatricians, the most likely health professionals to see parents in the early family-making years, who offer more than a suggestion that the parents "try to relax."

Some parents wind up seeking professional help from a counselor or therapist, almost always for what they feel is an individual problem. Our concern with this approach is that the natural strains of new parenthood may be borne mostly by one of the parents, who sees it as her or his personal problem. While one of the partners may be in need of help to sort out what has triggered his or her distress, individual counseling neglects the fallout of the distress on the couple's relationship.

Peggy sought therapy and found it helped her "get a little clearer about why becoming a mother has been so anxiety-provoking for me," but without Bill there the trouble she and he were having seemed only to get worse. Like all the potential sources of support we have mentioned, individual therapy for only one partner can actually add to the strain that the parents are under *as a couple*. Our hope is that health and mental health professionals will become more aware of the common issues for couples in this major family transition. Since we know that 12.5 percent of the new parents in our study who had no intervention separated or divorced by the time their babies were eighteen months old, the need for help during this crucial period in a marriage cannot be overestimated.

Do friends, family, community services, and health professionals actually help to buffer or protect new parents from life stresses during the transition to parenthood (Nuckolls, Casell, and Kaplan 1972)? Our Important People questionnaire (Curtis-Boles 1979) provided a measure of how often the men and women in our study were in contact with important sources of support, and how satisfying that contact felt. We also obtained a general estimate from a Recent Life Events questionnaire of how much stress each man and woman was contending with based on the sum total of changes in their lives. We presented a long list of potentially stressful events including having a miscarriage, surgery, or major illness; moving to a new home; having problems with alcohol or drugs; losing a close friend or parent; getting promoted; and reentering school.[6] The list included positive and negative life changes on the assumption that both are stressful (Holmes and Rahe 1967).

Given the changes parents were reporting in our interviews and couples groups, we were surprised to find that despite a range of life stress levels among couples who became parents, there was no significant difference between stress in new parents as a group and stress in childless couples. According to this estimate, then, becoming a first-time parent is not accompanied by any more overall life change and stress than being a partner in a comparable childless couple in the first decade of married life.

Does this mean that parents' level of life stress is unimportant in their adaptation during the transition to parenthood? Quite the contrary: New parents who reported more life change (from which we inferred more stress) described lower marital satisfaction at six and eighteen months after their child was born. Furthermore, as their child grew older, parents' social supports became less effective in buffering the impact of life stress on their marriage.

We expected couples with low life stress and high social support to be at an advantage, partners with high life stress and high social support to be doing fairly well, but couples with a great deal of life stress and little support from others to be at risk for serious marital distress (Heming 1985). When their babies were six months old, couples with the most favorable life stress/ social support balance were satisfied with their marriage, even if they were contending with many stressful life events besides having a baby.[7] At this point, a kind of Goldilocks principle seems to be operating: when couples' stress level was not too high, not too low, and their level of social support was just right, they were better able to master the expectable stress of becoming parents and keep their marriage on track. But by the time the babies were one and a half years old, partners who reported more stressful life events were less happy with their marriages regardless of the amount of social support they were receiving. Support from others, then, can be especially helpful to couples during the first months of parenthood, but it cannot ultimately prevent the stresses of becoming a family from taking their toll on the marriage.

We have been discussing stressful life events and social support as if they are forces totally outside the couple's control; yet we found that men and women who are more satisfied with their marriage before they have a baby are better able to keep positive ties with people outside the family over the next two years. By contrast, couples who are already in distress as they begin the transition to parenthood may become preoccupied with the baby and their own turmoil, leaving them unwilling or unable to reach out to others.[8] Since support from other important people can make the early strain of transition more manageable, we encourage new parents to line up resources they can count on in the early months, before the cumulative stress of the transition sends them on a downward marital slide.

CHAPTER 7

Legacies from Our Parents

JACKSON: In the family I grew up in, the women always did the household work, regardless. My grandmother never worked. My grandfather worked and brought home the money, so she took care of everything at home. My mother worked, but she still came home and fixed dinner and everything, and then later with my stepmother, it was the same.

Then I marry *this* woman [*laughs affectionately*] and she wants to divide the work at home in half! Well, I say, "This half's buying paper plates!" I can now see that how you deal with your wife and kids is affected by the things that you saw growing up—it sounds obvious now that I've thought about it, but I just didn't realize it before.

TANYA: I grew up in the same kind of family that Jackson did. My mother did it all—looked after me and the kids and my father *and* she had a job too—but I was determined that it wouldn't be like that in our house.

We heard many comments like Jackson's and Tanya's. The couples in our study made it clear that their parents have bequeathed legacies to their children and grandchildren that are powerful and often invisible. In this chapter, we explore how new parents learn about their family legacies. We describe examples of some parents who repeat the nurturing or painful family patterns they grew up with, and others who find ways to break their families' negative cycles.

One major challenge for a couple creating a new family is to figure out how both of their dreams can fit together. How can two people with different experiences in their families of origin create a family in which they can repeat the things each found important and supportive and change the things that hurt them or hampered their development?

Most of the evidence shows that, in general, there is more continuity than discontinuity between the generations: The relationships in the generation we create tend to have more positive outcomes for those of us who felt nurtured by our parents and whose families functioned adequately, and more negative results for those of us who grew up in families with significant rejection, loss, strain, or dysfunction. Nevertheless, there are some compelling exceptions in which individuals and couples with painful early family experiences manage to avoid being bound by the chains of the past, establishing nurturing, effective, and satisfying relationships in their own generation, sometimes by putting the difficult memories into a perspective that allows them to move beyond them. Some manage to accomplish this on their own. Others use the help of friends, religious leaders, or mental health professionals, passing on the benefits through the relationships they create with their partners and their children.

Generational issues are with us always, but at few times are they more salient than when the generational cycle is about to begin again. A first child and grandchild brings the relationships between the parents and their parents into bold relief. There seems to be a reaching out from both generations, especially between mothers and daughters. When the relationships are going well, these close ties can be a great comfort for both generations, although the grandparents' well-meaning attempts at providing help do not always succeed.

For some couples, frequent contact with their parents around the time of the baby's birth is a natural continuation of close and loving relationships. For a few, the older generation's attention is experienced as new and is not easy to manage. When their son, Avi, is six months old, Pauline, thirty-one, and Mel, thirty-three, explain how a new child can provide an opportunity for closeness between generations that have been separated by years of physical and emotional distance:

PAULINE: My relationship with my parents was very much on hold before Avi was born. I moved away from home about fifteen years ago. We kept in touch, but I didn't spend much time with them. Now they have lots of really strong feelings about Avi, some positive and some negative. It upset my parents a lot that Mel and I chose to not marry. But they came out to see him when he was a month old and then again when he was five months old. They've been here more since he was born than they have in the past ten years.

The visits have been both stressful and intense for Pauline and Mel, but there seem to be a few roses among the thorns:

PAULINE: They were really glad to see the baby and to share in the joy. And that made me very happy. But they are angry, real angry, at us for not getting married. I say it's none of their business, and we certainly don't need that negative atmosphere while we're trying to find our own way with Avi. Mel and I tend to have our worst fights right before they come and right after they leave. I think they are trying to accept the situation. They are very mixed about Mel, but they are accepting me more now.

MEL: My parents also went through a period of being really disappointed and angry that we weren't getting married, but once Avi was born I think they put that aside. My father has really warmed up a lot around the baby. It's hard for me to understand how that changed our relationship, because in some ways he's still the same and in some ways he isn't. He seems warmer when he's with everyone else. With Pauline's parents, I'm not sure where we are. When they left this last time I was shaking my head. I don't feel very close to them at the moment. And when they're here, *we* sure aren't very close to each other, either.

Avi's grandparents' attitudes about their children's lives creep into their relationship with their children and with their grandson. The conflict and distress between the generations spills over into the communication between Pauline and Mel, and into the atmosphere in which Avi first learns about family relationships. While his parents were speaking tensely of these family dynamics, Avi cried vigorously, a common response when a baby picks up on the parents' discomfort.

Pauline and Mel have some recognition of these generational patterns, which bodes well for their eventually being able to deal with their distress as a couple. New parents who do not see the connections between their struggles with their own parents and their distress as a couple are less likely to feel that they are on the same side when they tackle difficult issues in their life together.

A second theme that shows up as Pauline and Mel talk is that the birth of a baby can force some parents and grandparents to grapple once more with issues they have not successfully resolved. The distance between Pauline and her parents did not begin over their disagreement about whether she and Mel should get married so that their grandson would have a "proper" family. Similar disputes about how Pauline was going to live her life played a part in her decision to leave her parents' home at sixteen. Now, with a new baby on the scene, the generations are back in frequent contact. They have an opportunity to put some of the old issues aside and go on with their relationship, though it is possible that the process could get derailed by the unspoken tensions between the generations, tensions that Pauline and Mel talk about endlessly with each other.

As we talk with friends, colleagues, and the parents in our study, we can see how commonly we all make repeated overtures over the years to our children and parents to try to patch up earlier misunderstandings or rifts. One of our findings—something we certainly did not know in our early years of family making—is that all relationships across the generations have set-backs at times, but some of us are lucky enough to make some progress toward mending them.

Occasionally, new parents' attempts to renew closeness with their parents go painfully awry. You may recall Henry from chapter 3, who talked about his and Anna's painful experiences with his unresponsive father. A first-generation Arab-American who had promised his grandfather that he would not marry out of his faith, Henry wound up marrying Anna, an Italian-American. Henry's father refused to see Anna once he learned that she was going to have a baby. By the time their second daughter was born, Henry could tolerate this painful impasse with his father no longer:

> HENRY: Last spring I realized how much I was hurt by the way my father treated me all my life. And I just felt that it was time to let go. I don't want to carry around any more of this pain and anger with me. I've been such an angry young man after all of these years of rejection. Feeling like shit. Not desired. I kept making overtures, taking the baby to see him, and getting shut out. It was just hurting too much. I finally let go and decided I could not see him anymore.

Some grandparents must see their children's moving away or doing things differently as an indication that they no longer care about them or value their way of life. From our conversations with the parents in our study we can say unequivocally that, regardless of the state of their relationships with their parents, adult children not only care about what their parents think and feel but continue to long for their love and approval even when the generational bonds feel strained. Given the many difficult childhood experiences many people have undergone, it is a testimony to the strength of these bonds that so many new parents want to maintain relationships with their parents and create families of their own.

Repeating the Generational Cycle

A widespread belief, supported by a wealth of evidence, is that "good things" and "bad things" cycle through the generations. One of the most negative examples of this tendency can be seen in studies of child abuse, in which parents who abuse their children physically and psychologically tend to have been victims of abuse when they were growing up (Finkelhor, Hotaling, and Yllo 1988; Main and Goldwyn 1984). Patterns replayed down generational lines are not limited to extremes of abuse, of course. Difficult relationships with parents, both past and present, can take their toll on the relationships that couples are trying to create in their new families.

Henry, now the father of two daughters, five and a half and three years old, is explaining that in the same year in which he felt compelled to let go of his father, he and Anna decided that they could not make a go of their marriage:

HENRY: I keep thinking about the fact that my parents also divorced when I was young, and how I vowed that I was going to be so different. And here I wind up in the same boat. I think in some ways, I was a lot like my mother, and Anna was a lot like my father—in the quickness of her mind, her quick wit, her sharp tongue in arguments. I don't think either Anna or my father have ever lost an argument! In the beginning, I held Anna in some awe. There was a kind of comfort too, to have her in my life as a father substitute because I couldn't have him. So, she was kind of disciplinarian for me too but, like my relationship with my father, what I got from my wife had a lot of negative aspects to it. Eventually, it became too much for me.

The legacy of strong admonitions from Henry's grandfather and father to their children and grandchildren has led to painful and severed relationships: between Henry's father and grandfather, between Henry's father and mother, between Henry and his father, and now between Henry and his wife. Despite his determination to stay connected to his father, Henry has not been able to overcome the generational rifts in his family.

Although the generational ties have been hurtful for Henry throughout his lifetime, becoming a parent opened old wounds that had never healed. Feeling deeply attached to his children pushed him to sever his relationship with his father and eventually to end his marriage with Anna, his "substitute father," as he came to see her.

As Dolores, his and Anna's first-born, goes through kindergarten, we hear hints that some of the generational pain may be playing out in Henry's relationships with the younger daughter, Rose. He and Anna are separated, but his daughters are with him almost half the time. Rose is very much like him, he says—so much so that six months ago she rejected him the way he says he rejected her mother. She just didn't want to have anything to do with him, only with her mother. Henry cried in front of Rose and told her why he was hurt. "I think she understood: Since then, she has been sharing with me at such a deeper level—much more than Dolores. We have this intuitive sense of each other. We spend many hours just sitting curled up together, watching out the window of the house, listening to music together. Not talking or doing anything else. That's quite amazing to me."

Henry feels that he has had to pay a price for straying from his grandfather's and his father's directives, and that he has failed by repeating his parents' divorce pattern, which he had vowed to avoid. Although he can articulate the similarities in his father's and Anna's personalities that played a role in his attraction to Anna and his distress with her, he is unable to avoid the negative effects on his marriage. Despite the earlier rifts, Henry has created a very close relationship with both daughters. His thoughtful musings about Rose's difficulty in relating to him illustrate how similarities between parents' and children's personalities can complicate the ways in which the generational patterns play out.

A great deal has recently been written about the mental health of adults whose parents had serious problems with alcohol (Brown 1985), suggesting that alcoholic parents' dysfunction affects their children's development as they are growing up. Our study indicates that there may be long-lasting effects when adult children of alcoholics become parents themselves.

Twenty percent of the parents in our study had childhoods clouded by their fathers' and/or mothers' struggles with alcohol. None reported having current problems themselves with alcohol or drugs, but a few acknowledged that they had had drinking problems in the past. We were frankly surprised at the large number of study participants who had come from alcoholic families, and wondered what special problems they faced as new parents.

What we found was most disturbing: On *every* index of adjustment to parenthood—symptoms of depression, self-esteem, parenting stress, role dissatisfaction, and decline in satisfaction with marriage—men and women whose parents had abused alcohol had significantly greater difficulty (Cowan, Cowan, and Heming 1988). There is no doubt that adult children of alcoholics have a harder time creating a family that satisfies their ideal. Families with serious problems of alcohol use and abuse have been described as placing a premium on keeping negative emotions in check (Steinglass et al. 1987). Family members tend to hold on to secrets, deny any problems, and avoid talking about their inner feelings. This makes life very unpredictable for a child, as the family atmosphere varies markedly depending on whether a parent is sober or intoxicated. Little wonder that when these children become adults creating families of their own, they find it difficult to manage the tension and maintain good feelings in their intimate relationships.

What is even more disturbing about this generational legacy is that by the time their children are preschoolers, these parents describe them as having fewer developmental successes, although our observations show that their children are doing just as well developmentally as the children of the rest of the parents in the study. This suggests that parents who grow up with troubled and ineffective parenting develop unrealistic expectations of what they can expect of their children and, as a result, have difficulty seeing their children's behavior in a positive light.

The plight of these grandchildren of alcoholics did not end in preschool. When they were in kindergarten, we asked their teachers to describe all the children in the classroom (using a checklist of children's behaviors adapted from the work of Earl Schaefer [Schaefer and Hunter 1983]). Without knowing which children were in our study, the teachers more often described the grandchildren of alcoholics as shy or aggressive, and as performing less well in their academic work.

Families with alcohol problems create a legacy that is passed on through successive generations. Even if their children do not abuse alcohol or drugs themselves and are determined to do things differently in their own families, they may find themselves inexorably repeating at least part of a pattern they had vowed to change.

Since we were not able to observe what happened in the parents' families while they were growing up, we do not have firsthand information about how generational cycles recur or get interrupted in these new families. There are hints about how family dynamics recur from one generation to another in a study of four generations by Avshalom Caspi and Glen Elder (1988). The cycle starts with an irritable, unstable child who grows up, marries, and generates tension in the marriage. The husbands and wives in such marriages tend to be less warm and effective parents, and in the next generation their children tend to have behavior problems and to grow up as irritable, unstable individuals. When they become involved as adults in conflictful marriages and have children of their own, the negative cycle begins again.

Despite the aura of Greek tragedy in Caspi and Elder's report, there are two optimistic implications of their formulation. First, they and we have been focusing on the families at the end of the spectrum with problematic legacies. At the other end are adults who grew up with fairly competent, effective, and affectionate parents who recreate this positive atmosphere in their new families. Second, if men and women can break the negative chain at any point—as individuals, in their marriage, or in their relationships with their children—it is likely that they can avoid carrying over such unsatisfying relationships into their new families.

Breaking the Generational Cycle

Most of us have had the experience of having a familiar, hurtful phrase pop out of our mouths in the heat of a struggle with a spouse or child. Can we keep from repeating our painful childhood experiences with our own mates and children? Our results suggest that some men and women manage to come to terms with very painful early experiences in ways that allow them to create new and more adaptive patterns. Some do this difficult work with the help of professional counselors or therapists, and others appear to do it on their own or with their mate. We focus here on continuity and discontinuity across the generations, primarily as the early growing-up years affect present-day couple relationships, with a brief look at how parents' legacies from the past affect their relationships with their children.

CONFLICT IN THE FAMILY OF ORIGIN

Before their memories could become colored by their experiences with their children, we asked the expectant parents in our study about the level of conflict in their families of origin.[1] We grouped the couples into four patterns: (1) both husband and wife described low conflict in their families of origin; (2) both husband and wife described high conflict in their families of origin; (3) his family had high conflict, hers had low conflict; and (4) his family had low conflict, hers had high conflict. The forty-eight couples assessed in pregnancy fell approximately equally into each of the four groups. Did those patterns make a difference to how satisfied couples were with the quality of their marriage during the transition to parenthood?

Couples with the first pattern—low conflict in both partners' families of origin—showed the least drop in marital satisfaction from pregnancy to eighteen months after the birth of their first child. These parents were able to avoid some but not all of the marital tension and conflict that couples tend to experience as they become parents. When both partners came from high-conflict families, they experienced a substantial decline in their satisfaction with marriage over the same period of time. For better or for worse, both groups of couples showed continuity from generation to generation.

What intrigued us was what happened when new parents' families of origin had different levels of conflict. When the husband grew up in a high-conflict family and the wife recalled little conflict in hers, both partners, particularly the wives, became increasingly dissatisfied with their marriage as they became parents. Following Caspi and Elder's formulation, we speculate that when men from high-conflict families experienced the stress of becoming fathers, they expressed more irritability and anger to their wives. Their wives, whose family models left them unprepared to deal with this level of irritability or conflict, reacted with disappointment or distress, which is reflected in their increasing disenchantment with the marriage. In this case, the negative cycle from the husband's family gets replayed, overriding the wife's more benign early experience.

The fourth group of couples managed to avoid repeating the patterns of *her* negative past. When wives from high-conflict families married men from low-conflict families, their slight decline in marital satisfaction during the transition to parenthood was virtually identical to the low-conflict pairs in the first pattern. Our speculation is that the women in these couples may express their irritability or anger during the tense weeks and months of becoming a family, but their husbands do not respond in kind. We know from a number of other in-depth studies of couples that marital satisfaction is affected not so much by the amount of anger either partner expresses but by the spouses' tendency to respond in ways that escalate the irritability, anger, or criticism between them (Gottman and Levenson 1986; Markman and Notarius 1987).

RELATIONSHIPS WITH PARENTS IN THE FAMILY OF ORIGIN

It seems that when partners come from backgrounds with similar levels of conflict, they tend to repeat the patterns they knew in their original families. When they come from different backgrounds, negative cycles are more likely to be repeated if they come through the husband's family line rather than the wife's. We explored these difference patterns by examining in more detail parents' recollections of their early relationships with their parents.

Both John Bowlby in England and Mary Main and her colleagues (Main et al. 1985) in the United States talk about memories of the central relationships in our early family life as providing us with "working models," or pictures of what we expect intimate family relationships to be like. Main has found that when adults describe what are called insecure attachment relationships with their parents, their children are more likely to have insecure attachments to *them* (Main and Goldwyn in press; Main, Kaplan, and Cassidy 1985). We were interested in new parents' models of their early relationships because they may help us understand what we see in the relationships they develop with each other and with their own children.

We used a structured interview created by Mary Main and her colleagues to stimulate parents to think back in some detail to their childhood relationships with their parents.[2]

Interviews and questionnaires can provide only a brief sketch, of course, of what is a very long and complicated process of growing up, becoming adults, and developing intimate relationships, but they help us to explore both continuity and discontinuity between generations.

If parents say, with conviction and supporting detail, that their parents were loving, involved, and comforting to them when they were anxious or upset as children, they can be described as having a model of secure relationships between parents and children. Even if they experienced one or both parents as rejecting, neglectful, or overinvolved, their model would still be described as secure if they talk about both the positive and negative aspects of those relationships in a lucid, free-flowing, coherent manner, giving examples that clearly illustrate their descriptions and not getting lost in intrusive or incoherent thoughts about early difficulties.

Len and Connie originally entered our study as a couple who hadn't yet decided about having children. Connie became pregnant about a year later, and almost four years after that, when little Sam was three and a half, we spoke with both of them about their childhoods. Len provides an example of someone who has managed to gain a perspective on his childhood experiences. He says that he was "a difficult little baby who became a pain in the ass as a kid." His mother was extremely critical, but she spent a great deal of time with her children and Len felt comforted by her when his friends rejected him. His father had a terrible temper. Although he would roughhouse with Len on occasion, he tended to be "either away at work or yelling at home." His parents got along when he was young but their relationship became stormy and they separated for a while later on. Len's childhood memories are mostly about conflict with his parents, but in late adolescence, after his parents got back together, the family drew closer together.

Typical of many men and women who were described as having a secure model of relationships between parents and children, Len's childhood was not ideal. But from his perspective as an adult, he can see that his parents were limited by their own family experiences; he feels that both his mother and his father had been severely deprived as children and that "they were doing the best they could with the resources they were given."

Main and her colleagues are clear that while the traumatic effects of very difficult childhoods may be forever etched in memory, a person can develop a model of relationships that makes it possible to break the links that chain us to the negative patterns of the past. This is dramatized by the fact that two-thirds of the parents in our study who were classified as having secure models of parent-child relationships described very difficult relationships with one or both parents while growing up (Pearson et al. 1991). Several had parents who were physically abusive or mentally ill, or who committed suicide during their childhood. Others experienced their parents' divorce or the death of a parent while they were growing up.

Connie describes a very difficult early family life. An only child, she recalls years of bickering between her alcoholic parents, followed by her father's sudden exit from the family one night when she was ten. She never saw him again. Three years later, she came home from school to find that her mother had committed suicide. Soon after their son, Sam, was born, Connie found herself preoccupied with memories of her parents. When we talked with her about her childhood, she was still struggling to deal with her feelings about these traumatic experiences: "I can't get over the feeling that both my parents abandoned me. When I see how great Len usually is with me and Sam, I get even more upset about what went on while I was growing up." As we do with each parent, we ask Connie why she thought her parents were the way they were. The question stumps her. She is so upset with them for what they did to her, it has not occurred to her to wonder why her parents' lives were in such turmoil.

As individuals with either secure or insecure models of intimate relation-ships grow up and marry, can their choice of partner affect their sense of security? Using the twenty-seven couples for whom we have complete data on both parents' childhood and their current relationships as couples and as parents, Deborah Cohn helped us explore the possibility that a nurturing marriage can modify the effects of early negative experiences on the parents' relationship as a couple (Cohn et al. 1991).

There are three kinds of pairings that couples can fall into: Both he and she have secure working models of relationships (as did twelve couples in our study); both he and she have insecure working models (five couples); and one parent has a secure working model and the other has an insecure working model (ten couples).

Observing the parents as they work and play together with their three-and-a-half-year-old (see chapter 8), we found that insecure/insecure pairs showed much less cooperation and warmth and expressed much more nega-tive emotion to each other in front of their child than the other two couple pairings. Not surprisingly, in their separate visits, both parents with insecure models were much less warm, engaged, and structuring than other parents in the study.

The secure/secure pairs showed much more positive emotion to each other: They were warm; they talked amiably, and they were cooperative. In their separate visits with their child they were significantly warmer and more effective in helping their children to cope with difficult tasks. Thus, in couples with similarly insecure or secure models of family relationships, continuity prevails across the generations.

Perhaps the most encouraging and provocative finding was that the insecure/secure pairs—in all but two of which it was the wife who had an insecure model of relationships—showed just as much warmth and cooperation with each other during the family visit as the secure/secure pairs did. Furthermore, when women with unresolved feelings about their growing-up years were married to men with a coherent view of even the most difficult early family experiences, the women's parenting was as warm, structuring, and engaged as that of the mothers described as securely attached.*

Something about the quality of the couple relationship appears to be providing a buffer that interrupts the potential carryover of the women's early negative experiences into the relationship with their husbands. And, despite the fact that these mothers had not yet been able to come to terms with their own difficult childhood experiences, the positive relationships with their husbands appeared to be helping them establish nurturant and effective relationships with their children.

In Connie and Len's case, both experienced conflict and difficulty in their families of origin, but they are at different stages of coming to terms with those experiences. The effect of early legacies on their couple relationship now stems not just from the negative experiences themselves but from how each partner has come to understand their effects. Len has not only reestablished a positive relationship with his parents as he moved into adulthood but also come to a more tolerant and understanding view of his mother's and father's earlier relationships with him and with each other. Through his affectionate and understanding relationship with Connie, and his active involvement with their son, Sam, he has helped to make it easier for Connie to avoid replaying the extremely negative relationship she observed during the stormy years of her parents' marriage. Perhaps it is this curative power of the marriage that has enabled Connie and the other women in the insecure/secure couples to establish warm and effective relationships with their children. We will discuss the connection between the quality of the marriage and the quality of the parent-child relationship more in the next chapter.

How do these links between generations operate? Our speculation is that there is a process much like the one we described earlier between husbands who come from families with little conflict and much warmth and their wives who come from families with much conflict and little warmth. The men in these pairs seemed able to de-escalate the conflict between them with

---

*Michael Rutter (1987; Quinton, Rutter, and Liddle 1984) showed this pattern in a well-known study of British families. When mothers who had been reared in institutional homes were able to form positive and satisfying marital relationships, the quality of their parenting did not reflect their own earlier deprivation.

warmth or humor. Since their wives experienced less nurturing in their early relationships, perhaps they found the warmth and responsiveness in their marriages so nurturing that they learned more positive ways of relating by example and worked even harder to maintain the harmony in their marriages.

We are left to wonder whether women with positive early experiences can buffer the effects of their husbands' troubled childhoods on their marriage and life as a family. We did not see enough couples with this pattern to examine what happened to their relationships. Are women with secure models of relationships less willing to marry more troubled men? Are men with insecure models of relationships less willing to commit themselves to women with more nurturant pictures of intimate relationships? The two couples in our study who fit this pattern expressed less warmth to each other during the family visit than did the average couple in the study. It looks as though it is particularly difficult for wives to keep the marriage on an even keel when their husbands have difficult and unresolved relationships with their parents, even if the wives themselves have more positive models. This may be an example of the general phenomenon that men's moods and behavior tend to affect the quality of the marriage more than women's moods and behavior do (Boles 1984). The central issue here may be that men who had difficult childhoods are likely to be either angry or inexpressive. Wives may find either of these extremes more difficult to tolerate in a spouse than husbands do.

From what we have learned about the effects of alcoholism, family conflict, and children's attachment to their parents in the past generation, we draw several general conclusions. There is clearly a tendency for positive or negative experiences from the past to be carried over into the partners' relationship as a couple. The risk of negative carryover is especially strong when both partners bring painful and unresolved family issues to their marriage. These early family difficulties tend to increase the risk that men and women will become more disenchanted with their marriage during the transition to parenthood, which leaves them more irritable and angry and less cooperative with each other and with their children.

What are couples to do when they want to have children of their own but their family histories are bleak? Our findings show that some partners can overcome painful and even traumatic early experiences by creating a more nurturing and satisfying relationship with a spouse. Connie and Len seemed to do well because his view of relationships and his caring of her provided some of the nurturance that she had lacked in her own family. This seemed to lay a foundation for Connie to begin to modify her notion of intimate relationships. Many men and women find this task less formidable with the help of a professional counselor or therapist.

What if neither partner has examined or come to terms with his or her early experiences? We find that many couples tend to work earnestly but silently to create a family environment that will nurture their children. Each attempting to avoid different family traumas, they find to their surprise and disappointment that their plans and goals do not mesh. It seems important for both partners to let each other know about the baggage they feel they are carrying. A collaborative approach may help couples to safeguard the positive legacies and reject the negative legacies from the past as they attempt to build nurturant family relationships with each other and with their children.

CHAPTER 8

Parenting Our Children

BILL: In my house, when I was growing up, any kid who got into danger, like going near a light socket or running out on the road, got a swat on the bottom. I'm not talking about child abuse. I'm talking about a clear warning that some things are not OK to do.

PEGGY: When Bill says that, my heart sinks. Hitting is one of my absolute taboos. In my family, kids got seriously smacked around when my parents got angry. I hope I will never, *ever,* touch Mindy in anger. I'm trying to be patient with Bill, but when I see him swat Mindy, I feel like swatting *him*.

BILL: But you're letting her get away with murder.

PEGGY: I feel like I have to protect her.

BILL: You're protecting her too much. She doesn't know what to do if she can't get her own way. When I picked her up at nursery school last week, I found her standing alone in a corner of the yard both days. The teacher explained that the other kids were starting to avoid her because she wouldn't share the toys or the play equipment.

Legacies from their childhoods have left Bill and Peggy with qualitatively different notions about how to be effective parents. Some couples handle these differences by agreeing to find a middle ground; others, by accepting each other's parenting style with an attitude of "you do it your way and I'll do it mine." But when the marriage is full of conflict, as we have seen in the case of Peggy and Bill, child rearing becomes a prime target for dissension. Strong disagreements between Mindy's parents drive them to take extreme positions with her. Bill is even more determined than he might ordinarily be not to let Mindy "get away" with anything, because he wants to offset what he regards as Peggy's tendency to spoil her. Peggy is more reluctant to set limits than she might normally be, "to make up for Bill's harshness." We don't know whether Mindy is confused by her parents' different strategies or disturbed by their bickering, but we do know that she is having difficulty getting along with the other children at nursery school.

Peggy and Bill illustrate one of our major findings. Everything we have described about parents' transition to parenthood—their ability to make sense of their own childhood experiences, their satisfaction or distress as a couple, their level of stress and support, and their internal conflicts as individuals—seems to come together in their ways of being parents. We see variations on this theme when we talk with Sharon and Daniel. Sharon tells us that she went through a troubled stretch about six months ago when Amy was three. She was depressed, preoccupied with the possibility of returning to work, and feeling guilty that she couldn't seem to pay attention to Amy's needs. Daniel says that he and Sharon kept fighting about how to handle Amy's tantrums when they left her with a baby-sitter. He wanted to be more helpful to Amy when she was upset, "but I got so distressed and frazzled by what was going on with Sharon that I found myself matching Amy yell for yell." The struggles between Amy and her parents are a result of some spillover from Sharon's depression. The tension between Mindy and her parents stems from the fact that Bill and Peggy are reacting to different childhood experiences, which leads to different inclinations about how to handle Mindy. These individual and three-generational issues make parenting especially problematic because they stimulate tension between the parents and give the child conflicting messages about what to expect.

Parenting Styles

In previous chapters we focused on what happened to the parents as they made their journey from couple to family. Here we show that how they cope with their transition to parenthood, and especially with their couple relationship, has short-term and long-term consequences—for the quality of their relationships with their children and, ultimately, for the children's academic and social adjustment at school.* When the transition is difficult for the parents, there tend to be difficulties for the children as well.

*We are not claiming that all of the responsibility for the child's developmental progress can be attributed to the parents' behavior. Many forces, including genetics, the child's temperament, the presence of siblings, and events outside the family, will affect the course of a child's development. What we are focusing on here is the fact that parents' well-being or distress contributes both to their parenting style and to their children's developmental successes and difficulties.

WORKING AND PLAYING WITH PRESCHOOLERS

To get a sense of the relationships between parents and their three-and-a-half-year-olds, we invited each family to our project playroom for three forty-minute visits: one for mother and child, one for father and child, and one for both parents and the child.[1] With the family's consent, we videotaped each visit. In a playful, unstructured part of each visit, we provided a sand tray and a cabinet of miniatures and invited each parent and child to "build a world together in the sand." We also had the parents introduce a number of challenging tasks that would be difficult for children of this age to do: to repeat to their parents a story that we had told the children outside the playroom; to classify shapes or use blocks to match a model we provided; and to make their way through a maze game. The parents were invited to be as involved and helpful as they typically would be at home (Cowan and Cowan 1990; Pratt et al. 1988).

The videotapes of these family visits reveal an amazing variety of reactions between parents and preschoolers. While fiddling nervously with a toy tea-cup and saucer, Mindy tells her father that she can't remember the story she just heard. He becomes increasingly insistent and tense: "Put that away, Mindy. No play until I find out what the story is. Do it *now!*"—and he takes the teacup away rather forcefully. By contrast, when Willie says, "I forget," his father, Paul, gently leads him: "Was the story about a little kid or a big kid?" "Big." "Boy or girl?" "Girl." "Did she ride an elephant in her pajamas?" "No! A bike."

Members of our staff observed and rated the parents' behavior in the different visits.[2] We use our ratings to summarize two central dimensions of parenting that follow Diana Baumrind's (1979, 1991) scheme for describing parenting style. The first is warmth and responsiveness. Some parents responded warmly to their child's behavior, reacting in a positive way to the child's attempts to get through the maze or to select play materials for the sand world. A few parents reacted to the child in an angry, critical, or threatening tone. A very few were cold and disengaged, and others seemed emotionally removed and preoccupied despite invitations from the child to become involved.

The second major dimension of parenting style has to do with the parents' tendency to provide structure, to set limits, and to encourage the child to try tasks even if they seem difficult. Some parents tended not to help structure the situation even when the child was floundering. Others might say, "I know the puzzle looks confusing, but why don't we start with this part?"

We based our summary descriptions of parents' styles of working and playing with their children on a combination of both the warmth and structuring dimensions: Parents who showed a high degree of warmth, responsiveness, and structure were described as *authoritative;* those at the other end of the continuum, who showed little warmth or structure, were described as *disengaged;* parents who showed little warmth and a lot of anger, structure, and limits were described as *authoritarian;* and those high in warmth but low in structure and limit setting were called *permissive*.

We know from many studies that children of parents with an angry or a cold, demanding, authoritarian parenting style appear to be in the most developmental difficulty, whereas children of parents with a warm but firm authoritative style tend to be more competent both socially and cognitively (Hetherington and Parke 1986; Maccoby and Martin 1983; Mussen, Conger, and Kagan 1984). The children of authoritative parents did better in our study, too; they showed more developmental progress in some laboratory tasks we gave them when they were three and a half, and they had higher achievement scores at the end of their kindergarten year.

We looked more closely to see what else the authoritative parents were doing when they worked or played with their children. Along with our colleague, Michael Pratt (Pratt et al. 1988), we found that parents with an authoritative style supported their children's learning in two ways. First, when their children were confused or having difficulty, authoritative parents modified their help and instruction to meet the children at their level of understanding. Then, once the children grasped the idea of what to do, the parents stepped back and let them proceed on their own.

THE TRANSITION TO PARENTHOOD AND PARENTING STYLE

We found that how parents had managed their lives during the transition to parenthood had a great deal to do with their parenting style when their children were three and a half. Parents with less conflict in their families of origin, greater marital satisfaction during pregnancy, less life stress six months into parenthood, and less depression and marital distress when the children were eighteen months old were more likely to be warm, responsive, structuring, and limit setting with their preschoolers.[3] Conversely, parents who were not feeling good about themselves and their marriage during the transition were more cold, angry, unresponsive, and unable to set limits during the parent-child visits later on (Cowan, Cowan, Schulz, and Heming in press).

We found continuities between how men and women viewed themselves and their lives in pregnancy, how they managed their transitions to parenthood, and the quality of their relationships with their children two to four years later. For couples who began the journey in good shape and who managed to maintain a positive relationship as a couple, these results are reassuring. For couples like Peggy and Bill or Sharon and Daniel, who started their journey in difficulty and experienced additional hardships along the way, individual and marital difficulties tended to spill over into their relationships with their preschoolers.

Because much of the information about the parents in this analysis was obtained after the children were born, one could argue that it is not parents' well-being but children's temperament that affects their parenting style:

When babies are difficult to manage, mothers and fathers have more difficulty making the transition to parenthood and dealing with the children as preschoolers. We conducted a more stringent test of our idea that the transition to parenthood provides a context for the development of parent-child relationships. The information parents provided about themselves during pregnancy, before their children's personalities could have influenced their parenting behavior, was highly related to the kinds of relationships we observed between the parents and their children almost four years after they became a family. Women who were most satisfied with themselves and with their family division of labor before their babies were born were warmer and more able to set limits with their preschoolers.[4] A woman's positive feelings about herself and about the way she and her partner shared the family work seemed to create a positive climate for her to become a more effective parent.

When we looked for links between a man's life before he became a father and his parenting style almost four years later, we came up with both intriguing and puzzling results: Expectant fathers with positive memories of their parents, higher self-esteem, greater involvement in household tasks, and lower outside-the-family stress before their babies were born were more authoritative with their sons four years later, but these qualities of men's lives did *not* seem to carry over to the tenor of their relationships with daughters.[5]

Why? Our attempts to answer this question led us to two troubling findings. First, parents, especially fathers, react to boys and girls differently; girls typically receive less positive treatment. Second, we can trace the origins of these gender differences in parenting to the fact that couples' marital difficulties during the transition to parenthood amplify men's tendency to treat daughters less sympathetically than sons. From our data, it looks like father-daughter relationships are at risk when the parents' marriage is in trouble during the early years of becoming a family.

GENDER MAKES A DIFFERENCE

In this age of egalitarian, nonsexist ideology, many parents are trying hard to defy the old gender stereotypes. Most men and women assured us that the gender of their child would not make a difference to their style of parenting. In contrast with past generations, they are more likely to consider buying a toy truck for a little girl and a doll for a little boy. They are a little less likely to think that girls need to be protected and boys taught to defend themselves. Yet our observations of fathers with their three-and-a-half-year-old sons and daughters showed a familiar theme in studies of parent-child relationships: Gender makes a difference.

Mothers of sons did not differ as a group from mothers of daughters in the way they interacted with their preschoolers on any of our parenting style observations: Some mothers were authoritative, some more disengaged, some more authoritarian, and some more permissive, but women's parenting style was not related to the gender of their child. But we observed that fathers of daughters were a little less authoritative and a lot more authoritarian than fathers of sons.[6] As a group, fathers of girls were more likely than fathers of boys to react to their children in a colder, more critical manner, to set more limits, and to give them less encouragement to do things their own way. These results are consistent with Jeanne Block's summaries of earlier studies of parents' treatment of boys and girls (Block 1976a, b; 1983).

Our attempt to understand the salience of gender in the relationships between parents and young children led us to see once again the central importance of the parents' marriage and how it changes during their transition from partners to parents. We found one missing piece of the puzzle in our observations of the couple's relationship during the family visit. When the couple worked together cooperatively and responsively, the fathers' separate visits with their daughters went positively too.[7] When we saw conflict and hostility between the parents in front of the child, we were likely to find that the father and daughter were having a difficult time in their separate visit.[8] What startled us about these results was that the state of the marriage did not tend to intrude on the relationship between fathers and sons.

We are concerned about the consequences of the close tie between parents' marital distress and fathers' tendency to react to their preschool girls in a more irritable, cold, angry, authoritarian manner. In a more detailed analysis of the videotaped family visits, Patricia Kerig (1989; Cowan, Cowan, and Kerig in press) looked closely at the parents' specific responses to the children's behavior in our playroom.[9] She found that, overall, girls tended to receive more positive comments from their parents than boys did. Boys got rewarded with positive responses for their independent behavior when they were working at the tasks in our playroom, but girls were more likely to be overridden and negated.

The quality of the parents' marriage plays a crucial role here. Mothers who were more unhappy with their relationships with their husbands tended to be more authoritarian and less authoritative with their children, girls or boys, but *especially when daughters asserted themselves*. The parents who responded most negatively to daughters were fathers who were more distressed in their relationships with their wives. These fathers gave the most negative responses of any parents in the study, no matter what their daughters did. This means that a young daughter whose parents are in conflict is less likely than a son to have even one parent available to be warm and responsive, to be able to structure tasks that are difficult, and to be observant enough to step back when she gets her bearings.

We now have at least a partial answer to why there are such complex patterns in father-son and father-daughter relationships. How a father engages with his preschool-age daughter depends not so much on how he feels about himself and his life, but on how his relationship with his wife turns out in the first few years of raising a family. A father's relationship with his son seems to be tied to how he has been feeling about himself and his life while becoming a parent, quite independent of the atmosphere in his marriage.

A follow-up question is more difficult to answer. Why does a daughter so often become the target of the negative fallout from a conflictful marriage?

We think that this is easier to understand if we look more generally at how the parents' marital quality is related to the tenor of their relationships with their children. Given parents in a marriage with a good deal of unresolved conflict, it seems understandable that some of their frustration will spill over into their relationships with the children. Indeed, the parents in highly conflictful relationships showed colder, more critical, authoritarian parenting styles in three of the four gender combinations: mothers with sons, mothers with daughters, and fathers with daughters. What prevents the spillover from marital to parenting difficulties for fathers of sons?

Although most parents spontaneously mentioned that they would be equally happy to have a son or a daughter, several facts support our hunch that boys are the favored sex for fathers. First, although there were no differences in the self-descriptions of prospective fathers of sons and daughters before their babies were born, two years later, men who had sons used significantly more of the favorable items on the Adjective Check List to describe themselves than men who had daughters.[10] Second, if their first child was a girl, couples were more likely to have a second child by the time the first was eighteen months old.[11] Although there may be many reasons for this phenomenon, it means that many families with first-born girls go through a second transition to parenthood sooner and are subject to more strain than families whose first-born are boys. Third, in the first four years of our study, couples were more likely to separate if their first child was a girl. This is consistent with the results of a much larger study of a national sample by Morgan, Lye, and Condran (1988) and of two in-depth family studies by Jeanne and Jack Block (Block, Block, and Gjerde 1986) and Mavis Hetherington (Hetherington and Anderson 1989).

Joan and Rob are talking with us about this phenomenon just after their son, Chuck, has entered kindergarten. They are describing a very stormy period in their relationship that started when Chuck was about four and lasted almost a year.

ROB: It was very touch and go for a while. Some of the things we talked about in our couples group were helpful, but after about a year of fighting we found it hard to remember anymore what we could do to make it better. What kept me hanging in there was Chuckie. I know too many men who get divorced and just lose their kids. I wasn't going to let my son go.

JOAN: It's really better now. At the worst times, when I'd almost lost hope, I'd imagine Chuckie growing up without his father there. I know Rob would've been there for him in many ways, but it's not the same . . . especially for a boy.

Mothers and fathers perceive boys as more vulnerable than girls during a separation or divorce: Mothers feel that boys are difficult to rear alone, and a marital split usually deprives sons of having their fathers around full-time. Our hypothesis, then, is that both parents make active efforts not to let marital and other family difficulties erode the quality of the relationship between father and son. Unfortunately, unhappily married men do not generally make the same efforts to safeguard their relationships with their daughters. Fathers tend to treat their young sons fairly well, regardless of how the marriage feels, but their relationships with their daughters are often as troubled as their relationships with their wives.

Our impression is that when the relationship between the parents is tense, a mother and daughter may form a kind of alliance that plays into the father's tendency to see "his women" as a twosome united against him. Bill expressed it directly in a moment of frustration: "I can't deal with either of the women in my family." A mother may be less likely to form this kind of alliance with her son, but even if she does, the father is not as likely to withdraw and leave the parenting of a son to his wife.

We are not suggesting that fathers consciously allow their marital difficulties to erode the relationships with their daughters. As we see it, gender issues become heightened in the natural course of becoming a family. As we have shown, the initial differences between men and women become magnified as they navigate the transition to parenthood. Partners take on more divergent family roles, they report more conflict and disagreement, they feel more distance between them, and a majority become at least somewhat more dissatisfied with their overall relationship. Particularly for couples who have no satisfactory ways of resolving their differences and impasses, this increases the potential for more conflict and criticism between them, which increases the likelihood of children's being exposed to their parents' disagreements. When differences between the parents increased between pregnancy and eighteen months after their child's birth, the parents were more likely to show marital conflict in front of their child when we observed them several years later.[12] The families in which fathers were most negative and ineffective with their three-and-a-half-year-old daughters had a history in which the parents had grown farther apart as they made their transitions to parenthood.

We want to emphasize that our findings are based on group trends and so will not apply in every case. But there is the potential for troubled relationships between parents and children, particularly between fathers and daughters, when the marriage is not going well. Unless parents find ways to buffer their relationships with their children from the effects of their marital unhappiness, it looks like their children will pay a price for the parents' disenchantment, even if, or perhaps especially if, they stay together.

In addition, parents' tendency to praise girls for compliance and to criticize them for asserting themselves may leave girls more vulnerable to depression in adolescence and adulthood (Weissman and Klerman 1977). Depression has been conceptualized by some as a condition of learned helplessness (Seligman 1975) and an inability to take actions in one's own behalf (Beck 1976; Lewinsohn et al. 1981). Our findings suggest that the seeds of girls' conflicts about asserting themselves may actually be sown during their parents' transition to parenthood, when gender issues become heightened because of the parents' distress about unresolved differences between them.

Parents' Well-being and Parenting Style

The gender of the child is an important ingredient of parenting style. How parents fare in other aspects of their lives, often in combination with how their marriage is going, also helps us understand the quality of their relationships with their preschoolers.

As a group, the parents in our study tended to be functioning fairly well, but between 20 percent and 30 percent reported enough symptoms to be at risk for clinical depression during their children's early years (Cowan et al. 1991).[13] Although we expected to observe less effective parenting styles in the parents who were more depressed, we found that parents' depression did not compromise their ability to be warm, responsive, and structuring with their preschoolers unless the marriage was also in difficulty. But parents who were depressed were the ones more likely to have conflictful and hostile interactions as a couple when they were with their child in our playroom (Miller et al. 1991). When there was more conflict between the parents, they were less likely to be authoritative with their child. So, the connections seem to go from depression in one parent, to conflict in the marriage, to less effective parenting. Parents' styles of reacting to their children were related to their feelings of depression when their marriage was also troubled, tense, and conflictful. A warm and cooperative marital relationship appeared to buffer the negative effects of one parent's depression on the relationship with the child (Cowan et al. in press).*

We should not forget the buffering effects of the marriage on parenting that we reported in the last chapter. When wives who had insecure models of parent-child relationships were married to husbands with secure models, the couple seemed to be doing well and both parents were warm, engaged, and structuring with their children. A positive marriage seems to help women break the negative generational cycle and react to their children positively and effectively.

Finally, we know that most women feel powerful conflicts about being home with the children or going back to their work outside the family (Harber 1991). This is another arena in which individual and marital issues play out in the parenting. We found that mothers and fathers who were more satisfied with their work (regardless of how many hours they worked), and more satisfied with the way the two of them resolved issues about child care

*In clinical samples of mothers who are seriously depressed (Cutrona and Troutman 1986; Field et al. 1990), researchers do find direct links between parents' depression and parenting style. As Hops, Sherman, and Biglan (1990) point out, however, it is hard to find seriously depressed young mothers with relatively harmonious marriages. It may be that the impact of clinical depression also plays out through tensions in the couple's relationship.

(regardless of their particular child-care arrangements), were more authoritative with their children.[14]

As Peggy and Bill tell us about the strain that is cycling throughout the relationships in their family, we see how this individual-to-marriage-to-parenting connection unfolds. They wind up discussing the issue of being strict or lenient with Mindy almost every morning before Bill leaves for work. Or they fight about whether Peggy should go back to work, whether she can help him solve his business problems, and whether or when they should be planning a second baby. Peggy explains: "We're not making much headway on any of these issues. By the time he closes the door, I'm a wreck. I want to be there for Mindy, but sometimes I'm just too crabby and impatient, especially when she starts getting upset."

Bill is distressed, too, and tries to calm down during the day. He usually feels that he wants to apologize when he gets home, but by then Peggy is often frosty and Mindy sulky. When he feels he can't deal with either of them, he slips into the den to sort out some of the business problems of the day. Peggy and Bill are quite aware that the atmosphere in their relationship is affecting their ability to be responsive to Mindy, but when they are not resolving some of their differences and not feeling taken care of by each other, it is hard for them to be nurturant to their child.

Long-Term Consequences for Children

As we followed each family through their first child's kindergarten year, some of the longer-term effects of the parents' transition to parenthood became evident. The better the parents felt they had managed their transition to parenthood, the better their children were managing their transition from family to school.

Beginning kindergarten is a big step for children and for their parents. Even if they are veterans of day-care centers or nursery schools, children enter the more formal elementary school environment with some apprehension. The school is large, there are children they don't know, and the teacher is a stranger. They don't know where to put their jackets, what the teacher expects, or what the rules are. For most, the challenge will be to make a shift from play and exploration to the more structured academic requirements. To accomplish these serious tasks, they will be asked to sit quietly, to pay attention, and to follow instructions for much of the day.

How did the children in our study adapt to this major transition? Our measures of adaptation focus on children's academic achievement and on their behavior in the classroom. Our information came from two sources: each child's score on the reading recognition and mathematics sections of the Peabody Individual Achievement Test, given by one of our staff members in the summer after kindergarten, and a ninety-one-item checklist that each child's teacher filled out once in late fall and again in late spring of kindergarten year.[15] Because teachers rated each child in the classroom without knowing which children were in our study, we have information about how the teacher perceived the social and academic adjustment of each child in our study relative to his or her peers.

Kindergarten children who are described by the teacher as disobedient, uncooperative, rule-breaking, and prone to fighting we described as *aggressive.* Boys and girls who are shy, prefer solitary activities, and don't make friends easily we described as *shy and withdrawn.* We say that kindergarteners who are restless, easily distracted, and unable to concentrate or work quietly at an activity are having *concentration problems.*

Using a complex statistical equation, we found that a number of measures combined to predict the child's adaptation to kindergarten: parents with less conflict in their families of origin; greater marital satisfaction during pregnancy; less life stress six months into parenthood; less depression and marital distress when the child was eighteen months old; more warmth and cooperation in the couple relationship; and more warmth and structure with the child at three and a half. We found that how the family was faring during the pregnancy-to-preschool period was related to the children's ability both to get along with peers and to accomplish the academic challenges of elementary school (Cowan et al. in press).[16] When families were in difficulty or distress in many aspects of their lives, their children were described by their kindergarten teachers as more aggressive or more shy, and more likely to have problems concentrating in the classroom. These children also had lower reading and mathematics achievement scores at the end of their kindergarten year.[17]

It will probably not be surprising to learn that Peggy and Bill's daughter had a difficult time in kindergarten. Her teacher's description implied that Mindy had a hot temper, hit other children, and was rarely chosen by others to play with. She had not yet mastered the rudiments of reading and arithmetic that had become the focus of classwork during the second half of the school year. Unfortunately, Mindy's difficulty became one more thing for her parents to fight about. Each was still blaming the other for being "too harsh" or "too soft," still defending his or her own parenting styles based on their experiences in their original families. Bill's business was still having problems, and Peggy had decided to get a job outside the house instead of helping Bill with his accounts because things were going so badly between them.

Willie was faring much better than Mindy during his transition to school. During the early parenthood period, his parents, Beth and Paul, spoke of the childhood experiences that had left them feeling vulnerable. They seemed to be using these painful experiences to understand each other's position, to thrash out their marital differences, and to parent Willie in a style that combined what was important to each of them. Willie's kindergarten teacher described him as a delightful, curious, outgoing child who was cooperative with the other children and doing well in his academic work.

It makes sense that parents' effectiveness at working and playing with their preschoolers plays a role in how their children acquire their social and academic skills. What we are learning from our study is that the quality of the parents' marriage has two important additional contributions to make to children's developmental progress. First, except for fathers of sons, marital conflict tends to spill over into most parent-child relationships in ways that lead maritally distressed parents to be less helpful and supportive of their children's development. Second, conflict between the parents has an even more direct and disruptive effect on the children, suggested by their teachers' descriptions of them as less able to concentrate on their classroom work. While we have known for some time that children tend to have difficulties at school when their parents divorce (Hetherington and Anderson 1989), our study is part of an emerging body of work that illustrates that children whose parents are together but in unhappy or conflictful relationships are also at risk for academic and peer relationship problems as they set out on their school careers.

We end our description of the journey to becoming a family at the beginning of a new transition—a fitting closing, we think, for the saga of modern families, who are always on the move, exploring challenging terrain toward individual and family milestones. The story of how parent-child relationships evolve resembles our accounts of family well-being in every chapter of part II. As men and women cross the great divide from couplehood to parenthood, they tend to get divided from each other. How they feel about themselves, their marriage, their work, their friendships, and their own childhoods is interrelated. The family atmosphere they establish before their children are born tends to be carried over into the early years of child rearing, shaping the tone of the relationships they develop with their children. Ultimately these family relationships become the models that the children draw on as they strike up relationships with other children and tackle the challenges of school.

As clinical psychologists, we are anxious to go beyond describing family dynamics. We can see that children benefit from the strengths their parents bring to the family-making venture and suffer when their parents find the journey perilous. What is both exciting and troubling about our results is that there is some degree of predictability about what will happen five to six years down the road of becoming a family. We have learned that it is possible to identify many of the couples whose marital and parenting relationships are at risk from the state of their relationships during pregnancy and the early family-making years. Our findings make it clear that there is an urgent need for early family interventions so that the parents' distress will not be borne by their children. In part III, we begin by describing a unique intervention for expectant couples. Then we discuss what we have learned from couples with and without the intervention about common pitfalls to effective communication between partners, in the hope that expectant and new parents can learn to help themselves and each other as they make their way along this rugged terrain. Finally, we look back briefly at the journey. We highlight the big issues, describe some warning signals for couples most likely to be at risk for distress, and offer suggestions for couples, health professionals, researchers, and policy makers that might bring more joy and less stress to the family-making process.

PART III

Protecting the Homestead

"The work being done on your marriage—are you having it done, or are you doing it yourselves?"

Drawing by Maslin; © 1989
The New Yorker Magazine, Inc.

CHAPTER 9

An Ounce of Prevention: Couples Groups

ANNIE: I don't know what to do. I'm so exhausted from getting up with Carrie two or three times every night for the past week, I can hardly function during the days. Mitch says he's willing to take a turn at least once a night, but he never hears her cry! I'm some mother—I don't even have the energy to smile back when Carrie gurgles.

MITCH: I can hardly believe it when she tells me in the morning that Carrie howled for an hour and a half. I truly don't hear a thing, but Annie doesn't believe me.

ROB: Joan and I had the same fight last week. I haven't been hearing Chuckie either.

JACKSON: And I don't hear Kevin. What is this—new fathers' hearing loss?

MARTIN: It must be genetic. Men aren't wired to hear babies' cries.

This is a conversation from one of our Becoming a Family Project couples groups. Four couples have been meeting weekly and talking with us since the women's seventh month of pregnancy. All have become parents at this point, and the four newborns are asleep either in an infant seat or in a parent's arms. We notice how rare it is for all of the babies to be asleep at once. All eight parents look exhausted.

Versions of this discussion emerged in almost all of our couples groups with new parents. The men are fascinated by their common problem, and the women's reactions range from humor to mild anger to serious distress. As each couple admits to struggling with variations on "new fathers' hearing loss," the tension level in the group lightens. Even though they are weary, both men and women are relieved to find that this is happening to almost everyone else. It seems to mute their consternation and feelings of distress with their partners and allows us to focus on the unexpected impasses between them.

When we ask Annie what happens when she tries to talk to Mitch about how tired she is, she says that he seems sympathetic but she is still the one who gets up at night. She begins to cry as she relates how distant she feels from Mitch. As if she has a direct line to her mother's emotions, little Carrie begins to whimper. Annie becomes distracted trying to soothe her. Without a word, Mitch reaches over to pick her up. "Frankly, I'm stumped," he explains. "If I don't hear Carrie, what am I supposed to do, stay up all night waiting for her to cry? I have to get up first thing to get to work, and I've been doing all the shopping and errands outside the house for weeks, so I'm feeling pretty much at my wits' end too. And when I hear Annie's critical tone . . . well, I just can't talk to her when she's so worked up." At this point Carrie is wailing and Annie moves toward Mitch, signaling that she wants to take Carrie back to her lap.

The rest of us in the room have the vivid impression that Carrie is mirroring her parents' tension and distress. Early on, then, all of the group members get a hint of how parents' emotional states can affect their babies. At the same time, the babies' reactions can keep the parents from taking care of their own needs by completing a conversation that might help them resolve the sticky issues in their relationship.

As we will show, the couples groups we conducted had a marked and profound effect on the parents in the first three years of becoming a family. Although the positive effects did not last forever, they did make a difference in the aspects of parents' lives we have been describing.

What's Out There? Then and Now

Before developing our idea of groups for expectant and new parents in the early 1970s, we scoured the professional literature on pregnancy, new parenthood, and couples therapy, certain that others must have thought of providing services for new parents. We found almost nothing. Since then, we have read of a few interventions for parents whose babies are at risk for difficulty because of the parents' health problems, the baby's prematurity (see Cherniss 1988; Parke and Tinsley 1982; Powell 1987), or retardation (Ramey et al. 1976), but the kinds of groups we developed for ordinary families—in which mental health professionals work with both men and women before their distress warrants longer-term counseling or therapy—simply do not exist.

Long after we had begun, we read about several small pilot studies (Aran-off and Lewis 1979; Colman and Colman 1971; McGuire and Gottlieb 1979; Myers-Walls and Sudsberry 1982) and two major experimental intervention projects in which health professionals worked with expectant parents—expectant mothers in the Washington, D.C., area (Shereshefsky and Yarrow 1973) and expectant couples in London (Clulow 1982). Clulow provides vivid descriptions of how each partner's dynamics play out in the relationship as the couple enters parenthood. By the time these projects were written up and published, however, the services were no longer available because the funding had run out.

Despite extensive documentation of the fact that "social support" is helpful for new parents (e.g., Gottlieb and Pancer 1988; Nuckolls, Cassells, and Kaplan 1972; Wandersman 1987), we have not found any other systematically evaluated groups for couples making the transition to parenthood, in which the leaders are trained to help with a full range of family issues and difficulties: individual, marital, parenting, three-generational, and outside-the-family.

Why We Work with Couples in Groups

Our findings about the central role of marital quality in men's and women's adaptation to parenthood certainly reinforce our strategy of targeting our intervention to couples. While the few existing services for new parents are offered to mothers, fathers' participation is the key to demonstrating that family making is a joint endeavor, not just during pregnancy, labor, and delivery but in the years to come. Men simply have little access to settings in which they can share their experiences about intimate family matters. Given how stressful family life is for so many couples, we feel it is important to help them understand how their increasing differences during this transition may be generating more distance between them.

Why intervene with couples in *groups?* We find that a group setting can provide the kind of ongoing support that contemporary couples often lack if they are creating new families far from their parents and extended families. Groups of people going through similar life experiences help participants "normalize" some of their strain and adjustment difficulties; they discover that other couples are in the same boat and that the strain they are experiencing is expectable at this stage of life (Lieberman 1981). This can strengthen the bond between husbands and wives and undercut their tendency to blame each other for their distress.

Couples rarely have an opportunity to watch and listen as other couples struggle with difficult marital or parenting issues. At best, they get edited versions of another couple's controversy once it has been resolved. In a group with trained leaders, we can provide a learning environment in which men and women can talk about what does and doesn't work and experiment with strategies tailored to their particular situation. Not childbirth preparation and not groups about parenting, our Becoming a Family Project groups are designed to provide couples with a safe environment in which husbands and wives can be encouraged to explore their expectations and realities, their hopes and anxieties, and their successes and disappointments *as they are happening.*

By inviting the babies to become part of the groups, we help parents feel less pulled to stay home with their newborns. Some women say that the groups provided their only contact with other adults in the first month or two of parenthood. Because of the potential isolation and exhaustion these weeks can bring, both parents, but particularly mothers, often feel blue or depressed. Having the babies right there in the groups not only allows the parents to show off their progeny but has the added benefit of allowing the tensions between the parents' and the babies' needs to become visible, as they did in Mitch and Annie's discussion of middle-of-the-night feedings.

We were extremely fortunate to find that the best candidates for staff couples in our longitudinal study were "real-life" couples. Harriet Curtis-Boles and Abner Boles III, and Ellen Garrett and Bill Coysh, married graduate student couples at the time, worked with the two of us for almost four years.[1] Five of the six leaders were clinical psychologists at the pre- or postdoctoral level and the sixth, Ellen, was a businesswoman.

The format for training the group leaders was drawn from our earlier experience with John and Lynne Coie, our collaborators in the pilot study to test our intervention approach (Cowan et al. 1978). At the beginning of the training, all of us completed the study questionnaires that the couples would eventually fill out, as a way to describe our own lives as individuals and as couples. Then, using the semi-structured format we would be using with the couples in the study to talk about our lives as couples, we met weekly as a group over a four-month period.

As we mentioned in the introduction, the twenty-four expectant couples invited to be in one of our couples groups were randomly chosen from all of the expectant couples entering the study. Each was interviewed by a staff couple to acquaint them with the project and with us. Each staff couple conducted two six-month-long groups. Once the groups were under way, we supervised the clinical work in our staff meetings on a weekly and then twice-monthly basis throughout the first and second years of the study. All of us on the staff monitored the process and progress of all six groups.

It is 7:00 P.M. on a Tuesday evening in mid-April, the first meeting of our group. Four couples—Annie and Mitch, Joan and Rob, Tanya and Jackson, and Sandi and Martin—have gathered in the conference room of the Psychology Clinic. The four women are beginning their last trimester of pregnancy. Three of them are still feeling nimble, but Joan says she feels "like a beached whale." We have met each couple in our initial interviews, but they are strangers to one another.

We tell the group members a little about ourselves and ask them what drew them to the project. Because each husband and wife in the group had completed a packet of questionnaires before the first meeting, they have already begun to think about the aspects of family life we will be discussing.

After the introductory session, our evenings usually start with an unstructured "check-in" that gives each person a chance to raise any current concerns and topics for future discussions in the group. A husband or wife faced with an urgent decision about a job or career move is encouraged to sort out the issues involved. The relationship with one man's parents may have become heated around choosing a name for the baby. His wife says she wants him to tell his mother that it is up to them to choose their own baby's name. We try to help both partners figure out what, if anything, they can do to take care of each person's needs.

The second part of each meeting is devoted to a topic that has been selected by us or by the group. During the six months of meeting together, we travel with the couples over our five-domain map of the transition to parenthood, helping them to see how the various territories are connected. In the early meetings, we focus on each of the partners as individuals. Then we move on to talk more about their lives and their dreams about their relationship, their work and family decisions, three-generational issues, and their pressing questions about being parents.

We scheduled the six months of meetings so that couples could spend the first three months *anticipating* how they will manage once they have a baby and the next three exploring their *actual* experience once their babies are born. Over the twenty-four meetings, the couples build a set of shared experiences and ideas.

ANTICIPATION

At first, some husbands seem less comfortable than their wives about volunteering their feelings, questions, or worries, but with the leaders' gentle encouragement the men in every group begin to talk. They describe their experience of the pregnancy, their anxieties about managing the labor and delivery, and especially their pictures about becoming fathers. Group participants soon discover how common it is for men and women to struggle with discrepancies between how they think they are supposed to feel and how they really feel. During late pregnancy, common themes emerge in each of the groups.

Individual Concerns About Pregnancy, Labor, and Delivery   Even though all of the couples in our study attended some kind of childbirth preparation together, both husbands and wives worry about things they cannot raise in such classes. Husbands talk about needing to be strong and protective of their pregnant wives; it would be selfish, they feel, to discuss their own fears and needs. Wives are concerned about what is happening to their bodies and how that makes them feel. Each person in the group gets to hear about his or her mate's worries and about a host of issues that couples do not usually discuss, yet obviously need to discuss. As we encourage this kind of talk, the group members learn from our reactions that we expect men and women to have some of these negative feelings and concerns.

Family Legacies   As we encourage couples to flesh out their pictures of life as a family, they begin to describe their childhood years. Sandi says that her parents are very traditional. Martin's politically radical parents consternate her: "I just assumed that when we got married, the home stuff was my department, but I can never do anything around the house without Martin mixing in. I can't tell whether he's doing it because he wants to or whether he feels he has to because his parents just did everything together." Joan, looking thoughtful, comments: "I'm just beginning to see something. With Rob and me, it's the other way around. He's the one from the family where the women did everything, and my folks were the odd ones who shared. Either way it can lead to things getting mixed up between you." Other couples' stories can help us take a fresh look at our own.

Ideas About Parenting   "Babies should be tended when they are upset so that they will be sure of their parents' love for them." This item from our questionnaire about parenting ideas (Heming, Cowan, and Cowan 1990) usually stimulates heated debate. Some expectant parents focus on the baby's sense of insecurity if left to cry; others are as passionate about not teaching a child to cry for everything he or she needs. Discussing some of these crucial parenting ideas before the baby arrives is one way of preparing for the real dilemmas that every couple will face. When partners discover that they have different notions of how to handle some of these common issues in a setting that is intended to entertain many points of view, there is less chance that they will find themselves startled to be on opposite sides of the debate when the baby is howling in the middle of the night. This initial sharing of expectations about parenting rarely leads to a resolution of partners' differences, but it initiates them into a process of problem solving that can stand them in good stead in the months and years to come.

Work/Family Issues   Every couple faces the problem of how to juggle the pulls between work and family life. Because our group discussions involve a wide range of situations, group members can see that their tension does not stem solely from their inability to fit everything in. We pay attention to each individual's and couple's needs and try to address the forces over which they have little or no control: no paternity leave, career demands, financial worries, and so on.

Marital Conflicts   One evening, Joan and Rob arrive looking tense, faces flushed. Joan looks as if she has been crying. No one comments. The group discussion goes on for a few minutes; then, during a remark about an argument between Sandi and Martin, Joan begins to cry. With our encouragement, she and Rob describe a fight they had on the way to the meeting. They had been at a wedding reception of a friend and were leaving early to be on time for our group. Rob said he wanted to stay. Joan wanted to stay too, but said nothing about that, only insisting that they must leave. We ask a few questions about what had been happening before the fight started. It seems that Joan had asked Rob on the way to the reception whether he had read the childbirth books she had bought. He had brushed off the question, implying that he would get around to it, but he didn't sound as if he was interested in reading them. Joan says she thought, "Uh-oh, he has cold feet about the baby and second thoughts about me, too. And then, when Rob said he didn't want to come to the group tonight, I felt—well, that's really it, he's jumping off the train."

Rob protests: "I don't know where she gets that stuff. I love her. I'm really excited about the baby. But every time I start one of those books, I start getting tight and anxious. I figure it's better if I just let it happen without thinking about it so much." As far as the recent conflict was concerned, he explained: "What I really wanted to do was to stay at that party for a few more minutes and then go off by ourselves. When you blew up, I thought, 'Well, I know what she says about wanting us to be together, but it doesn't sound to me as if she's really interested.' "

This interchange demonstrates how difficult it can be for two people to communicate with each other, especially when one or both of them are apprehensive or tense. One issue tends to spiral into another. Each partner sees the same event differently. Both make quick assumptions about what is going on inside the other without checking them out. Rob doesn't feel right about saying he's anxious, in part to avoid a fight but in part because he doesn't think men ought to feel that way. Joan blows up. Rob backs off. The sad part is that she doesn't let him know that she wants to stay longer too, and he says so little about what is going on inside him that she does not get to find out, until we ask him about it in the group, that he really wanted to be with her alone. By the end of the discussion, Joan and Rob have not resolved the differences that started their fight, but they are working together to figure them out. We can feel the relaxation of the tension between them, and they seem to feel a great deal better about each other.

Joan says she feels self-conscious because she and Rob have taken so much of the group's time. But Sandi says she is relieved to hear them struggle with something that they have not yet resolved: "Martin and I have been having some of the same kind of go-rounds lately, but we haven't had the nerve to bring them here. What we usually tell here is the cleaned-up version. I've learned a lot about how complicated one little spat can be."

AFTER THE BABIES ARRIVE

Soon after the women give birth, the couples bring their infants into the groups. They are eager to describe the details of their labor and delivery. "Old hands" who have been parents for weeks spontaneously bring prepared food and words of wisdom for the newest parents. Men talk animatedly about their ability to handle their wives' long labors and difficult births; they are astounded at the strength the women showed and, to a man, they are amazed at the intensity of their feelings for their newborns. Rob tells Martin, whose baby is due in several days: "You wonder and worry about whether you'll be ready when the time comes, and then you just are. When the doctor told us it would have to be a C-section, Joan and I just got in there and did it. They treated me just like one of the medical team. It was amazing to see that little boy emerge. They asked me to cut the cord! There's been no experience in my life to match it!"

Each of us becomes absorbed in the images of these "birth stories," as the couples come to call them. Throughout the weeks of sharing these experiences, we are continually impressed by how eagerly men, who generally do not find it easy to talk about intimate feelings, are opening up. Slowly, groups of former strangers have come to sound like trusted confidants. After the group meetings end, many participants express their surprise that it was easier to have some of these conversations in a safe setting with people they didn't know well than it is at home or with friends.

In the three months that follow, we return to many of the issues we had discussed before the couples became parents. The earlier discussions have prepared us for talking about how to deal with the stress points in life with a newborn. Some of the partners' joint preparation cushions them from the shock of finding that their fantasy plans do not meet the reality test. We cannot help couples to avoid the stresses of new parenthood, but we can help them to face them, to think about how to deal with them, and to use their strengths to cope more effectively.

Our work in the couples groups sensitizes us to an often ignored aspect of the delicate balance between partners. A father who has been at work all day offers to hold his daughter, to soothe her, to change her. Even though his wife has said that she wants him to become "involved" in caring for the baby, she cannot seem to resist showing him how to hold her when he shows the slightest hesitation at the baby's fussing. "She likes it better if you hold her this way," she encourages. When their daughter cries in the next few moments, he hands her back to his wife, saying to the baby, "Here, sweetie, let's give you back to the 'expert.'" This kind of exchange can leave men feeling like the "second-string" parent and women feeling that they are carrying the whole burden of responding to the baby. Couples can slip into a more traditional division of baby care than either wanted.

Men and women in the group learn to appreciate that each of the issues they explore is related to each of the aspects of life we have been discussing. He wants to be more involved with the baby than his father was with him. She wants a more egalitarian relationship than her parents had, but if he gets to be an expert as a parent *and* in his job outside the family, where will her special contribution lie? The legacies from their families of origin have not given them models to talk about these new concerns easily, and their inability to do so leaves them feeling more distant than they did when they first planned this baby. Each time we venture into new territory, they tie ideas from earlier group discussions to the topic at hand.

> ROB: Last week we were talking about what we wanted to carry over from the families we grew up in, and what we *didn't* want to happen in our families now. Then right now, as we were talking about why I didn't want Joan to go back to work, at first I couldn't figure out why was I so upset. Then I realized I was getting in touch with how much I hated it when my mom wasn't home for me.
>
> JOAN: I'm not sure whether that means it'll be OK with you if I go back, but I'm relieved that at least you're not saying that it's just my problem.

In the last weeks, the groups begin to mirror the couples' lives at home. A father begins talking about how distressed he is that he has had no time alone with his wife since their son's birth, and his wife and baby begin to cry. A mother becomes absorbed in feeding or diapering her daughter, and we all become totally distracted with her, focusing on the baby's whimpers and gurgles and losing our train of thought completely. Even with this lesson before us, partners express surprise at how easily their needs as individuals and couples get sidetracked as they try to cope with the addition of the extraordinary demands of a newborn into their busy lives.

OUR ROLE AS GROUP LEADERS

In the most general sense, we think about our role as leaders as one of encouraging partners to explore the complexity of the exciting yet anxiety-provoking aspects of their journey to parenthood, to talk about the things we had found so difficult to do when we were becoming parents. We help them recognize when unresolved tensions in one aspect of life seem to be spilling over into another aspect.

We do not pretend that we can resolve couples' dilemmas or offer prescriptions to reestablish the balance in their lives. Our task is to slow them down so that they don't simply rush past muddy trails or rocky crevices in hopes of skirting disaster. We know that tension gets stimulated between partners when one is troubled about how the conversation is going, does not let the other know, does not ask a clarifying question, and tries to keep the discussion or debate going. This is a quick route to feeling like adversaries. If partners can learn to explore each person's point of view by amplifying and understanding it, they are much more likely to come out feeling on the same side even if they disagree. If the process feels more equal and productive, the frustration of being at an impasse can sometimes be avoided even if the problem cannot be solved immediately.

When a couple uses the protection of the group to work on a problem they have been unable to resolve by themselves, we encourage both partners to describe their experience of the difficulty. As participants present their individual views, we draw them out, looking for the sources of their different views. Our questions and their answers help to highlight the unique perspectives that no amount of mind reading can unearth.

Few couples have settings in which they can get help in revealing, redefining, and negotiating their problematic differences. The group provides a regular and safe haven in which they are encouraged to explore the major issues and challenges that interfere with their communication. For many couples, the group time is the only time when they talk seriously with each other about anything other than managing tasks and arranging schedules.

SUPPORT OR THERAPY?

When we describe the Becoming a Family groups to professional and lay audiences, we are usually asked whether they are education, support, or therapy groups. We think the groups encompass the best aspects of support groups, consciousness-raising groups, group therapy, and couples therapy.

For fairly well functioning couples, drawing out the participants and working with them when they are stuck helps them to clarify issues, discover some new perspectives on a problem, and expand their repertoire of skills for living as a family. When couples are in serious distress, the discussion in the groups can be both tense and frightening for the members. At times over the years, we have seen a couple through a major crisis. Several months after their babies' births, mothers in two different couples groups had to be hospitalized for serious illnesses. In both cases, frightened, anxious, and sometimes angry fathers were left to care for their infants. We tried to help make sense of these dramatic events for the couple in crisis and for the others in the group as well. Despite their increased feelings of vulnerability, group members rallied, spontaneously offering material and emotional support to the distressed parents and babies.

In one poignant example, Dawn was unexpectedly hospitalized, leaving her husband, Peter, to care for three-month-old Bonnie just as the group meetings were coming to an end. This exceedingly stressful situation was made even more difficult by the fact that Bonnie had not yet learned how to drink from a bottle. Peter came to the next group meeting with the baby, looking exhausted and worried. Bonnie kept wailing frantically, and after several failed attempts to feed her, he felt ready to do the same. Spontaneously, several of the mothers in Peter's group suggested a plan to help until Dawn was well enough to return home. Margaret, one of the mothers in the group who was still breastfeeding her baby, came to the couple's apartment, sent Peter out for a walk, and calmed Bonnie down enough to nurse her. Bonnie soon ate hungrily and fell asleep, quiet for the first time that day. Later in the day, Jenny, another mother from the group, came to visit Peter and Bonnie. Because she had already begun the sensitive task of weaning her baby from breast milk to bottle, Jenny was pretty sure that she would be able to get Bonnie to cooperate with her to drink from a bottle. She worked patiently with Peter and Bonnie until both of them "got the hang of it," as she put it.

The bonds that developed among the members of the group grew very strong as we all weathered Dawn and Peter's crisis.

In both of the groups that experienced severe distress in one of its members, the participants suggested that the group continue meeting a little longer until the distressed couple was on a more even keel. The response was unanimous in each case, and everyone attended faithfully for an extra month beyond our expected ending. We heard recently that two couples in each of these groups have maintained friendships begun more than eleven years ago.

We have become less concerned about deciding whether the groups provide support or therapy. At times, they do both. Because the groups are led by mental health professionals, we can deal directly with new parents' crises and high levels of distress. Could groups without leaders accomplish this task? Of the six groups we conducted for this study, one decided to continue meeting on their own for an additional four months, another for almost a year. In both cases, the couples told us later, they decided to stop meeting regularly when one of the couples began to talk about serious marital difficulties. Without experienced leaders there, they explained, the group did not know how to encourage the safe exploration of one another's marital problems. As Annie told us, "without you, we didn't have what it takes to handle the level of intimacy we had established."

There is one central difference, though, between what goes on in our Becoming a Family Project couples groups and therapy. Couples have not come to us saying that they are in serious distress or that they need to change. We have made it clear that we will help them monitor their own comfort with revealing their thoughts and feelings. Some men and women say less than others, but all say at the end that they have gained something by attending the sessions. At the very least, the comradeship of couples going through a major transition together provides the support and comfort of knowing they are not alone.

Short-Term Effects of the Intervention

Even before interpreting the statistics, there were clear, qualitative signs of the impact the group meetings were having on the parents. In a follow-up interview almost fifteen months after the group ended, Rob said: "Our group got together a couple of weeks ago, and we're planning a reunion on the second anniversary of when the group began. There's something wonderful about all of us knowing each other's kids all their lives. It's like being part of a very special family." Joan added: "Sometimes I feel that it really saved our lives. Our fighting was getting out of control. You probably wouldn't be surprised that we still do it, but we're able to come back to each other when it's over and really work things out."

While we are gratified to know that the couples *say* the groups have been helpful to their adjustment as couples and families, we also want to know whether we can *document* the effects of the intervention: We compared the patterns of the group couples' responses to our questionnaires with those of the couples in our comparison sample before and after having their babies and before and after their group experience. Did couples' patterns of change over the transition to parenthood in each aspect of family life look any different with and without the help of a couples group?

We were amazed and pleased to find that, although we could not see the effects of the intervention on everything we measured, there were statistically significant differences in each aspect of family life between the parents who had participated in a couples group and those who had had no intervention.[2]

SENSE OF SELF AND IDENTITY

The couples groups did not affect men's and women's self-esteem as measured by the difference between descriptions of "Me as I am" and "Me as I'd like to be" on the Adjective Check List. This is consistent with the results of most other studies indicating that self-esteem is a very stable characteristic of adults' personalities (Gough and Heilbrun 1980). We also found no differences in the men's descriptions of themselves on the pie as Parent, Partner, or Worker as a consequence of being in a couples group.

By contrast, the groups did have an impact on women's investment in different aspects of their identity. From pregnancy to six months after birth, mothers with and without a couples group experience similar declines in the size of their Worker/Student identities, but by eighteen months after their first child's birth, mothers who have been in the intervention return to their previous psychological involvement in their Worker or Student self. By contrast, mothers with no intervention have Worker or Student pie pieces that are half the size they were in their pre-baby days. Not only do group mothers come back to their work-related identities earlier, they also show significantly less decline in the Partner/Lover aspect of themselves than mothers without the intervention. It looks as if the group discussions, by encouraging partners to keep a focus on their couple relationship, help the women maintain their identity as wives and partners while they are taking on motherhood and returning to their jobs and careers.

DIVISION OF FAMILY WORK

Group participation has different effects on men's and women's satisfaction with their division of labor in the family. When the babies are six months old, partners' actual division of caring for the baby is no different in the intervention and the nonintervention couples, but fathers who have been in a couples group are *less satisfied* with their involvement in the care of their babies than fathers with no intervention; they want to be doing *more* housework and child care than they actually do. Over the same period, however, their wives are *more satisfied* with the couple's division of labor than wives who were not in one of the groups.

From our discussions in the groups, it is very clear that men want to continue their involvement in outside-the-family work *and* to be significantly involved in caring for their babies. Over the six months of meeting together, as fathers became painfully aware of what it takes to manage a demanding job and the day-to-day care of a household with a baby, their frustration rises. Fathers who are in our intervention groups probably talk more about reconciling these two aspects of their lives than do most men in the first year of new parenthood.

While mothers in the groups feel these work and family pulls too, they are more satisfied than their nonintervention counterparts with the couple's division of labor. Their satisfaction may reflect their appreciation that their husbands are sharing their concern about running the household, raising their child, and keeping their relationship as a couple alive because we talk about these things regularly in the groups. This shared concern may leave the women feeling somewhat less burdened, even if they cannot turn the egalitarian division of labor they envisioned into reality. The group wives' satisfaction may also reflect the fact that they hear other husbands talking about doing less child care than they had expected.

The groups have been over for more than a year by the time the babies are one and a half. At this point, the intervention fathers' satisfaction with who does what has remained stable, whereas fathers without the intervention are becoming significantly *more dissatisfied* with how the family work is divided. Now, fathers from the intervention groups are more satisfied than the comparison fathers with their involvement in caring for the children. Here we see the delicate balance within partners affecting the balance between them. The group women have retained more of their Worker/Student and Partner/Lover identities *and* satisfaction with their division of baby care. This may be helping their husbands reconcile the discrepancies between what they had hoped they could do and what the reality of their lives permits. Some support for this idea comes from our data showing that by the second year of parenthood, husbands and wives from the couples groups are having more similar perceptions of their division of baby care, whereas spouses with no intervention show more discrepant descriptions of theirs.

THE MARRIAGE

Most fathers, in groups and not in groups, reported higher levels of marital conflict and disagreement during the transition to parenthood. An interesting twist here is that the fathers who have been in a couples group say that they have *more* marital conflict about two specific issues: the family division of labor and the quality of time they spend together as a couple. While it is possible that the group discussions contribute to arguments about these aspects of life, it is also possible that partners who have been in a couples group simply talk more about these issues. After the group meetings ended, we asked each couple whether they thought that participating in the study had had any effect on them. Often they replied that they learned they'd do better talking about what is bothering them rather than sweeping it under the rug. As Annie said, "If you don't deal with things directly, they tend to come out anyway. We used to ignore our differences for fear that we'd get into a fight about them. But we're finding that we can handle more conflict than we used to be able to do. We still don't like it very much, but we learned that even when you have a fight, life goes on and nobody dies."

Both husbands and wives from the couples groups report fewer negative changes in their sexual relationship than those without the intervention. The protected setting of the couples groups makes it possible for couples to exchange information about this private aspect of married life. One evening late in her pregnancy, Annie described how she and Mitch were having problems when they tried to make love: "Nothing quite fits together the same way anymore. Last night we were trying to get comfortable, and moving every which way trying not to put too much weight on the baby, and suddenly Mitch fell out of bed!" There was laughter and a few sighs of relief from other group members. We later learned that this was the main topic of conversation for all the couples on their way home.

Sharing personal information was common in every couples group we have led or supervised over the past fifteen years. It clearly relieves tensions for some couples and answers unasked questions for others. The reports of less negative change in the sexual relationships of the intervention couples are consistent with our impression that when group members describe their experiences of these largely unexpected shifts in their sex lives, they feel less worried that something is wrong with them and more hopeful about things getting back to normal. When the leaders who are asking these delicate questions have their own spouses in the room, it appears to give participants the message, "We know that these are intimate matters but we are not embarrassed talking to you about them, if you are comfortable talking with us."

Since moderate but significant increases in overall marital disenchantment are reported by almost every researcher who studies the transition to parenthood, we were especially interested in whether we could show any measurable effects of the intervention on partners' feelings about their marriage. As we described in chapter 5, the marital satisfaction of partners without the intervention declined from pregnancy to six months after birth, and dropped even more sharply between six and eighteen months postpartum. For the intervention group participants too, there was a slight decline from pregnancy to six months after birth, but it was less severe than that of the comparison couples. Then, in contrast to the couples with no intervention, the group couples maintained their level of marital satisfaction over the following year.

Two years after the study began, we learned that ten of the original ninety-six couples had separated or filed for divorce. Four were from the twenty-four originally childless couples; the other six were from the forty-eight couples who had become parents with no intervention. In other words, two years into the study the marriages of 16 percent of the childless couples and 12.5 percent of the couples who had become parents and had no special help had not survived. By contrast, more than a year after the groups ended, *the marriages of all of the couples group participants were still intact.*

Longer-Term Effects of the Intervention

All of the couples who participated in a couples group were still together when the children turned three. It looks as though our work with them as they were becoming parents helped keep their optimism about their relationships alive. Although the numbers are too small to determine the statistical significance of this difference, the trend is certainly an encouraging one. Because there are no other intervention studies of this kind with new parents, we have nothing to go on in terms of how long we can expect this early help for couples to last.

By the time we were ready to begin our follow-up interviews, when the children were three and a half, another couple in the sample of parents with no intervention had separated, bringing the total to 15 percent. (This figure is consistent with the findings of Eiduson in a Southern California sample of new parents [1983], and with the figures from several national samples of families in which it is possible to calculate the age of the children when their parents divorce [Bumpass and Rindfuss 1979; Cherlin 1977; Morgan, Lye, and Condran 1988]). At this point, the first of the intervention couples decided to separate (4 percent). Even so, couples were still more likely to be in intact marriages if they had participated in our intervention before they had their babies—96 percent compared with 85 percent—but there were almost no differences between the two sets of parents on their questionnaire responses.

We confess that we would like to be able to leave our story on a note of optimism, but when we returned to visit the families once again during their children's kindergarten year, the news was discouraging: Six years after the children were born, the divorce rate in families with or without our intervention was up to 20 percent. Five and a half years after the intervention had ended, we could no longer discriminate between the two sets of parents' on any of the measures of parents' sense of self, role arrangements, marital quality, or marital stability—the aspects of life in which the intervention had made a difference earlier. Nor did the parents appear to be significantly different in their interactions with their children. Consistent with this finding, children of intervention parents were doing no better and no worse in their adaptation to kindergarten than the children whose parents had had no intervention.

It is not realistic to expect the effects of a six-month intervention to be evident four or six years later on the parents' relationships as couples, their parenting style, or their children's adaptation to school. By then, couples have been dealing with the effects of having more children, job changes, moves, births, deaths in their extended families, and the strain of working and rearing young children.

How long can intervention effects be expected to last? In a consultation with Enrico Jones, an expert in research on the effects of therapy, we were reminded that very few therapy studies follow clients more than a year after therapy ends, virtually none do two-year follow-ups, and a five-year follow-up is unheard of. While this is not completely reassuring, it gives us some comfort to know that demonstrating intervention effects over a three-year period is something of an achievement.

We can see now that we initiated the Becoming a Family Project with a rather rosy view of preventive interventions. As in the public health disease-prevention model, we hoped we could eliminate, or at least reduce, the incidence of marked distress in fairly well functioning families. It is clear now that the kind of work we have been doing does not *prevent* couples from experiencing the typical changes and strains of new parenthood. Anticipating a particular change and discussing the discrepancies between expectations and reality do not prevent couples from having tense middle-of-the-night discussions after the baby is home, but do make their disagreements, even heated ones, come as less of a shock. Parents also see that other partners have differing opinions on a number of critical issues in their lives.

The groups do not seem to affect basic aspects of men's behavior in their families. In general, fathers in the couples groups do not become appreciably more involved in housework or caring for the baby than fathers without an intervention. But by eighteen months after birth, both men and women who have participated in a couples group are more satisfied with their role arrangements than parents in the comparison subsample, even though group fathers had been less satisfied one year earlier. One possible interpretation of these findings is that the groups function merely as a palliative to help parents feel more satisfied. Another possibility is that experiences in the group affect men's and women's *expectations* about their lives as parents and partners, leaving less discrepancy between what they expected and the reality of their lives (cf. Belsky 1984; Garrett 1983; Parke 1979).

Cognitive theories of stress and emotion (cf. Lazarus 1991) help us to understand what may be happening here. These theories argue that our experience of stress is not determined by specific events, but by whether we interpret these events as likely to cause us physical or psychological harm. In this view, how men and women understand what is happening to them as new parents can affect the way they feel about themselves, each other, and the baby. When group members learn that the shifts they are experiencing are common to this time of life, they are less likely to interpret them as a commentary on their adequacy as individuals or as a couple. They are more likely to be able to engage in collaborative problem solving rather than adversarial sniping. By helping partners take a new perspective on their experiences, mental health professionals can play an essential role in preventing future distress.

We found some support in our interviews for the notion that our intervention was affecting how men and women interpreted their experience. Although partners in both intervention and nonintervention subsamples often recounted difficulties or dilemmas they were experiencing, parents who had been in a couples group appeared to have a more optimistic attitude: "We haven't solved all the 'who does what' issues," Tanya says, "but we're working on them." Parents who had not been in a couples group tended to report changes that seemed to be happening *to* them. One father, for example, said in answer to a question about changes in their relationship, "We're just not spending as much time together as we used to, and when we do, we *find ourselves* bickering a lot." The lower divorce rate among the group participants in their first three years of parenthood suggests that they felt able to do something about the problems in their marriages.

We often hear researchers and clinicians say that it is difficult to get men to consider family issues. A number of men in our study were skeptical about joining the study or about participating in a group. The fact that the interviews and groups were always conducted by a couple seemed to help a great deal. Most of the men became active and responsive participants over the more than six years that we followed them, and no couple ever dropped out of one of our groups. Once in the groups, fathers functioned as ongoing models for one another; as some men became involved in discussion and active caretaking of their newborns, others followed. As they diapered, fed, and soothed their infants, they talked about how to handle their children and keep their marriages vital, defying the stereotype of the uninvolved father. The structure and process of the group reinforced the attitude that, regardless of the inequality of time spent with the baby, fathers and mothers were involved in a joint endeavor to keep their relationships alive as they created new families.

By providing a setting in which both parents can continue to paint their pictures of the kind of life they want to have as a family, the intervention appears to keep some men involved in ongoing talk with their wives about what is and isn't working well. In the second year of parenthood, the men from the couples groups became more satisfied with their own involvement in the care of their children, with their sexual relationships, and with their overall marriages. The work in the group appeared to make it possible for more couples to negotiate work and family balances that left the women feeling more like Workers and Partners in the second year of parenthood.

We mentioned that, in general, men and women tend to become more different from each other as they make the journey from pregnancy to parenthood and this difference seems to contribute to increases in marital conflict and distress. When we compared group couples with the nonintervention couples, we found that partners in the group couples showed significantly less divergence from each other in their roles and perceptions of family life during their transition to parenthood. It seems that our focus on each partner and on the relationship between them interrupts some of the processes that tend to draw husbands and wives apart. This finer balance between the spouses may be contributing to their sustained marital satisfaction and stability during their children's toddler years.

Despite the fact that the groups offer emotional support and that group participants are vocal about the groups' helpfulness, the data from our follow-ups at six months postpartum suggest that participation in a group may actually contribute to some dissatisfaction or distress at first. If our assessment of intervention effects had stopped at that point, we would not have seen any statistically significant differences between couples with and without the intervention. Most of the measurable positive effects appeared eighteen months after birth, more than a year after the groups had disbanded.

As we mentioned in chapter 3, developmental theorists like Erik Erikson (1968), Heinz Werner (1948), and Jean Piaget (1967) propose that conflict, disequilibration, and temporary disorganization are *necessary* for individuals to proceed from one developmental stage to another. The fact that the effects of the intervention were clearer in the second and third years of parenthood than immediately after the intervention suggests that the groups helped parents face the initial strains of the transition, rather than ignore them as unacceptable. By helping men and women slow down to focus on some of the hot spots, we may have temporarily increased the amount of turmoil that couples experienced. But because we also provided a safe setting in which to observe other couples' stress and try new alternatives, the couples may have felt less embarrassed by their own difficulties and stimulated to try some of the strategies we discussed until they experienced some degree of success. We are proposing that some disequilibrium in a protected environment that focuses on successful coping strategies may actually produce the positive effects that we found. The delays we found in the positive effects of the intervention may help explain why intervention studies with a one-time "outcome" measure—often quite soon after an intervention ends—find so few visible effects.

At our three-and-a-half-year follow-up, Joan talked about how grateful she felt for the time she and Rob had in the group to focus on their relationship as a couple. Now that they have had a second baby without a group, she understands even more about the early experiences:

JOAN: It was so lonely after having Scott, our second. It just wasn't the same and I couldn't figure out why at first. I finally realized that we were not in a group and we didn't have the time to sit down and talk—to each other or to other couples going through it. When the group met weekly, it helped us be more conscious of the issues that we should be talking about and working on. Sometimes it was a real pain, and Rob and I had some tough times then. But I'm not sure some of the problems we had to deal with would have come to our attention except through the groups. And then, after it was over, we continued to work at things for quite a while. But now, with everything happening in our lives, I feel we're getting lost again. There ought to be a group for couples having second kids!

Joan's comments are certainly consistent with our point of view and with our finding that the impact of our intervention declined over time. We feel that we need to extend our version of couples groups, beginning in late pregnancy and continuing with periodic "booster" interventions about every two years. This added assistance would reinforce couple's strengths, encourage them to keep building the skills they need to cope with being parents and partners, and prepare them for the inevitable challenges and crises of this complex and demanding period of family growth.

On the strength of our results showing that parents' ability to cope as individuals, couples, and parents in the preschool period is an excellent predictor of their children's academic and social adaptation to elementary school, we have mounted a new intervention study in which we work with parents during the years surrounding their first child's transition to elementary school. Our Schoolchildren and Their Families Project offers couples several kinds of group and individual consultation. By helping parents work on their confusing or troubling marital and parenting issues, we hope to increase their satisfaction and effectiveness as partners and parents and, in turn, reduce some of the burden that children can carry from their parents' stress and unhappiness. If our work with the couples helps them feel more competent and satisfied as parents and partners, this should free the children to cope more effectively with the academic and social challenges of the early school years. We hope that our work with families undergoing major transitions will encourage other health and mental health professionals to join us in developing these kinds of family-based preventive interventions.

CHAPTER 10

Talk to Me: Hidden Challenges in Couples' Communication

W E CAN IMAGINE A COUPLE who thinks they might be ready to start a family taking a deep breath after reading this book so far and saying to each other, "Okay, here's what we have to do if we're going to make sure that the children we bring into our lives have the right kind of family atmosphere to grow up in. We have to feel good about ourselves and our relationship. We have to work out the 'who does what' problems that we've been skirting. We should try to come to terms with some of what's been troubling us in our relationships with our parents. We need to figure out how we're going to arrange our work lives after the baby comes, where we'll get child care, and whether we can count on friends and family for extra support. And we'd better try to come to some agreements about what we think kids need and how we'll look after those needs. The parenting part might take care of itself if we just make sure that our relationship as a couple is in as good shape as it can be. Now, how do we do that by ourselves?"

This couple is probably concerned because when they try to talk about a disagreement, they typically find themselves becoming tense, angry, and frustrated. The more their tension rises, the less they understand how two people who love each other can be locked in an exchange that feels so terrible. At the height of their argument each would state that the other is the main obstacle to a solution, but inside they both harbor the fear that there is something wrong with them.

Most couples, we have learned, do not know that some conflict and tension are inevitable in any intimate relationship. Nor do they realize that the key to a satisfying marriage is not whether a couple has challenging problems or whether they always resolve them, but *how they talk to each other* about them. In part I, we described couples who coped well with the decision about whether to have a baby. We showed that their effective problem-solving process had positive consequences for their satisfaction with their relationship over the next two years. Videotaping the couples later on as they tried to resolve a difference or disagreement about a "who does what?" issue, Jessica Ball (1984) found that how partners felt about their overall marriage had to do with how they felt about the process of talking about the problem, not with whether the problem was resolved during the discussion. We have a good deal of evidence to show that when spouses' conversations about problems feel productive and satisfying to both of them, it colors the atmosphere of the family in warmer hues by contributing to each partner's sense of well-being and fostering more positive relationships throughout the family.

There are hidden challenges that keep partners from talking with each other in a satisfying way. These challenges exist in all couples and can hinder productive discussion even in the most mundane conversations. Couples are especially prone to stumble over them in the early years of becoming a family because so many decisions that had previously been made by one spouse alone suddenly require complex discussion. "I need to go to the store," a topic that may not even be raised before the baby is born, can require extensive negotiation afterward. Similarly, unless a job change involves a radical move, the decision can be made by one spouse independently in the pre-baby days. But when children are involved, the welfare of the whole family must be taken into account before such a decision can be made.

Spouses' styles of talking to each other are not the sole determinants of how their relationship feels or of how successfully they will adapt to change in each area of family life. However, when one parent is reading the newspaper at the breakfast table while the other is talking to her mother on the telephone, diapering the baby, and having an anxiety attack because she is late for work, we know that she will feel that their communication needs improvement.

The issue for couples is not simply "improving communication skills." The transition to parenthood raises so many issues simultaneously in so many aspects of couples' lives that they find it difficult to prevent the tension from any single topic from spilling over to other areas. Sharon and Daniel illustrate how quickly the spillover can occur if they have no stop mechanism:

SHARON: Last week I asked Daniel to make a call to *one* of the child-care centers. Just one. You would have thought I was asking him to go to the moon and back.

DANIEL: But I had just come home from work. I was tired. You were being totally nasty. I was playing with Amy, looking after her like you asked me to, and you wanted me to call right that second. Besides, you'd just told me that your mom had recommended this place, and you know what I think about *her* judgment.

SHARON: Daniel, this really pisses me off. Grow up for once. I needed some help that day. I really want to get going back to work, and to do that we need to line up some decent child care for Amy. I'm doing most of it and feeling really overwhelmed. You could have been civil about it, even if you couldn't or wouldn't make the call.

DANIEL: You weren't being civil to me then, and you're being downright mean now. And if you're so overwhelmed, how are you going to manage going back to work? Maybe we should wait a while.

If we hadn't proceeded with our interview questions, Sharon and Daniel would have continued to argue, bringing in new issues every few minutes but discussing none of them fully to either partner's satisfaction. Their conversation moved so fast, they did not realize that they had started discussing a child-related issue but moved immediately to Sharon's alleged "nastiness," her vulnerability, her mother's role in their life, Daniel's exhaustion, his civility, and his worry about Sharon going back to work. They were both so preoccupied with their own vulnerability and hurt feelings that they spent their time and energy reacting to the other's attack and defending themselves, getting distracted from trying to find a solution to any of the problems they raised.

We are not intending to say, "If only partners will sit down and talk to each other calmly, everything will be fine." Many of the barriers to effective and satisfying couple communication are deeply ingrained. Especially when partners come to their relationship with legacies of poor communication or angry, hurtful battles, it is difficult to change strategies overnight. Even when they know they must sit down together to face what is bothering them, many couples will have difficulty finding alternatives to the patterns that get them into trouble.

In this chapter we discuss what we have learned from the couples in our study about why communication is so difficult, particularly during their transition to parenthood. In the couples groups, we tried to help parents acquire the skills to spot the hidden challenges that interfere with satisfying communication. This did not necessarily help them avoid discouraging arguments or frosty periods of silence, but it gave both partners a way of thinking about how they might talk with each other in a more collaborative, less adversarial way. It encouraged them to come back together at a calmer time to figure out how they had become adversaries and to try again to work on the problem together.

Let's Talk About Communication

Why is communication between spouses such a problem? And how does the problem get magnified when couples have babies? Let's start with a basic definition. Communication involves an exchange of information. The information can be relatively impersonal and factual ("They're going to build a new freeway outside of town") or relatively personal and emotional ("I'm feeling very depressed today"). Messages sent by a speaker don't really become *communication* until a listener receives them and makes a response ("It's going to take me forever to get to work while they build the freeway"; "I'm sorry you feel depressed").

Communication doesn't rely solely on words. A shrug, a roll of the eyes, an almost imperceptible move toward or away from the other can serve as a commentary on what has been said or on the current state of the relationship. As Gregory Bateson (1972) has observed, "One can't *not* communicate." The husband who fumes silently while his wife describes her harrowing day with the baby is sending a forceful, if not a direct and clear, message about what he is hearing.

Researchers have generally investigated two kinds of couple communication: solving problems and expressing feelings. As we shall see, these two easily become intertwined. Many if not most expressions of anger occur when problem solving has reached an impasse or expressed feelings have not received a sympathetic response. The voluminous body of research and popular writing on marriage contains a wide variety of "explanations" of marital distress (see Jacobson and Gurman 1986). In almost all theories, communication difficulties are treated as deviations from some (usually unspecified) picture of healthy couple functioning. Dan Wile (1981, 1988) questions this premise. His point of view, which we find helpful, is that miscommunication and conflict are natural and inevitable in intimate human relationships and should be taken as signals that something in the relationship needs attention. Marriages become distressed when couples cannot find a way to have the conversations they need to have *after* the inevitable conflicts and frustrations occur.

In their attempts to establish satisfying communication, couples face three hidden challenges whether or not they are parents: striking a balance between individuality and mutuality; understanding that each partner can see things only from his or her own perspective; and dealing with the inevitable differences between the partners in how they talk to each other and regulate their emotions. We say that the challenges are hidden because they influence the tone and content of conversations in ways that couples rarely see. When partners become parents, they face a fourth hidden challenge: keeping discussions about the child from getting mixed up in their own individual and mutual conflicts. Unaware, for example, that a disagreement about whether to give in to their child's demands reflects unresolved tension about whether one spouse will give in to the other, couples often find that their conversations are taking strange turns and that they are feeling surprisingly upset.

Because daily decision making is now so urgent and necessary, these hidden challenges in couples' communication make it more likely that new parents will lose their balance in their struggle to reestablish their equilibrium.

BALANCING INDIVIDUALITY AND MUTUALITY: ME, YOU, AND US

Each of us is a separate individual who needs some degree of connectedness to feel secure in the world. The overarching issue for couples is the challenge of balancing these needs for individuality and mutuality. How can I develop in my own way, follow my own path, without becoming separated and isolated from my partner? How can we share our lives, enrich our sense of connection, and still be the kind of person each of us wants and needs to be? When maintaining connectedness and intimacy seems to demand that we give up something essential to ourselves, trying to pursue our own hopes and dreams can result in more conflict and less intimacy in our marriage.

Couples may have been struggling with this dilemma for months or years, but the need to resolve it feels urgent after the birth of a first child. Compromises that worked well before the child arrived must often be renegotiated. Both partners' energy is limited. Investment in their personal development feels like it comes at the expense of family relationships. Involvement in family relationships seems to leave fewer resources for creating time and opportunities to develop as an individual.

Mark is a twenty-six-year-old law student, and Ingrid, also twenty-six, sells computer software. Mark has been a part-time rock musician while in law school, playing gigs three or four nights a week. They tell us that he has cut back his time with the group to once a week, which he sees as a big sacrifice. But he feels he doesn't get any credit for it. Ingrid knows that music is important to him, but feels that she and Jason need him at home now. Before Jason was born, Ingrid worked hard at her job and didn't mind the evenings that Mark was out with the band. They gave her a chance to read, relax, or have dinner with her friends. They planned to have Jason and they love him, but his presence raises a dilemma that Ingrid and Mark did not have to think about before. In this conversation Mark is concerned with meeting his own needs, while Ingrid is focused on maintaining and enhancing relationships in the family. Given their different agendas, conflict between the two of them is virtually inevitable.

Each time they discuss this issue, the conversation gets more heated and a resolution seems farther away. Ingrid calls Mark selfish. Mark calls Ingrid possessive. Each is focused on the negative qualities of the other, unaware that both are struggling with a universal dilemma: The two sets of needs are both legitimate but difficult to satisfy simultaneously, especially when a baby has just been added to the mix.

We think that individuality and mutuality are both necessary for healthy relationships. The amount of individuality or mutuality in a relationship does not define how well that relationship functions. Rather than embracing either one, each couple must find the *balance* between the two orientations that creates an atmosphere conducive to the development of the individuals and the relationship. What does this balance look like in a couple? Wile (1988) describes the optimal situation as one in which individuals who differ with each other share the same platform, from which they are willing to have discussions about their relationship not only when things are going well but also, and especially, when things are not going well. Jessica Ball (1984) found that when partners feel that they are "on the same side of the net" even when they disagree, they feel better about the resolution of discussions of specific problems and better about their overall marriage.

Who are the parents most likely to achieve such a balance? Our impression is that they combine three important qualities. First, both partners seem to have a firm sense of themselves as individuals; they feel separate from their parents, from each other, and from their children, and yet they are connected with all of them. Second, the partners seem to be able to tolerate their own ambivalence so that they can understand both sides of an issue or problem. They do not feel that they have to fight to change their partner's outlook on life, though they are willing to fight to change their partner's mind on a given issue. Third, they have a *process* for discussing issues; they don't avoid conflict and they don't prolong fruitless stalemates. We asked Beth and Paul about how they dealt with a conflict or disagreement between them in the past year. They looked at each other and laughed:

PAUL: Is it safe to discuss?

BETH: I think so, but you never know what's left over. It was important for me to take the kids in my class to an out-of-state drama festival. They'd won the regionals here, and it was a very big deal for them—and for me. But it was going to be a week long, and Willie was barely weaned. Because of how the festival runs, I just couldn't take him with me. Looking back on it now, I'm not sure why it was so important, but it was—absolutely. And it was just the wrong time for Paul, because he was coming up for his qualifying exams.

PAUL: You're being kind. Time wasn't really the issue. I just wasn't ready to look after Willie on my own for a week.

BETH: But you started by giving me all sorts of reasons why it was a bad idea for *me* and for *Willie* if I went.

PAUL: Well, that was just the first two weeks of our negotiations.

BETH: We had one really bad fight. And then—I have to give you credit for this—you came to me and you said, "I know this is important to you, and I don't understand why. But it's important to me that you get to do what really matters to you. So let's work out some way to do it." And once the pressure was off, you started to talk about your own concerns about looking after Willie, which I could understand, so I phoned my mom and asked her if she could come and stay here while I was away. She gave me a bit of a hard time about going, but she had to admit that

if Willie wasn't going to be with his mother, being with his grandmother was almost as good.

Many couples might have begun as Beth and Paul did, on opposite sides of
the fence because their individual needs at the moment are colliding, but
after two weeks of unresolved tension, they might have either escalated the
fight into a full-fledged battle or backed off in hurt silence. Together, Beth
and Paul were able to find the resources to keep coming back to the problem
until each of their needs could be recognized and addressed.

Are we simply saying that couples who balance individuality and mutuality come to the transition to parenthood in good shape? No. Some of the
couples in our study who did not start off that way managed to get clearer
about these issues by struggling with them together. In a few cases, it took
the help of a therapist. And some of the couples in our intervention groups,
with guidance from the leaders and examples from other couples, became
more able to integrate these two important aspects of family life over time.
What we are saying is that when the dilemma of reconciling individual and
mutual goals can be discussed directly, couples like Beth and Paul can shift
from a debate about whether she should go on the trip to a more collaborative discussion about how both partners can get their legitimate needs met.

WE ARE STUCK WITH OUR OWN UNIQUE PERSPECTIVES

A second existential dilemma at the heart of our efforts to communicate can
never be completely resolved. Each of us, as independent beings, can never
know for certain what is going on in the mind and heart of another person.
Two individuals, even if they have a high level of social skill and empathy,
cannot be sure that they understand fully what is meant by what someone
says or does. When Sharon tells Daniel that he is ignoring the fact that Amy
needs a lot of attention, she is really thinking about how often her own
parents left her alone when she was growing up. When Daniel says that he
is giving Amy more than enough attention, he is thinking of his overprotec-
tive parents, who rarely left him on his own. Sharon and Daniel tend to distort
each other's comments because each sees the world through different lenses,
colored in this case by their experiences in earlier relationships. Neither
partner really knows what the other means by "a lot of" or "enough" attention, and neither one asks a clarifying question.

More often than not, we assume that we know what others mean—they
mean what *we* would mean if we used the same words or actions. We may
not realize that there is a difference in interpretation until an argument
erupts. ("I didn't know that you meant *two hours*. I consider *fifteen minutes*
of Amy's crying a long time.") Because partners often give words different
interpretations, it might be useful to assume that communication between
spouses, like negotiations between countries at the United Nations, can
benefit from the help of a translator.

Two problems described by marital researchers and couples therapists—"mind reading" and "negative attributions"—can be traced to the fact that we can never completely transcend our own perspective. Both seem to increase during couples' transition to parenthood.

Mind Reading   In our naïve assumption that we know what our partner is thinking and feeling, we act as if we can read his or her mind. In intimate relationships we frequently *can* guess what our spouse is thinking or feeling. Each partner develops a kind of shorthand understanding of what his or her spouse needs, what pleases, and what angers. The problem is that some mind reading is, inevitably, off base and can lead to unexpected and inappropriate behavior.

We have described Peggy and Bill's stormy relationship, after a pregnancy in which Peggy was vulnerable and in discomfort. Eighteen months after giving birth, she has not officially gone back to work, but she is directly involved in taking care of Bill's business accounts. The day after one of their fights, they tell us, Bill stops to buy flowers for Peggy. On the way home he remembers that the last time he bought flowers, Peggy was suspicious that he was covering something up. On the way home, he wonders, "Why can't she trust me? Here I am, working hard, being a faithful husband, trying to do something nice, and when I get home she's just going to jump on me. She doesn't appreciate me for what I am. I wanted this to be a nice evening, and she's going to ruin it with her nagging." He opens the door, thrusts the flowers angrily at Peggy, and marches off to the den. Like many of us, Bill has indulged in mind reading: He gets angry at what he thinks Peggy is thinking and feeling before he has checked out his assumptions.

Bill is not the only mind reader in the family. Both he and Peggy assume that they know what is in each other's minds and hearts, especially when it comes to discussing their interactions with Mindy. The following day, still smarting from the aftermath of their fight and Bill's strange behavior, Peggy explained, she saw the following scene: "There's Bill, locked in his office next to our back bedroom, and Mindy bangs on the door, shouting 'Daddy, Daddy,' and Bill doesn't respond. Mindy bangs louder, and Bill gets furious, because he thinks Mindy is trying to manipulate him. I see it so differently. Mindy was missing her dad and wanting to talk to him. I think Bill was just trying to get back at me, because of the fight the other night." Bill's interpretation? "No, no, no. *I* was trying to teach Mindy that she just can't barge in whenever she wants. I don't think this is really about Mindy. You're just trying to make me feel guilty."

New parents are vulnerable and uncertain. They often assume that there is a right way to do things with their children, if only they could know what it is. They see their partner doing something that surprises, displeases, or even frightens them. Given rushed schedules and high tension, they may read their partner's mind in an attempt to understand what is going on—and easily come up with an interpretation that leads to misunderstandings and hurt feelings.

Negative Attribution   A human tendency, described by "attribution theorists" in social psychology (Kelley et al. 1983), is to ask ourselves why people
do what they do. We tend to explain *other people's* troubling behavior as
reflecting their personality or motives, while we tend to explain *our own*
troubling behavior as due to positive motivation or to circumstances beyond
our control (Baucom, Sayers, and Duhe 1989).

When Peggy sees Bill do something that she wouldn't do, she attempts to
figure it out in her own terms. Initially, she can't understand why Bill would
ignore Mindy's cries. She would never shut Mindy out of a room, unless,
perhaps, she was so upset with Bill that she did it in retaliation. She is making
an assumption about Bill's motivation. Bill, on the other hand, sees himself
as involved in fulfilling his role as a father and teaching his daughter not to
intrude when he is working. Since the intensity of Peggy's feelings leads him
to question his own strategy with Mindy, he accuses Peggy of trying to make
him feel guilty.

The issue here is not only that Peggy and Bill are mind reading. Each is
also attributing negative motivations to the other's behavior. And nothing we
know of gets spouses angrier than being accused of harboring negative
motivations—even if, or especially if, the accusation hits home. In the process of trying to understand what is happening to them, Peggy and Bill are
focusing on what Wile (1988) calls "character flaws" in their partner and not
on their own behavior. Partners tend to feel righteous about their own
actions and skeptical about the actions of the other. The attribution problem
usually cuts both ways and escalates the level of marital conflict.

Barbara Epperson's study (Epperson, Cowan, and Cowan 1991), based on
data from our Becoming a Family Project, shows that negative attributions
made by husbands and wives may have important implications for predicting
the fate of their marriage. Surprisingly, partners' level of satisfaction with
marriage when they entered our study did not predict who would later
divorce. The best predictor was the number of negative adjectives (aggressive, fussy, nervous, sarcastic) one partner chose from the Adjective Check
List to describe the other. That is, marital dissolution was predicted not by
the kind of marriage couples believed they were in, but by the kind of
partners they believed they were married to. The connection between partners' negative attributions and marital dissolution was stronger for couples
who became parents than it was for the nonparent couples in our study.

Partners in transition to parenthood are especially prone to forget that
other people have different points of view. As they gain confidence interpreting their infant's cries, smiles, and body movements, they begin to assume
that they know what he or she feels and needs. When partners talk to each
other, they make the same assumption. They may be wrong about both their
baby and their partner, but only the partner can fight back verbally. As the
stress of this life transition mounts, it becomes increasingly difficult for each
partner to tell the difference between "this is what I'm hearing" and "this is
what he/she is saying." Conflicts between partners multiply in the resulting
confusion.

DIFFERENCES BETWEEN PARTNERS ARE INEVITABLE

Given the fact that husbands and wives are trapped in their own perspectives, that they have different personalities and different legacies from the past, it should come as no surprise to find that they are likely to perceive, remember, and react to the same events quite differently and to have different styles of talking to each other and expressing their feelings. The dilemma contributing to communication difficulties is this: Part of what attracts us to a partner is the way that person is different from us. But as the relationship unfolds, those intriguing differences grow larger and increasingly problematic.

It really doesn't matter what kinds of questions we ask couples—simple factual ones about their incomes or whether they experienced any job changes in the last six months, or questions that call for complex evaluations of emotion-laden issues—husbands and wives often have different perceptions of reality.

Memories   Particularly vexing differences occur in partners' recollections of past conversations. Alice and Andy, one of the Yes-No couples who were still struggling late in the pregnancy with the decision about having a child, recalled their first conversation about the pregnancy:

ALICE: The first time I told you I was pregnant, you swallowed hard, but you said that you'd support me all the way.

ANDY: Alice, I never said anything like that.

ALICE: You did too, Andy. We were at dinner, remember? In that little restaurant with the pink tablecloths.

ANDY: I remember the restaurant, but. . . .

This conversation went on for quite some time, both partners becoming increasingly insistent that their memory of the event was the correct one. But in the absence of a videotaped record of their life together, there is no way for couples to arrive at the "truth" of who said or did what five minutes, five days, or five months later.

It is not only the past that provokes disagreements between partners about the perception of events. Is the house picked up? Yes, according to one partner; no, according to the other. Is the baby dressed warmly enough? Maybe/Maybe not. Is your mother intruding on our lives? Yes/No. Is your work demanding too much of your time and energy? I don't think so/ Definitely.

How We Talk   The sociolinguist Deborah Tannen, in her recent best-seller, *You Just Don't Understand* (1990), claims that men and women speak different languages and approach conversations in different ways. Men talk to exchange information ("report talk"), and women talk to extend intimacy ("rapport talk"). Men try to maintain a one-up position, rarely revealing their vulnerabilities. Women try to increase symmetry, revealing their vulnerabilities as a way of keeping the relationship even. Men value their autonomy; they don't like to ask for directions or to be told what to do. Women search for connectedness; asking for help and checking what others want helps to enrich their relationships.

In Jessica Ball's (1984) study of husband-wife differences in communication style, twenty-seven of the Becoming a Family couples were invited to discuss a "who does what?" issue in front of a videotape camera. She then invited each partner separately to watch the tape and comment on the interaction. She found that wives raised problems more often, talked more in the first few minutes of the discussion, and were generally perceived by both partners as having more influence over the way the discussion went as a whole. These findings might lead to the interpretation that women have more conversational control, at least in the initial phases of talks about problems. When they watched and commented on the videotape, however, the women tended to say that they saw themselves as being in an entirely supplicatory position throughout these talks. As one woman explained: "It *looks* like I'm running the whole show here, but all the while I'm going on and on, I'm waiting on edge with suspense. What if he doesn't want to work on this with me? I'll feel totally crushed and helpless."

Fifty-nine percent of the men and 81 percent of the women elaborated their perceptions that, regardless of the wife's activity level or the floor time she occupied, the husband typically had veto power over the discussion as a whole: He controlled whether there would be a dialogue at all and under what terms and circumstances it would occur, as well as having final say over the outcome. In our study, men were described as exerting their control largely through either nonresponse or angry outbursts.

This gender difference in communication style leads to many conversational impasses. When problems are raised, as we've seen mostly by women, their partners tend to jump into the problem-solving mode with quick solutions. Men's well-intentioned responses often backfire for several reasons. First, husbands' solutions are often presented prematurely, before their wives feel that they have been understood. Second, when a husband offers a quick solution, he sends a message that conveys: "Oh, this problem is easy to solve; here's what you do," as if his wife can't see the obvious. The couple's conversation often shifts abruptly to a debate on the merits of "his" proposal to solve "her" problem. This restricts the possibility of exploring a number of alternatives and choosing the best available one. In our group meetings we often asked couples to "have a discussion, not make a decision" until both partners had completed exploring the problem. Given this framework, men were able to hold back on their initial tendency to make proposals because they knew that the decision phase was built into the process.

Regulating Feelings   Recent research by the psychologists John Gottman, Robert Levenson, and others supports and extends the notion that men and women deal with problem-solving discussions in different ways (Gottman and Levenson 1989; Markman and Notarius 1987). Using videotape of couples discussing a "hot issue," these psychologists have found that women take the initiative and that men tend not to raise issues that will lead to conflict. When conflict does arise, husbands tend to become more rational and avoidant as their wives become more emotional and engaged. In marriages that are already in trouble, this combination of mismatched styles leads to an escalation of the conflict by wives and withdrawal by husbands (Gottman and Levenson 1989).

Women's tendency in conflictful exchanges, it has been observed, is to become more expressive, while men's is to "stonewall" (Levenson and Gottman 1985). Under what he perceives as attack in conversation, a man tends to talk less, to make his face impassive and his body unexpressive, and to offer fewer head nods and less eye contact to his partner. In the face of this reaction, the woman becomes more directly expressive and more upset about the interaction. In happily married couples, men tend to engage in the discussion without withdrawing to this extent, but in distressed marriages, if husbands' attempts to withdraw are followed by wives' pursuit of them, the men respond to the women's anger or sadness with their own anger, or contempt. The wives, in turn, then become even more angry. This escalating pattern is typical of spouses whose marriages are distressed now, and it also predicts decline in marital satisfaction over the next few years (Gottman and Krokoff 1989).

We believe that the tendency for women to raise potentially explosive issues for the couple is amplified after a baby arrives. Mothers are primarily responsible for either looking after the child during the day or making the necessary child-care arrangements. When the couple comes together at the end of the day, the child-related problems are most likely to be brought up by the wives. Husbands sometimes feel that if their wives did not raise problems about the child, there wouldn't *be* any. As the messengers, wives are often the targets of their husbands' anger for being the bearers of bad news.

In the research just mentioned, partners discussing "hot" marital issues were hooked up to equipment that measured their level of physiological arousal—heart rate, pulse, blood flow, and so on. When the conversation heated up, women tried to keep it going and men, as just explained, shut down (Gottman and Levenson 1989; Markman and Notarius 1987). But, in contrast to their impassive exteriors, men became highly aroused during the conflict, a physiological arousal that lasted much longer than that of their wives. Men's stonewalling, it seems, may be an attempt to avoid the uncomfortable consequences of the physiological disruption. Not only did the women's physiological arousal during the argument not reach as high a level as their partners' but, once women expressed their feelings, their physiological responses shifted more quickly back to normal.

What these studies point out is that, although it looks to women as though their husbands are unfeeling or uncaring during important discussions, they may in fact be feeling a great deal. Unfortunately, men's self-protective maneuvers, combined with women's active pursuit of upsetting issues, can have debilitating effects on the relationship between them.

How Differences Create Communication Pitfalls   The researchers whose work we have been describing make very broad generalizations about differences between men and women. In our view, the essential importance of their work is not that women are always ready to engage in conflict and men always to stonewall. In some couples, the reverse pattern can be found at least some of the time. What is central, we believe, is that differences between partners in their styles of communicating and regulating their emotions present particularly powerful obstacles to satisfying couple communication. Partners begin a conversation, find that they disagree, and are drawn even farther apart by the clash in their characteristic ways of attempting to resolve the problem.

The picture we get from Gottman and Levenson's research is that as a husband and wife talk with each other, sending words and nonverbal signals back and forth, each is focused on three channels of information: the words, the tone, and the feelings or reactions. First, they attend to the meaning of the words, trying to interpret from their own perspective what their partner is literally saying. As we have seen, this in itself can be a difficult task. Second, they are paying attention to tone of the message: Is it hostile, loving, complaining, complimentary? If one partner's tone turns negative, it gets harder for the other to track the content of what is being said. *But they continue the conversation anyway.* In the meantime, a third channel, the physiological system, is bouncing around, sending messages of arousal—excitement, tension, anxiety—into an already complex exchange. One partner may need to damp things down just when the other is letting feelings out at full tilt.

All of this monitoring makes it hard to have a relaxed conversation. When the marriage is not going well, the differences between husbands' and wives' strategies are exaggerated, making an unsatisfying exchange more likely. When a baby comes along and the initial differences between husbands and wives are magnified, there may be more exaggerated discrepancies in their communication styles. In an atmosphere heated up by frequent marital conflict or cooled down by withdrawal in hopes of avoiding a fight, partners are less likely to talk to each other about their deep and private feelings. While this strategy may reduce fighting temporarily, it also tends to reduce the feeling of intimacy. One or both partners may conclude that they are not entitled to feel the way they do, even if the feeling is not expressed.

Looking back at Mindy's birth, Peggy and Bill described just such a situation. Bill was supposed to be the "coach," the strong one, when Peggy was in labor. He was terrified but tried not to let it show. As Peggy instructed and requested him to do various things, he became more and more closed and sarcastic. She got more and more angry. It wasn't until Mindy was nearly six months old that they talked about it. Peggy asked Bill why he didn't tell her what he was going through, and he said, "As the labor got more intense, I kept feeling more and more frightened and that's just not what was supposed to be happening. It was just the worst time to say anything like that to you."

Pauline and Mel described an argument they have very frequently. Every time Pauline's parents come to visit, she is reduced to tears. Her mother criticizes how Pauline and Mel handle Avi, how the house looks, their neighborhood, and on and on. Mel shrugs it off, but Pauline takes it to heart. "I want her to tell her mother either to shut up or to stay away," he told us. But Pauline said that she could never do that: "It would just tear her away from us and her grandson, just when we're reconnecting after all these years. Besides, she has so little in life. She did the best she could with me and my sister. It would be ungrateful and immature of me to get angry with her now."

The problems go deeper than the simple facts that Bill does not want to admit his fear and Pauline feels she cannot tell her mother what she thinks: One spouse does not feel *entitled* to express the negative but very human feelings he or she is experiencing. Keeping quiet rarely works. Negative feelings tend to pop out indirectly, increasing the distance between the two people in the relationship and decreasing the probability of dealing constructively with the problems that led to the feelings in the first place.

The early months of parenthood provide fertile soil for "unentitlement." Parents have many notions of how they're supposed to feel. Friends, neighbors, and family smile at the baby and tell new parents how proud and happy they must feel. But sometimes new parents are overwhelmed and frightened. Can they admit it to themselves? Can they tell each other? Trying to "protect" their partners from worry, they often deprive them of emotional support. What a relief it usually is when a husband admits that he is having a hard time of it, and his wife says, "I thought it was only me." Or when a wife admits that she doesn't always know what to do when the baby keeps crying, and her husband is relieved that he is not the only one at a loss.

When emotional regulation is out of balance in a marriage, the partners may not be able to tell whether they are being heard, especially if one partner stonewalls. Much of the force and repetition in a couple's arguments may come from partners feeling they have not been heard, or have not gotten their point across, so they make the point again, louder and more forcefully (Wile 1988). Wile advises couples who are saying things for the second or third time at ever-increasing decibel levels to take this as a signal that their communication process is not working. Rather than continuing the escalation, it is time to back up and check out whether the messages are getting through.

With these examples of heated exchange and conflict between spouses, it would be easy to get the impression that new parents argue all the time. Most don't. What's more, after the heat of an argument, most hesitate to return to the issues that upset them. Each partner fears that bringing it up again will just mean they will fight again, and hopes that if they don't talk about the problem, it will go away. These fears have some validity. Returning to unresolved issues does sometimes start up the unpleasant cycle again. Not rocking the boat becomes an even more urgent goal when a family is already sailing on choppy seas. New parents have little uninterrupted time for each other, and little surplus energy. "Why ask for trouble?" they might think, and we certainly understand their reluctance to get back into a conflict. But unless they reopen contentious issues during a period of calm, they will not be able to create ways of recovering from fights or profiting from them so that the next time they will not be as devastating.

BRINGING THE CHILD INTO THE STRUGGLE

Many of the examples we have given in this chapter show that discussions about the child figured largely in the communication problems of the couples in our study. How could it be otherwise? Differences between partners' points of view, communication styles, and ways of regulating emotion are inevitable. Even when their fundamental values are fairly similar, parents' reactions to the child are bound to highlight some areas of difference between them. We find that differences between husbands and wives about their children generate much more heat than most other topics of conversation or argument. The parent role occupies a central part of their identity. Many, but not all, parents believe that how the child "turns out" is ultimately a reflection on them. This places high stakes on the resolution of even minor disagreements.

We are concerned in this section with the subtle ways in which children become enmeshed in conflicts between their parents that are not really of the children's making. There is an inherent possibility that parents might "triangulate" the child into their overt or hidden conflicts, a notion that has several connotations, all of them negative (see, for example, Bowen 1978). In one meaning, the parents cannot distinguish between what they each want and need for themselves and what they believe the child needs. Their differences of opinion or arguments about the child are difficult to resolve because they are not really talking about what they think they are are talking about.

For example, Tanya says that Kevin needs to be cuddled more, and Jackson says that Kevin needs room to breathe. Tanya may want more cuddling for Kevin, but she may also need more cuddling for herself. She doesn't feel entitled to ask for it, but it remains a salient issue for her and she raises it at every opportunity. Jackson probably feels the need for some freedom for himself. Not feeling entitled to ask for it, instead he ardently defends his son's need for breathing space.

A second way couples triangulate their child into their relationship is by fighting about the child as a way of avoiding their own issues. Peggy and Bill have used this mode a great deal, arguing about Mindy and how each one should treat her while avoiding some of the more difficult problems in their communication with each other.

A third variety of triangulation looks different from the first two, but serves the same function. Some parents become almost totally involved in their children's lives, neglecting the issues in their relationships as couples. Based on the results of the development of the children in our study, these devoted parents might do better to redirect some of their energies. Focusing on the marriage to the detriment of the child would, of course, be just as bad.

We are guided here by the findings we have already made clear: When parents feel satisfied about themselves and their relationship as a couple, their relationships with their children seem to be more effective, and their children wind up better equipped to handle the challenges of their lives inside and outside the family.

Communication and Family Breakdown

We have shown what a challenge it is for men and women to communicate effectively and how the arrival of a child seems to make miscommunication and conflict more probable. Alice and Andy are one of almost 20 percent of the couples who were not able to maintain their marriages through the child's transition to elementary school. While they spoke positively about their relationship when we first met them, they continued to be in pain over their serious altercation about the unintended pregnancy. Here is a case where the individual needs of both partners clearly clashed with their mutual goals, but because they loved each other, Alice and Andy tried to patch over their differences and went ahead and had the baby. Over time, they forgot that each of them must be experiencing the transition to parenthood differently. Their relationships with Jessica were genuinely warm and adoring, but when they were in difficulty about issues in the couple relationship, Andy became angry again and this created a good deal of tension between them. As more time passed and other life stresses confronted them, Andy began to feel that Alice was not the person he thought he knew.

Given their large age difference, and very different experiences of growing up, it is not surprising that each had different perceptions and feelings about what it would mean to become a parent. Although they appeared to have been successful in calming the conflict that had erupted when Alice told Andy she was pregnant, the events that followed suggested that they never truly came to terms with their different experiences of the decision making.

About three months after Jessica was born, Andy began to have serious difficulty in controlling his anger with Alice. The earlier wounds that they had covered over began to fester. Each felt that their hard-won agreements in pregnancy had been violated, but they did not feel safe enough to talk to each other directly about their disappointment or their fear. Rather than confront their distress or ask for help, they decided that a move across the country to a less hectic setting might reduce some of the pressure they were feeling.

Over the next several years, they vacillated between periods of optimism and serious distress. They had pulled themselves away from the support of their friends, and it took a long time for both of them to find work they found rewarding. When their relationship was not going well, each of them felt somehow unmoored. Their best times seemed to revolve around Jessica, but that did not help them to work out the unresolved issues in their relationship to either one's satisfaction. Looking back, they felt that it all began to unravel soon after the move, when Alice became ill and her mother died within a month's time. As Alice withdrew from Andy to tend to her emotional and physical wounds, he felt abandoned again, as he must have felt when she insisted on having a child so early in their relationship.

By the time Alice pulled herself together, this time with some professional help, she and Andy had decided that they needed to separate. Both of them were distressed about splitting up their family and tried on more than one occasion to reconsider the plan, at least for Jessica's sake. But the magic had gone out of their marriage. Around the time of Jessica's fourth birthday, they separated for good.

For her part, Jessica appears to be doing quite well. Andy and Alice have maintained their devotion to her, arranging shared custody and visitation. At our kindergarten assessment, Jessica seemed shy, a little withdrawn, but able to use fantasy play to express her feelings when her mother was nearby. When she is in familiar territory she seems to cope well with the demands of other adults, and from her teacher's point of view, she is making a relatively good adjustment to both the academic and social demands of kindergarten. Because both of her parents have continued to communicate with her warmly and responsively, while building a reliable structure for her life with each of them, she will probably be able to concentrate enough to meet the challenges of school fairly well. Much later on, when it comes to working out the most painful parts of her intimate adult relationships, she may experience some difficulties (Wallerstein and Blakeslee 1989).

Communication and Family Adaptation

Our chronicle of the hidden challenges to effective and satisfying couple communication can be used to tell a more optimistic story. It is not a story without conflict, miscommunication, or withdrawal to neutral corners. The couples who come through the transition to parenthood on their feet are those who have been able to treat their problems in connecting with each other not as a failure or a deliberate attempt at sabotage by their partners but as a signal that something is not working. They have found ways to return to rocky territory, joining forces to figure out how they lost their way. They manage, then, to feel on the same side even while they are in the process of resolving their differences.

These couples are not saints or Pollyannas. They fight when they have something to fight about. Occasionally, when they try to understand a blow-up, the process goes awry and the fight starts again. But they have taken some risks to develop ways of thinking and discussing what happens when they talk to each other. They recognize the problem of balancing their individual and mutual needs with the needs of their children. They know that their unique perspectives will at times contribute to their misunderstandings.

And they have developed the ability to tolerate their different styles of dealing with emotionally loaded issues.

In these couples, it is not always the wife who raises the difficult issues. The husbands try to overcome their distaste for trouble or conflict, and attempt to engage rather than withdraw when something needs to be dealt with. Both partners work to avoid escalating angry or hurtful exchanges. Some of the time, they are able to express their negative feelings and to tolerate some distress in the other. They try to listen and to let each other know they are being heard. When they get upset about something their spouse is doing, they consider whether that raises an issue *they* should be dealing with before they try to get their spouse to do things differently. Perhaps most important of all, they are willing to rock the boat by stopping escalating arguments between them or by coming back to discussions that became hurtful or unproductive, in order to figure out what went wrong. Finally, the couples who communicate effectively are able to avoid triangulating their children into their marriage. They can disagree about child-rearing issues and argue vociferously, but these disagreements do not become substitutes for attending to their own relationship.

Let us assure you that we do not know any couples who can do all this all the time. But those who can express their views and feelings, and do not feel as though their negative feelings are going to escalate out of control, feel more energetic and optimistic about themselves and their relationship.

CHAPTER 11

Who Is at Risk and What Can Be Done?

SINCE THE BEGINNING OF OUR PILOT STUDY eighteen years ago, we have followed more than 100 couples through their transition to first-time parenthood. The experience has been both inspiring and sobering. We feel great admiration for these new pioneers, making their journey to parenthood in a world that was transformed while they were growing up. Not always knowing which way to turn, they have managed to show great determination, fortitude, and optimism—and surprisingly good humor.

We also come away with great concern about the burdens contemporary parents and children are shouldering. Our results show that the natural processes of becoming a family place women, men, and their relationships as couples at risk for increased disenchantment and strain. When parents are in distress during the children's preschool years, the children are at risk for academic and social difficulties as they begin their academic careers. Let us be clear: "At risk" does not mean that depression, marital distress, ineffective parenting, difficulty with peers, or academic problems are inevitable. Some individuals and families in the most adverse circumstances show surprising resilience. What we mean is that a majority of couples becoming new parents can expect to encounter increasing strain and distress in their intimate relationships during the family-making years.

In our attempts to understand this troubling phenomenon, we made some unexpected discoveries. Despite the fact that medical checkups are offered from the beginning of pregnancy and childbirth preparation classes are available during the last trimester, couples begin to be at risk even earlier—as soon as they start considering whether and when to start their family. Medical and childbirth services help partners focus on the physical aspects of pregnancy, labor, and delivery, but they miss the subtle and complex psychological changes that begin to affect the couple long before their baby is born.

We had underestimated the salience of the differences between men and women in this family-making period. We found that during the process of becoming parents, men and women experience qualitatively different psychological changes. They describe different shifts in the parent aspect of their identities and make different arrangements for their work inside and outside the family. These differences are accompanied by more disagreement and arguing as a couple, a feeling of more distance between them and less satisfaction with their overall marriage. Hoping to feel closer by creating a family together, partners get discouraged when the process of moving from partners to parents pushes them farther apart.

We should have been prepared for the fact that the most problematic issue for men and women in the early family years is who cares for the children. Neither the traditional male/female division nor the new egalitarian sharing arrangements stand out as ideal: Modern couples get penalized either way. When one parent brings home the bacon while the other stays home to look after the child, both can feel underappreciated and strapped economically, which burdens the marriage and the children. When both parents work outside the family, they tend to feel better about themselves and about their contributions to the family economy, but parents and children are breathless, often missing the opportunity for intimate moments. Although each of these alternatives has costs and benefits, we find that when men are more involved in the care of their children, they feel better about themselves, their wives feel better about themselves, and they both feel better about their marriage. Even more important than who actually does what is how the arrangements are negotiated and how both partners feel about the outcome. This makes it clear that each couple must find the balance that works for them.

We certainly knew from our own lives that having a baby can reawaken issues from one's childhood, but we found that the power of these legacies catches most parents off guard. We did not fully appreciate the magic that babies provide to link the generations of a family. The birth of a baby gives new parents an opportunity to reconnect with their parents and grandparents. A baby can give one partner a chance to teach the other about caring relationships between parents and children. It looks as if a warm, collaborative couple relationship can help some partners with inadequate parenting to break the generational cycle of dysfunctional relationships. Nevertheless, there is disquieting evidence that unless men and women are able to come to terms with the difficulties of their growing-up years, or to marry a spouse who has, their family patterns tend to be replayed across the generations.

Although we expected anxieties and conflicts about support or stress from work, child care, and friendships to spill over into both the marriage and the parent-child relationships, the pervasiveness of parents' struggles around these issues was a surprise. It has been eye-opening for us to see the paradox inherent in a country that professes to care so much about the development of its children and the preservation of the family unit offering virtually no resources to deal with these issues.

We are convinced that most new parents are doing the best they can against tremendous odds. Some of their tensions are generated by their attempts to follow strong but conflicting societal prescriptions. On one hand, we are surrounded by powerful messages about individualism: Each of us should make every effort to develop as fully as we can. There is some degree of governmental and educational support for acting on this message, and hard work toward self-fulfillment, individual achievement, and advancement pays off. On the other hand, our society sends us messages about the importance of enhancing the quality and sanctity of family life—to maintain the family as a "haven in a heartless world." But with no support from government or business and little support from medical and mental health services, which focus on individuals, couples who share this priority are on their own.

What the couples in our studies have shown us is that keeping a marriage viable while creating a family requires a delicate balance—within each partner, between the spouses, and between family and work. Each man and woman comes to the family-making enterprise with a particular set of strengths and vulnerabilities in the central aspects of their lives. As they become parents, each aspect of life requires rethinking and readjustment—a tall order, as we have seen. The combination of strengths and vulnerabilities that each couple brings to the transition affects the ease or difficulty of their journey from couple to family.

Who Is at Risk?

The changes associated with parenthood take place within a context of consistency and predictability. Individuals and couples who are doing well in pregnancy will probably continue to do well after the baby arrives; those in difficulty in the early phases of the transition tend to be struggling later on, with each other and with their children. Distress before the baby is born in any of the arenas of family life we studied should serve as a warning that there may be trouble ahead—for the marriage and possibly for the children's development.

How parents feel about themselves plays an important role in their experience of early parenthood. If they are disappointed with themselves before they have a baby—depressed or with low self-esteem—partners are likely to feel disappointed in their early years as parents. We have illustrated how parents' negative feelings about themselves foreshadow more symptoms of depression and higher levels of parenting stress, as well as greater conflict as a couple and with their children during the preschool period four years later.

Many aspects of the parents' marriage can put them at risk in the early parenthood years. The atmosphere of their journey to becoming a family is affected by the partners' approach to deciding whether to have a baby. Spouses who describe their general decision-making process as unproductive and unsatisfying are more likely to make their decision to become a family without working through one or both partners' hesitation or ambivalence. As we have seen, the greatest risk for the stability of the couple's marriage was going ahead with a pregnancy over the continuing objection of a husband who did not feel ready to become a parent: All of the couples faced with this agonizing dilemma had divorced by the time their first child entered kindergarten.

During pregnancy, other aspects of a couple's relationship serve as early warning signals: partners' negative views of each other; distress about the division of family labor; discontent with their arrangements for the care of their child; pessimism about their ability to make family decisions that meet both spouses' needs; dissatisfaction with how the overall marriage feels. All of these signals predicted expectant mothers' and fathers' later difficulties in managing their relationship as a couple.

As we have noted, men and women whose own childhoods were clouded with painful experiences—absent, rejecting, abusive, or alcoholic parents—tended to have more difficulty with each other and with their children. Although the stresses of pregnancy and the first few months of parenthood inevitably lessen, couples who begin their journey from partners to parents contending with a great deal of additional life stress from relationships, illness, or problems at work were more likely to be grappling with more strain later on.

We found that risks for couples pose risks for their children. Strain within the marriage during the transition to parenthood was reflected in parents' responsiveness or tension two years later, as they worked and played with their three-and-a-half-year-olds. Parents who were in the most unhappy marriages treated their sons and daughters in a cold, critical, more authoritarian manner. Here again, gender differences took center stage. Fathers who were unhappy with their wives reacted most harshly to their preschool daughters. We are especially concerned about the risk for girls' development when their parents, particularly their fathers, are distressed about the marriage. Children whose parents were unhappily married during pregnancy and the preschool period had more difficulty adjusting to elementary school two years later.

We all "know" that communication is central to couple relationships. What has become clear to us in the course of our study is the variety of ways in which ordinary problems in communication between partners can be exaggerated in the turmoil that follows the birth of a baby. If we think about parents' communication skills and impasses as laying the foundation for children to learn about solving problems, the links between the state of the parents' lives in pregnancy and the children's adjustment to kindergarten almost six years later become more understandable.

We have shown that hard times in the life of a family with young children do not come out of the blue. The transition to parenthood seems to act as an amplifier, tuning couples in to the resources they have, and turning up the volume on their existing difficulties in managing their lives and family relationships. We were able to predict with some accuracy how couples would fare as parents of young children, based on the interview and questionnaire information they gave us during the pregnancy. This means that we have the tools to identify potential distress and to help couples prevent at least some of this distress before it begins to tear their families apart.

Implications of Our Results

FOR COUPLES

We have noted that outside of couples counseling or therapy, there are currently no systematically evaluated services that offer expectant couples a protective setting in which they can begin to take stock of what works well and what doesn't before they become parents. Based on what we have learned both from the couples in our group intervention and from those who did well without the help of a couples group, we have compiled a list of things that expectant couples and new parents can do on their own to reduce the expected strain and enjoy more of the positive side of becoming a family. Although some of these ideas may sound very simple and obvious, we have found that many partners *think* of them without actually trying them. We believe it is never too late to give them a chance.

Share expectations. Many husbands and wives who are expecting a baby neglect to share their notions of the ideal family. They seem to assume that once they have decided to have a baby, their ideal family picture will take shape spontaneously. Others are understandably reluctant to talk about their hopes and anxieties because they are afraid that disagreement or conflict might result from finding they differ on important issues.

Much will depend on the nature and disposition of the child and on the parents' own reactions once the baby finally arrives, but it is our impression that men and women who can talk to each other about what they hope will happen, and what they are concerned might happen, begin their lives as parents feeling better prepared to deal with both the positive and the negative realities.

Give yourselves regular "checkups." Many couples who were *not* in the intervention groups in our study told us that filling out our questionnaires independently and then talking about their responses together had a powerful impact on their transition to parenthood. Some called our questionnaires and interviews their "checkups" because they offered an opportunity to take stock of how they were doing and to think about where they might make some adjustments before their disenchantment got the better of them.

Some of the questions that we describe throughout the book may be a starting point for couples to talk about how they feel they are doing in the major parts of their life together. These checkups should never begin in the middle of a fight, however; they require quiet, uninterrupted time when both partners feel free to explore their reactions.

Make time to talk with each other. New parents have very few opportunities for quiet time together. Most will be unable to spend an idyllic weekend away by themselves and many will not be able to afford to go out to lunch or dinner, with the new expenses of hospital bills, baby equipment, and child care. We suggest that partners try to make a regular time each week to go for a walk, to talk with no interruptions—to touch base with each other.

Many husbands and wives say that the day gets away from them. By the time everything is cleaned up at night, they are too exhausted for intimate conversation. It sounds terribly artificial, but making an appointment or a date can be useful—even if the laundry or dinner dishes have to wait or if the "date" must be rescheduled because of a crying baby or their own fatigue. Parents say that just knowing that they will have a time to be together can make a difference and get them through a strenuous week.

Negotiate an agenda. Spouses sometimes have a hard time agreeing on whether a particular issue is a problem. She feels overloaded with family work and wants to talk about his doing more. His evaluation of the situation is that she is wasting some of her efforts, and he has a plan for how she can be more efficient with her time or more effective as a parent. Besides, he feels that they are not getting out enough and wants to discuss that, whereas she knows that she will have difficulty finding a sitter she can feel comfortable with and fears that he will not understand her point of view. It is easy to see how either partner might want to skip such discussions.

Our general rule for ourselves and other couples is this: If one partner feels that something is a problem, at least for the moment it is a problem. And, because one partner's problem can raise a difficulty for the other, we recommend discussing only one problem at a time, however difficult it may feel to limit the discussion, with an explicit agreement that other difficulties will be addressed at the next opportunity. If they can trust that both of their issues will be addressed in time, they are less likely to sabotage today's discussion.

Adopt an experimental attitude. There are two important principles involved in this single point. First, life changes rapidly with a growing infant. "Solutions" that worked well for some weeks or months can suddenly seem totally ineffective. This is not a sign that the original plan was inappropriate or that one partner has not kept up his or her end of the bargain, but rather that something has shifted. An attitude that says, in effect, "let's try this and see if it works," can be helpful—whether it be a variation on the baby's feeding schedule, a new way of responding to her crying, or a plan for talking to the baby-sitter.

Couples find it useful to adopt this kind of experimental attitude toward problems in their relationship, too. When things go wrong or tempers run hot, many of us are quick to blame our partner for our distress. The idea of taking a fight as information that something is wrong in the relationship is quite helpful (Wile 1988). The trick is not to worry that you are having a struggle, or to avoid a fight; every couple has both trivial and important issues to work out. It helps to take a step back and shift from a "What are you doing wrong?" position to a "What's going on in our lives that this is happening now?" attitude. The recovery from these kinds of conversations after fights have erupted can be both healing and productive.

Don't ignore sex and intimacy. Women's physical changes and the couple's exhaustion typically lead to a decline in the frequency of sex both in pregnancy and after the baby arrives. The absence of sex can feel like a longtime drought. We have read advice columns that support the "if you're even partially ready, go for it" attitude. It seems to us that there is a territory between total deprivation and a return to the old pattern of more frequent and satisfying lovemaking. If partners are able to discuss it at all, and some find sex an awkward and difficult topic at this time, they can recognize that there are opportunities for nonsexual intimacy: touching, hugging, cuddling. This is often what is being missed most. Sometimes, the discovery that your partner is missing the intimacy, too, results in increased feelings of closeness.

Line up support in the early stages. Our finding that support from other people is helpful in alleviating parents' stress in the early months as a family suggests that couples should consider arranging for people or services who can provide support and relief when the going gets rough. This is difficult to do at the height of the transition, when most of the parents' attention is focused on how to juggle everything they used to do *and* take care of the new baby.

Talk with a friend or co-worker. As we described in chapter 9, participating in an ongoing group with the help of trained mental health professionals and other couples becoming parents can buffer men's and women's dissatisfaction and keep their marital disenchantment from getting out of hand, at least for the first few years. Although these kinds of groups are not available at this time, the kind of sharing of experiences and information that our groups provided might come from special friends or co-workers who are willing to talk about their experiences of being partners and parents. While we believe that working with mental health professionals increases the odds of making headway on difficult relationship issues, some new parents find that there are people with whom they can broach some of their questions and concerns.

For partners who are experiencing a fair amount of strain or impasse— about deciding to have children, about resolving conflict or differences in their relationship, or about how to handle confusing dilemmas with their children or parents—help is available in the mental health community. If you do not know where to begin to find competent help, start with your medical doctor, your child's pediatrician, your rabbi or minister, or a trusted friend or co-worker. You may be surprised to find that people you know are knowledgeable about helpers in your own or a neighboring community.

Often a local college or university will offer counseling or therapy in a clinic, and your local Mental Health Association will usually be able to direct you to help in your area.

Find the delicate balance. Understandably, the primary item on the agenda of most expectant and new parents is making things right for the baby. Yet what parents do directly for and with their children is only part of what it takes to create healthy children and family relationships. How parents feel about themselves, each other, their parents, their work, and their friendships all plays a part in creating a family environment that promotes or interferes with the children's ability to cope with new tasks and form satisfying relationships.

We certainly do not advocate the "me-generation" stereotype of parents ignoring their children's needs in order to pursue their own happiness, but many of the couples we spoke to appeared to be at the other extreme, ignoring opportunities to satisfy their own basic relationship needs "for the sake of the children." Especially when both parents work, they may hesitate to take the time to nurture their relationship as a couple because they are away from their children so many hours a week and want to spend all their nonworking hours with them. Although it clearly takes ingenuity and juggling, we believe that the children will ultimately do best in their development when their mothers and fathers find ways to balance their own needs with those of their children.

This is by no means an exhaustive list. It is meant to convey that the modern journey to parenthood, exciting and fulfilling as it is, is beset with many roadblocks. We are finding that even couples who do not ordinarily need the services of mental health professionals experience stress in the early years of family life. If this applies to you or someone you know, take heart. Most men and women need to muster all the strength and skills they have to make this journey. Almost all parents say that the lessons they learn along the way are well worth the effort. They are learning not to give up their dreams but to redefine them based on today's realities.

FOR CHILD AND FAMILY RESEARCHERS

In the past decade we have seen the beginning of a rapprochement between family researchers who study children's development and investigators interested in families with at least one member in psychological or physical distress. Studies of parent-child relationships no longer look only at mothers and children. Fathers have "become" important in psychological studies of children's development.

Even so, it is time to think about fathers' active role in the family not as "mothers' helpers" but as full-fledged parents with independent needs, agendas, and points of view. In two-parent families, even when the parents are divorced, it will never be possible to understand how one parent affects the child's development without knowing something about what the other par-

ent is doing. Almost two decades ago, Barclay Martin (1975) pointed out
that even when both parents are included in the same study, researchers
rarely look at their combined impact on the child. Sadly, this situation has
not changed appreciably since then.

The time is ripe for an even more systemic look at the way in which family
functioning affects children's development. As we have shown throughout
this book, the quality of the parents' marriage is an essential ingredient of the
tone and quality of life in the family. We have seen that how mothers, fathers,
and children cope with their early family transitions depends in large part on
how the couple is managing their relationship. It seems that the parents'
marriage can magnify the difficulties in each of the family domains when it
is in trouble as well as acting as a buffer, protecting couples from additional
strain when it is going well.

For a very long time, psychologists have been studying the development
and adaptation of *individuals*. Our study and several other recent investigations (Hinde and Stevenson-Hinde 1988) remind us that most growth and
development, of children and grownups, occurs in *relationships*. Our research
methods, assessment tools, and concepts are still very bound to the perspective of the individual. We must continue to search for both methodological
and theoretical breakthroughs to do justice to the complexity of understanding what makes relationships work.

FOR HEALTH PROFESSIONALS

Our results also contain a message for obstetricians, pediatricians, and family
medicine practitioners and their patients. As we have pointed out, the focus
of medical care for pregnant women is almost entirely on the physical health
of the mother and fetus. Later, as pediatricians and family doctors take over
the family's care, the focus of care shifts to the child's physical health. We are
concerned about the fact that fathers must make their own adjustments to
pregnancy and parenthood. When fathers adapt poorly, particularly when
the quality of their relationships with their wives is unhappy or stormy, the
well-being of the entire family is affected.

We often lament that, in addition to the rest of their burdens of work and
family, mothers end up in charge of the family's health. Instead of casually
allowing men to come along on their wives' visits to the obstetrician or their
child's appointments to the pediatrician, health care professionals might
consider offering fathers a formal invitation to accompany their wives and
children or to visit on their own. We have noticed that a few medical
practitioners in our area (Northern California) have begun to hold some
regular evening office hours to make it possible for men with nine-to-five
work schedules to take part in their family's health care. Only if we make it
possible for men to become involved are they likely to ask questions, discuss
their concerns, and gather their own information.

As part of an effort at screening and prevention, medical doctors could
think of each visit as an opportunity for a *family* checkup. We are not
suggesting a total revamping of the health delivery system, but one or two

questions about how the family is doing at regular visits. Medical doctors are probably in the best positions to help pinpoint family difficulties before they reach that critical stage when problems become very difficult to treat.

Finally, even if doctors do not pose these family-oriented questions, patients can raise their own questions or concerns. If doctors seem reluctant to broach these psychological family issues, they can at least be helpful in suggesting other resources.

FOR MENTAL HEALTH PROFESSIONALS

We hope that the results of our study will be useful to counselors and therapists. In reading the psychotherapy literature, we have been struck by the number of case histories in which it is mentioned in an aside that the patient has recently become a parent; the discussion of the patient's "problem" proceeds, and the issue never seems to be referred to again. Even if the adult's adaptation to parenthood is not the focus of the therapy, the therapist might pay attention to whether the focal issues could have been exacerbated by the natural stress and vulnerability that accompanies this major adult transition.

It is our hope that therapists working with mothers, fathers, couples, children, or families will be able to use the information here to reassure their patients that even if it is unwelcome, some stress in the family-making years may be normal and expectable. Our experience in working with couples in groups is that this kind of information can help parents put their distress in perspective, and buffer their feelings of helplessness or depression about being in over their heads or alone in their distress.

Finally, we hope to stimulate some mental health professionals to consider more active, preventive work with new families. We believe that the transition to parenthood is an optimal time to provide services for couples who are planning to have a baby. If there were more preventive services for couples like the one we have described here, men and women would get the idea that family making is a challenge for any couple and that there are things partners can do to be better prepared. In talking with other professionals in the United States, Canada, England, and Scotland, we have received very enthusiastic comments about the kind of groups we created, but with the exception of several colleagues who have told us they are pilot-testing similar interventions,* we are not aware of anyone attempting to develop similar groups to help couples with their marital and parenting dilemmas. We would be glad to talk with other professionals interested in trying this kind of intervention.

FOR FAMILY POLICY

We are sadly aware that the millions of parents who are rearing their children in poverty and countless others who are mentally ill constitute a vast under-

*Ed Bader, Toronto; Kuno Beller, Munich; Alan Bennett, London; and Howard Markman, Denver (personal communication, 1991).

served population at risk of repeating dysfunctional cycles in the next generations. At the same time, we have become alarmed by the millions of average families with poor to barely adequate financial and emotional resources who are creating families under unnecessarily stressful conditions. They too are underserved.

We believe that the results of our longitudinal research and intervention study document the costly consequences of disenchantment and distress in the early family years for each parent, their marriage, and their children's emotional, social, and academic development. Governments have an obligation to provide both mental health and prevention services to reduce the present level of family distress and promote the well-being of their citizens. There is much to be done with limited resources. Services for partners becoming parents will be expensive, but we are convinced that providing *no* services will be more costly in the long run—to all of us.

Parental leave policies and more flexible work schedules for mothers and fathers are essential to parents' ability to start their families on sound footing. If parents and children in dual-worker families are to flourish, decent, affordable child care is a necessity. There is no single prescription for the best balance of work and family for the optimal development of young children. The policies that politicians propose must allow for a great range of diversity in families, so that parents are supported in choosing the arrangements that make sense *for them*.

Specific policies have the potential to improve the quality of family life, but a fundamental change in outlook will be necessary before most of them can be enacted. The overarching concern of government and business with fostering the development of the individual is contributing to the burdens of parents and children. The philosophy, psychology, and economics of the American dream are personified by the Horatio Alger myth, not by a real commitment to building satisfying relationships in families and communities. The irony is that failure to provide real incentives for strengthening family relationships may be contributing to our children's inability to develop either the motivation or the skills needed to survive in our complex world.

A Final Word

We have been moved by our journey—our personal one and the one we took with the generous couples who allowed us into their lives. Like us, all of them would make the journey to parenthood if they had to decide again. Our own children have enriched our lives immeasurably. Each one has played an extraordinary role in our development and our understanding of what it means to be partners and parents.

We have emphasized the most difficult parts of becoming a family because the conspiracy of silence that surrounds this period leaves couples feeling that they are the only ones having a hard time. While we believe that difficulties and challenges are necessary for the growth of parents and children, we urge that more attention be given to those who need some assistance along the way. Our warnings are intended as weather advisories—not to advise couples to stay home, but to set out with the necessary gear to withstand the storms. We hope that parents, researchers, and health and mental health professionals will feel better equipped to understand the becoming a family journey so that couples can come closer to building the homestead of their dreams.

NOTES

CHAPTER 2   TO BE OR NOT TO BE A PARENT

1. The coding scheme was created by Jessica Ball who, with Frank Jaffe, rated the responses. The ratings revealed that husbands and wives showed substantial agreement in their problem-solving accounts ($r = .65$).
2. Although men do not have a monopoly on ambivalence about or opposition to parenthood, we were not likely to encounter women who still had a *strong* negative reaction to becoming a parent in the third trimester of pregnancy. Warren Miller's study (1978) shows that as the pregnancy progresses, women shift increasingly toward wanting the baby, regardless of whether conception was intended. In our study, men's ambivalence during pregnancy about becoming a parent was one of the strongest predictors of their own and their wives' later symptoms of depression, parenting stress, and marital dissatisfaction (Heming 1985, 1987).

CHAPTER 4   WHAT'S HAPPENING TO ME?

1. We use a standardized questionnaire created for our research called The Pie (Cowan and Cowan 1990a) with circles 4 inches in diameter.
2. Analyses of change from pregnancy until eighteen months after birth are based on data from forty-seven couples who became parents (twenty-three couples who participated in groups and twenty-four couples who filled out questionnaires both before and after the birth of their babies) and fifteen couples who remained

married and childless over the same period of time. Because they did not provide before-baby information, the twenty-four couples who filled out questionnaires only after the birth of their child were not included in the results reported in this chapter.

3. At six months postpartum, the correlation between the Parent piece of the pie and self-esteem for men was r = .21; $p < .05$) and for women r = −.25; $p < .05$). The discrepancy between partners in the size of the Parent piece of the pie and its relation to decline in marital satisfaction was determined by two multiple regression equations, one for men and one for women. As a predictor of eighteen-month postpartum marital satisfaction, we first partialed out prebirth marital satisfaction scores on step 1 of the equation. Then we entered a measure of between-partner difference in size of the Parent piece at six months after the child's birth. This measure accounts for a significant 17 percent of the decline in men's marital satisfaction during the transition to parenthood (F change = 12.3; df = 2/45; $p < .001$) and 11 percent of the decline in women's marital satisfaction during the same period (F change = 9.30; df = 2/45; $p < .001$).

4. There are thirty-two personality trait subscales on the Adjective Check List including adjustment, autonomy, aggression, counseling readiness, dominance, nurturance, need for achievement, masculinity, and femininity. There are fewer statistically significant changes over time on these scales than we would expect to occur by chance (only in two of thirty-two scales, one for men and one for women).

5.

| | Correlations Between Pie Pieces in Pregnancy and | | | |
| | 6 months after birth | | 18 months after birth | |
Pregnancy	*Men*	*Women*	*Men*	*Women*
Partner	.46*	—	.41*	.36*
Worker	.51*	.58*	.47*	.61**
Leisure	.33*	.49*	.42*	.56**

*$p < .01$
**$p < .001$

CHAPTER 5   WHAT'S HAPPENING TO US?

1. In the pregnancy version of the section on caring for the baby, there were twelve questions. In subsequent follow-ups the number of items was increased to capture some of the new tasks associated with the care of toddlers, preschoolers, and school-aged children.

2. Item correlations between spouses' ratings on household and child-care tasks averaged between .72 and .85 over all assessment periods. Item correlations between spouses' ratings of decision making were lower, averaging .35 to .42, probably because the range of ratings on these items was quite restricted.

3. Ratings of the father's involvement and satisfaction with his involvement were correlated with well-being in four domains:
   Individual: self-esteem (Adjective Check List [Gough and Heilbrun 1980]) and symptoms of depression (CES-D [Radloff 1977]);
   Couple: marital satisfaction (Short Marital Adjustment Test [Locke and Wallace 1959]) and family cohesion (high warmth, high expressiveness, and low conflict—Family Environment Scale [Moos 1974]);

Parent-child: parenting stress (Parenting Stress Index [Abidin 1983]); and *Outside the Family:* life stress (Recent Life Events [Horowitz et al. 1977]) and social support (Important People [Curtis-Boles 1979]). Our index of the balance between stress and support gives the highest scores to people with low life stress and high social support.

4.

When Fathers Participate More in Child-Care Tasks

Measure of Well-being	Pregnancy		6 months after birth		18 months after birth	
	Fathers	Mothers	Fathers	Mothers	Fathers	Mothers
Self-esteem			.26*	.27*		
Parenting stress			−.27*	−.20*	−.27*	−.29*
Depression					−.29*	−.27*
Marital satisfaction		.26*	.30**	.32**		.33*
Family cohesion	.33*	.32**	.23*	.26*		.22*
Positive balance between social support and life stress			.24*	.34**		

*$p < .05$
**$p < .01$

5. The connection between fathers' involvement and change in marital satisfaction was assessed in two multiple regression equations, one for fathers and one for mothers. As a predictor of eighteen-month postpartum marital satisfaction, we first partialed out prebirth marital satisfaction scores on step 1 of the equation. Then we entered a measure of fathers' involvement at six months after birth (either fathers' ratings or mothers' ratings). We find that fathers' daily involvement with the child-care tasks, as they perceive it, accounts for a statistically significant 6 percent of the increase in his marital satisfaction from pregnancy to eighteen months postpartum (F change = 3.80; df = 2/45; $p < .05$). His involvement as *she* perceives it accounts for 12 percent of the variance in her marital satisfaction change over the same period (F change = 9.66; df = 2/45; $p < .003$).

6. "Who does what" issues take second place as a subject of marital arguments when children are three and a half, yielding to conflictual issues about the marriage. They reemerge as the top contender for creating conflict by the time children are in kindergarten.

7. The range of conflict and disagreement change is from a 1.5-point-per-item average reduction in conflict to a 3.7-point-per-item increase on this 7-point scale.

8. There are more psychometrically elegant measures of marital satisfaction, but as Gottman (1979) points out, they are all highly correlated with one another and the Locke-Wallace has the advantage of brevity.

9. In our study, as in many others, the spouses' scores show correlations of about .60.

10. The multiple correlation was R = .64 for men's marital satisfaction and .61 for women's.

11. To test this idea statistically, we constructed a difference index, giving higher scores to couples in which he and she had greater differences between their scores on our key measures. The index included differences between husbands' and wives' reports of the state of things in each of the family domains: the size of the Parent piece of the pie chart; their satisfaction with who does what; the positive changes in their sexual relationship; their ideas about parenting; their description of their families of origin; and their balance of life stress and social support.

CHAPTER 6   BEYOND THE DOORSTEP: NEW PROBLEMS, NEW SOLUTIONS

1. In a multiple regression equation predicting mothers' symptoms of depression on the Center for the Epidemiological Study of Depression scale (Radloff 1977), we entered women's self-esteem scores in pregnancy on the first step. Their self-esteem accounts for about 9 percent of the variance in their depression scores two years later. On a second step, we entered women's work status (full-time home, part-time work, full-time work). Mothers' work status accounted for an additional 10 percent of the variance in their depression scores, over and above their earlier self-esteem (adjusted R-squared = .18).
2. Six months after giving birth, wives' employment is correlated with husbands' involvement in household tasks ($r = .22$; $p < .03$) and child care ($r = .51$; $p < .001$). Eighteen months after having a baby, wives' employment is no longer correlated with husbands' involvement in household tasks, but the more she works, the more child care he does ($r = .42$; $p < .01$).
3. Disagreement in their "How I would like it to be" ratings of bringing in family income on our Who Does What? questionnaire.
4. The more "other care" for the child, the smaller the Mother piece of the pie (six months: $r = -.32$; $df = 31$; $p < .08$; eighteen months: $r = -.44$; $df = 31$; $p < .004$).
5. The questionnaire is called Important People (Curtis-Boles 1979). We do not instruct people about whether they can or should put their spouse on the list. Some do, some do not. New parents' important people usually include current friends, co-workers, childhood friends, sisters, brothers, mothers, fathers, aunts, uncles, and a few important acquaintances. Each person named is given a score that combines frequency of contact multiplied by the parent's satisfaction with that relationship. Our index of positive social support is calculated by adding the scores for all four people to make one index.
6. Our Recent Life Events questionnaire is adapted slightly from Horowitz et al. (1969). Life change items are weighted based on estimates by mental health professionals of the stress-inducing qualities of those events, with more recent events given higher weighting.
7. Multiple regression equations indicate that the life stress/social support balance accounts for a significant proportion of the variance in men's and women's marital satisfaction, over and above their level of life stress or social support. The balance index adds a significant 9 to 12 percent of the variance in marital satisfaction for both parents (increase in R-squared) at six and eighteen months after birth.
8. The correlation between marital satisfaction in pregnancy and positive social support at eighteen months after birth was $r = .35$ ($p < .01$) for women and $r = .27$ ($p < .05$) for men.

CHAPTER 7   LEGACIES FROM OUR PARENTS

1. Conflict in the parents' childhood families was assessed by their descriptions of their families of origin on the conflict subscale of the Family Environment Scale (Moos 1974).

	Decline in Marital Satisfaction (average number of points)	
Conflict Pattern in the Family of Origin	Men	Women
Both partners recall low conflict	6	7
Both partners recall high conflict	17	13
His family had high conflict; hers had low	15	21
Her family had high conflict; his had low	9	9

2. The Adult Attachment Interview (George, Kaplan, and Main 1984) stimulates parents to think back in some detail to their childhood relationships with their parents. Men and women are asked to think of five adjectives that would describe their relationships with their mothers and their fathers. They are asked what their parents did when the children were hurt, and how they as children handled their own feelings of rejection, of feeling threatened, and of separations or losses of important people while they were growing up. Have their relationships with their parents changed in any major way between their childhood and now? Why do they think their parents behaved as they did? How do they think those past experiences affect their lives now?

CHAPTER 8   PARENTING OUR CHILDREN

1. Because a number of the original seventy-two families with children moved out of state, we were able to visit with only fifty-two (72 percent) when the children were three and a half. We have whole family observations on only forty-six because six of the families were divorced by then.
2. The male-female staff team in charge of the parent-child visits rated a number of qualities of the parents' behavior: pleasure/displeasure, coldness/warmth, responsiveness, interactiveness, confidence in the parental role, anger, respect for the child's autonomy, limit setting, maturity demands, structure, creativity, activity level, respect for the child's autonomy, and clarity of communication.

   The ratings are grouped into five categories or factors (for details, see Pratt et al. 1988) and the factors are combined into two summary scores. Parents with high scores on the *authoritative* index show pleasure, warmth, and responsiveness and are very highly engaged with the child during the visit. They also structure the tasks to help the child, express very little anger, and convey their expectation that the child will *try* most of the tasks. By contrast, parents with low scores on these qualities—little pleasure and responsiveness, and little structure and encouragement to try the tasks—appear to be fairly uninvolved or disengaged. They do not react to their child very much either positively or negatively.

   The same summary ratings can be regrouped to reflect *authoritarian* parenting style. Parents with high scores on this index show little pleasure, warmth, or responsiveness, and a fair amount of anger, limit setting, and expectations that the child do the tasks. Parents with low scores on the authoritarian index show warmth and responsiveness but do almost no structuring or limit setting; they can be described as permissive. They are generally warm and allow the children to do what they wish.

Baumrind describes authoritative, authoritarian, permissive, and disengaged styles as types. Here we treat them as bipolar continua: authoritative-disengaged and authoritarian-permissive.

3. The data presented here are derived from a latent variable path model (Cowan et al. in press). Latent variables are statistical combinations of two or more variables assumed to measure the same construct. We constructed latent variables in pregnancy, and six and eighteen months after birth, to predict parenting warmth and structure when the child was three and a half. Each latent variable contained measures from both husbands and wives. In pregnancy we assessed couples' marital satisfaction (Locke and Wallace 1959) and conflict in the family of origin (Family Environment Scale, Moos 1974). At six months postpartum we combined his and her life stress events (Horowitz et al. 1977). At eighteen months postpartum we included a measure of his and her symptoms of depression (Center for Epidemiological Studies in Depression Scale, Radloff 1977) and also measured their marital satisfaction again.

When children were three and a half, we assessed both parents' observed warmth and responsiveness to the child (mothers and fathers in separate visits) and their observed structure and limit setting with the child (mothers and fathers in separate visits). The measures from the transition to parenthood (pregnancy to eighteen months after birth) combine to predict 53 percent of the variance in parents' structuring and 28 percent of the variance in parents' warmth to the child. If we add to the equation the observed interaction between parents in the whole family visits when the child is three and a half, the combined variables account for almost 70 percent of the variance in parents' warmth during the separate parent-child visits.

4. Women's self-esteem (Adjective Check List) and satisfaction with division of family labor (Who Does What?) in pregnancy were correlated with authoritative parenting style (boys and girls combined): Self-esteem ($r = .52$; $df = 42$; $p < .001$); satisfaction with division of family labor ($r = .51$; $df = 42$; $p < .001$).

5. More authoritative fathers of three-and-a-half-year-old sons, previously assessed in pregnancy, showed more positive memories of their parents on the Family Relationships Questionnaire (Cowan and Cowan 1983; $r = .39$; $df = 19$; $p < .05$); higher self-esteem ($r = .44$; $df = 19$; $p < .05$); greater satisfaction with the division of family labor ($r = .42$; $df = 19$; $p < .05$) and lower outside-the-family life stress scores on the Recent Life Events scale (Horowitz et al. 1977; $r = -.43$; $df = 19$; $p < .05$).

6. Fathers of girls were observed to be marginally less authoritative ($t = 1.50$; $df = 45$; $p < .07$) and significantly more authoritarian ($t = 2.26$; $df = 45$; $p < .01$) than fathers of boys.

7. We combined our ratings of the parents' style of interacting as a couple during the whole family visit into two summary scores. The first describes positive interaction and the second captures conflictful interaction between the parents in front of the child. Couples high on the positive interaction index showed more warmth, responsiveness, and pleasure between them than couples with low scores. Couples with high scores on conflictful interaction showed more disagreement,

anger, and competitiveness and less cooperation with each other during the family visit.

8. When the couple was rated as higher in conflict in the family visit, fathers were more authoritarian (cold, critical, structuring, limit setting) with their daughters in the separate father-child visit ($r = .60$; df $= 21$; $p < .001$).

9. Unlike most studies that report correlations between average levels of parents' and children's responses across a whole observation period, Kerig's (1989) provides a microanalysis of how each parent responds when the child shows a specific behavior, providing even stronger evidence of the links between parents' and children's behavior.

10. Boys were coded 0; girls were coded 1. Correlation between sex of child and favorable items for fathers describing themselves on the Adjective Check List: $r = -.32$; df $= 44$; $p < .05$.

11. Correlations between having a girl and having a second child before the first was eighteen months old: $r = .25$; df $= 44$; $p < .05$.

12. Increasing discrepancies between the size of his and her Parent piece of the pie ($r = .34$; $p < .01$) and his and her satisfaction with their division of labor ($r = .57$; $p < .001$) from pregnancy to eighteen months after birth predicted greater conflict between parents (observed) when the child was three and a half.

13. Symptoms of depression were measured by the Center for Epidemiological Studies in Depression Scale (Radloff 1977) and by the Hopkins Symptom Checklist (Derogatis, Lipman, and Covi 1973).

14. Satisfaction with work involvement was measured by the discrepancy between the size of the Worker piece of parents' actual and ideal pie. Parents who were more satisfied with their psychological involvement with work outside the family were more authoritative with their children (fathers: $r = .47$ df $= 45$; $p < .001$; mothers: $r = .30$; df $= 45$; $p < .05$). Parents more satisfied with their process of resolving child-care issues (Leventhal-Belfer 1990) were more authoritative (fathers: $r = .28$; df $= 45$; $p < .05$; mothers: $r = .52$; df $= 45$; $p < .001$).

15. Our Child Adaptive Behavior Inventory is a modification of Schaefer and Hunter's inventory (1983). We added items concerning peer relationships and behavior problems.

16. Because our statistical analyses could not include well-being in each domain at each time period, we were forced to be selective. Except for the assessments of marital functioning in pregnancy and eighteen months and three and a half years after birth, we chose measures from one additional aspect of family life at each time period.

    We selected pairs of measures of family functioning from each aspect of family life—one for mothers and one for fathers. We began with both parents' remembered conflict in their families of origin and low marital satisfaction in pregnancy. We added information about parents' life stress six months after birth, and their symptoms of depression and low marital satisfaction when their child was eighteen months old. This is the same information that helped us predict the level of conflict between the partners in the family visit and low levels of warmth and structure in the separate playroom visits for the parents and their child (see p. 153).

17. The combined family model from pregnancy to preschool accounts for 60 percent of the variance in kindergarten teachers' ratings of children's aggression, 42 percent of the variance in teachers' ratings of concentration problems in the classroom, and 47 percent of the variance in children's academic achievement

(reading and math scores) on the Peabody Individual Achievement Test. (For details, see Cowan et al. in press.)

CHAPTER 9   AN OUNCE OF PREVENTION: COUPLES GROUPS

1. While there are some clear advantages to having married couples as leaders, we have trained graduate student male-female teams to lead groups for couples with young children (Chavez et al. 1988). For our new intervention study with parents of children making the transition to school, we have recruited eight mental health professionals, two couples in which the partners are married to each other, and two others in which the co-leaders are not related.
2. Mean differences and statistical tests of the intervention effects can be found in Cowan et al. (1985). Additional details concerning intervention effects are in Cowan and Cowan (1987b) and C. Cowan (1988).

REFERENCES

Abidin, R. (1983). *Parenting stress index manual.* Charlottesville, VA: Pediatric Psychology Press.

Alexander, K. L., & Entwisle, D. (1988). Achievement in the first 2 years of school: Patterns and processes. *Monographs of the Society for Research in Child Development, 53* (2, Serial No. 218).

Aranoff, J. L., & Lewis, S. (1979). An innovative group experience for couples expecting their first child. *American Journal of Family Therapy, 7,* 51–55.

Ball, F. L. J. (1984). *Understanding and satisfaction in marital problem solving: A hermeneutic inquiry.* Unpublished doctoral dissertation, University of California, Berkeley.

Barnett, R. C., & Baruch, G. K. (1988). Correlates of fathers' participation in family work. In P. Bronstein & C. P. Cowan (Eds.), *Fatherhood today: Men's changing role in the family* (pp. 66–78). New York: Wiley.

Baruch, G. K., Barnett, R. C., & Rivers, C. (1983). *Lifeprints: New patterns of love and work for today's women.* New York: McGraw-Hill.

Bateson, G. (1972). *Steps to an ecology of mind.* New York: Ballantine Books.

Bateson, G., Jackson, D. D., Haley, J., & Weakland, J. (1956). Towards a theory of schizophrenia. *Behavioral Science, 1,* 251–264.

Baucom, D. H., Sayers, S. L., & Duhe, A. (1989). Attributional style and attributional patterns among married couples. *Journal of Personality and Social Psychology, 56,* 596–607.

Baum, F., & Cope, D. R. (1980). Some characteristics of intentionally childless wives in Britain. *Journal of Biosocial Science, 12,* 287–299.

Baumrind, D. (1979). The development of instrumental competence through socialization. In A. D. Pick (Ed.), *Minnesota symposia on child psychology* (Vol. 7).
Minneapolis: University of Minnesota Press.

Baumrind, D. (1991). Effective parenting during the early adolescent transition. In
P. A. Cowan & E. M. Hetherington (Eds.), *Family transitions: Advances in family
research* (Vol. 2, pp. 111–164). Hillsdale, NJ: Lawrence Erlbaum Associates.

Beck, A. (1976). *Cognitive therapy and the emotional disorders*. New York: International Universities Press.

Bellah, R. N., Madsen, R., Sullivan, W. M., Swidler, A., & Tipton, S. M. (1985). *Habits
of the heart: Individualism and commitment in American life*. Berkeley, CA: University
of California Press.

Belsky, J. (1984). The determinants of parenting: A process model. *Child
Development, 55,* 83–96.

Belsky, J. (1988). The "effects" of infant daycare reconsidered. *Early Childhood Research Quarterly, 3,* 235–272.

Belsky, J. (1990). Parental and nonparental child care and children's socioemotional
development: A decade in review. *Journal of Marriage and the Family, 52,* 885–903.

Belsky, J., Lang, M., & Rovine, M. (1985). Stability and change across the
transition to parenthood: A second study. *Journal of Personality and Social Psychology, 50,* 517–522.

Belsky, J., & Rovine, M. (1988). Nonmaternal care in the first year of life
and the security of infant-parent attachment. *Child Development, 59,* 157–167.

Belsky, J., & Rovine, M. (1990). Patterns of marital change across the transition to
parenthood. *Journal of Marriage and the Family, 52,* 109–123.

Belsky, J., & Steinberg, L. (1978). The effects of day care: A critical review. *Child Development, 49,* 929–949.

Belsky, J., Steinberg, L., & Walker, A. (1982). The ecology of day care. In M. E. Lamb
(Ed.), *Nontraditional families* (pp. 71–116). Hillsdale, NJ: Lawrence Erlbaum
Associates.

Belsky, J., Ward, H., & Rovine, M. (1986). Prenatal expectations, post-natal
experiences and the transition to parenthood. In R. Ashmore & D. Brodzinsky
(Eds.), *Perspectives on the family*. Hillsdale, NJ: Lawrence Erlbaum Associates.

Benedek, T. (1959). Parenthood as a developmental phase. *Journal of the American
Psychoanalytic Association, 7,* 389–417.

Benedek, T. (1970). Parenthood during the life cycle. In E. J. Anthony & T. Benedek
(Eds.), *Parenthood: Its psychology and psychopathology*. Boston: Little, Brown.

Bernard, J. (1972). *The future of marriage*. New York: World.

Bittman, S., & Zalk, S. R. (1978). *Expectant fathers*. New York: Hawthorne.

Block, J. H. (1976a). Debatable conclusions about sex differences. *Contemporary
Psychology, 21,* 517–522.

Block, J. H. (1976b). Issues, problems, and pitfalls in assessing sex differences: A
critical review of *The psychology of sex differences*. *Merrill-Palmer Quarterly, 222,*
283–308.

Block, J. H. (1983). Differential premises arising from differential socialization of the
sexes: Some conjectures. *Child Development, 54,* 1335–1354.

Block, J. H. (1984). *Sex role identity and ego development*. San Francisco, CA:
Jossey-Bass.

Block, J. H., & Block, J (1980). The role of ego-control and ego-resiliency in the
organization of behavior. In W. A. Collins (Ed.), *Minnesota symposia on child
psychology* (Vol. 13). Hillsdale, NJ: Lawrence Erlbaum Associates.

Block, J. H., Block, J., & Gjerde, P. F. (1986). The personality of children prior to divorce: A prospective study. *Child Development, 57,* 827–840.

Block, J. H., Block, J., & Morrison, A. (1981). Parental agreement-disagreement on child-rearing orientations and gender-related personality correlates in children. *Child Development, 52,* 965–974.

Boles, A. (1984). *Predictors and correlates of marital satisfaction during the transition to parenthood.* Unpublished doctoral dissertation, University of California, Berkeley.

Bombardieri, M. (1981). *The baby decision: How to make the most important choice of your life.* New York: Rawson Associates.

Bowen, M. (1978). *Family therapy in clinical practice.* New York: Jason Aronson.

Bowlby, J. (1969–80). *Attachment and loss* (Vols. 1–3). London: Hogarth Press.

Bozett, F. W. (1988). Gay fatherhood. In P. Bronstein & C. P. Cowan (Eds.), *Fatherhood today: Men's changing role in the family* (pp. 214–235). New York: Wiley.

Bradburn, I., & Kaplan, J. (in press). Continuity and change in the transition to parenthood: A tale of two families. In P. A. Cowan, D. Field, D. Hansen, A. Skolnick, & G. E. Swanson (Eds.), *Family, self, and society: Toward a new agenda for family research.* Hillsdale, NJ: Lawrence Erlbaum Associates.

Brodzinsky, D. (1987). Adjustment to adoption: A psychosocial perspective. *Clinical Psychology Review, 7,* 25–47.

Bronfenbrenner, U. (1979). *The ecology of human development.* Cambridge, MA: Harvard University Press.

Bronfenbrenner, U., & Crouter, A. (1982). Work and family through time and space. In S. Kamerman & C. Hayes (Eds.), *Families that work: Children in a changing world.* Washington, DC: National Academy Press.

Brown, S. (1985). *Treating the alcoholic: A developmental model of recovery.* New York: Wiley.

Bumpass, L., & Rindfuss, R. R. (1979). Children's experience of marital disruption. *American Journal of Sociology, 85,* 49–65.

Caspi, A., & Elder, G. H., Jr. (1988). Emergent family patterns: The intergenerational construction of problem behavior and relationships. In R. A. Hinde & J. Stevenson-Hinde (Eds.), *Relationships within families: Mutual influences* (pp. 218–240). Oxford: Clarendon Press.

Catalyst (1988). Workplace policies: New options for fathers. In P. Bronstein & C. P. Cowan (Eds.), *Fatherhood today: Men's changing role in the family* (pp. 323–340). New York: Wiley.

Chavez, D., Corkery, L., Epperson, B., Gordon, D., Kline, M., McHale, J., Soulé, C., Sullivan, C., Weinberg, G., Cowan, C. P., & Cowan, P. A. (1988, April). Parents and partners: A preventive intervention for parents of preschoolers. Workshop sponsored by Prevention Section of American Orthopsychiatric Association, San Francisco.

Cherlin, A. (1977). The effect of children on marital dissolution. *Demography, 14,* 264–272.

Cherniss, D. S. (1988). Stability and growth in parent-support services: A national study of peer support for parents of preterm and high-risk infants. In C. F. Z. Boukydis (Ed.), *Research on support for parents in the postnatal period.* Norwood, NJ: Ablex.

Chodorow, N. J. (1978). *The reproduction of mothering.* Berkeley, CA: University of California Press.

Clarke-Stewart, A. (1989). Infant day care: Maligned or malignant? *American Psychologist, 44,* 266–273.

Clulow, C. F. (1982). *To have and to hold: Marriage, the first baby and preparing couples for parenthood.* Aberdeen: Aberdeen University Press.

Cohn, D. A., Cowan, P. A., Cowan, C. P., & Pearson, J. (1991). Mothers' and fathers' working models of childhood attachment relationships, parenting styles, and child behavior. Unpublished manuscript.

Cohn, D. A., Silver, D., Cowan, P. A., Cowan, C. P., & Pearson, J. (1991, April). Working models of attachment and marital relationships. Paper presented in a symposium chaired by D. Cohn on Working Models of Attachment and Couple Relationships at the meetings of the Society for Research in Child Development, Seattle, WA.

Colman, A. D., & Colman, L. L. (1971). *Pregnancy: The psychological experience.* New York: Herder & Herder.

Cowan, C. P. (1988). Working with men becoming fathers: The impact of a couples group intervention. In P. Bronstein & C. P. Cowan (Eds.), *Fatherhood today: Men's changing role in the family* (pp. 276–298). New York: Wiley.

Cowan, C. P., & Cowan, P. A. (1983). *Family relationships questionnaire.* Becoming a Family Project, University of California, Berkeley.

Cowan, C. P., & Cowan, P. A. (1987a). Men's involvement in parenthood: Identifying the antecedents and understanding the barriers. In P. Berman & F. Pedersen (Eds.), *Men's transitions to parenthood: Longitudinal studies of early family experience* (pp. 145–174). Hillsdale, NJ: Erlbaum.

Cowan, C. P., & Cowan, P. A. (1987b). A preventive intervention for couples becoming parents. In C. F. Z. Boukydis (Ed.), *Research on support for parents and infants in the postnatal period* (pp. 225–251). Norwood, NJ: Ablex.

Cowan, C. P., & Cowan, P. A. (1988). Who does what when partners become parents: Implications for men, women, and marriage. *Marriage & Family Review, 13,* 105–132.

Cowan, C. P., & Cowan, P. A. (1990a). The Pie. In J. Touliatos, B. F. Perlmutter, & M. A. Straus (Eds.), *Handbook of family measurement techniques* (pp. 278–279). Newbury Park: Sage.

Cowan, C. P., & Cowan, P. A. (1990b). Who Does What? In J. Touliatos, B. F. Perlmutter, & M. A. Straus (Eds.), *Handbook of family measurement techniques* (pp. 447–448). Newbury Park: Sage.

Cowan, C. P., Cowan, P. A., Coie, L., & Coie, J. D. (1978). Becoming a family: The impact of a first child's birth on the couple's relationship. In W. B. Miller and L. F. Newman (Eds.), *The first child and family formation* (pp. 296–324). Chapel Hill, NC: Carolina Population Center.

Cowan, C. P., Cowan, P. A., & Heming, G. (1988, November). Adult children of alcoholics: What happens when they form new families? Paper presented to the National Council on Family Relations, Philadelphia, PA.

Cowan, C. P., Cowan, P. A., Heming, G., Garrett, E., Coysh, W. S., Curtis-Boles, H., & Boles, A. J. (1985). Transitions to parenthood: His, hers, and theirs. *Journal of Family Issues, 6,* 451–481.

Cowan, C. P., Cowan, P. A., Heming, G., & Miller, N. B. (1991). Becoming a family: Marriage, parenting, and child development. In P. A. Cowan & E. M. Hetherington (Eds.), *Family transitions: Advances in family research* (Vol. 2, pp. 79–109). Hillsdale, NJ: Lawrence Erlbaum Associates.

Cowan, P. A. (1988a). Becoming a father: A time of change, an opportunity for development. In P. Bronstein & C. P. Cowan (Eds.), *Fatherhood today: Men's changing role in the family* (pp. 13–35). New York: Wiley.

Cowan, P. A. (1988b). Developmental psychopathology: A nine-cell map of the territory. In E. Nannis & P. A. Cowan (Eds.), *Developmental psychopathology and its treatment: New directions for child development* (Number 39, pp. 5–30). San Francisco: Jossey-Bass.

Cowan, P. A., & Cowan, C. P. (1988). Changes in marriage during the transition to parenthood: Must we blame the baby? In G. Y. Michaels & W. A. Goldberg (Eds.), *The transition to parenthood: Current theory and research* (pp. 114–154). Cambridge: Cambridge University Press.

Cowan, P. A., & Cowan, C. P. (1990). Becoming a family: Research and intervention. In I. E. Sigel and G. H. Brody (Eds.), *Methods of family research: Biographies of research projects I: Normal families.* Hillsdale, NJ: Lawrence Erlbaum Associates.

Cowan, P. A., Cowan, C. P., & Kerig, P. (in press). Mothers, fathers, sons, and daughters: Gender differences in family formation and parenting style. In P. A. Cowan, D. Field, D. Hansen, A. Skolnick, & G. E. Swanson (Eds.), *Family, self, and society: Toward a new agenda for family research.* Hillsdale, NJ: Lawrence Erlbaum Associates.

Cowan, P. A., Cowan, C. P., Schulz, M., & Heming, G. (in press). Prebirth to preschool family factors predicting children's adaptation to kindergarten. In R. Parke & S. Kellam (Eds.), *Exploring family relationships with other social contexts: Advances in family research* (Vol. 4). Hillsdale, NJ: Lawrence Erlbaum Associates.

Cowan, P. A., & Hetherington, E. M. (Eds.). (1991). *Family transitions: Advances in family research* (Vol. 2). Hillsdale, NJ: Lawrence Erlbaum Associates.

Coysh, W. S. (1983). *Factors influencing men's roles in caring for their children and the effects of father involvement.* Unpublished doctoral dissertation, University of California, Berkeley.

Crnic, K. A., Greenberg, M. T., Ragozin, A. S., Robinson, N. M., & Basham, R. B. (1983). Effects of stress and social support on mothers and premature and full-term infants. *Child Development, 54,* 209–217.

Crockenberg, S. B. (1981). Infant irritability, mother responsiveness, and social support influences on the security of infant-mother attachment. *Child Development, 52,* 857–865.

Curtis, J. L. (1955). A psychiatric study of 55 expectant fathers. *U.S. Armed Forces Medical Journal, 6,* 937–950.

Curtis-Boles, H. (1979). Important people. Becoming a Family Project, University of California, Berkeley.

Cutrona, C. E., & Troutman, B. R. (1986). Social support, infant temperament, and parenting self-efficacy: A mediational model of postpartum depression. *Child Development, 57,* 1507–1518.

Daniels, P., & Weingarten, K. (1982). *Sooner or later: The timing of parenthood in adult lives.* New York: W. W. Norton.

Daniels, P., & Weingarten, K. (1988). The fatherhood click: The timing of parenting in men's lives. In P. Bronstein & C. P. Cowan (Eds.). *Fatherhood today: Men's changing role in the family* (pp. 36–52). New York: Wiley.

Derogatis, L. R., Lipman, R. S., & Covi, L. (1973). SCL-90: An outpatient psychiatric rating scale. Preliminary report. *Psychopharmacology Bulletin, 9,* 1–25.

Dura, J., & Kiecolt-Glazer, J. K. (1991). Family transitions, stress, and health. In P. A. Cowan & E. M. Hetherington (Eds.), *Family transitions: Advances in family research* (Vol. 2, pp. 59–78). Hillsdale, NJ: Lawrence Erlbaum Associates.

Ehrensaft, D. (1987). *Parenting together: Men and women sharing the care of their children.* New York: Free Press.

Eiduson, B. T. (1983). Conflict and stress in non-traditional families: Impact on children. *American Journal of Orthopsychiatry, 53* (3), 426–435.

Epperson, B., Cowan, C. P., & Cowan, P. A. (1991). Predictors of divorce: A small-sample prospective study. Unpublished manuscript.

Erikson, E. (1950). *Childhood and society.* New York: W. W. Norton.

Erikson, E. (1959). Identity and the life cycle. *Psychological Issues, 1,* 1–171.

Erikson, E. (1968). *Identity, youth and crisis.* New York: W. W. Norton.

Fawcett, J. T. (1988). The value of children and the transition to parenthood. In R. Palkovitz & M. B. Sussman (Eds.), *Transitions to parenthood* (pp. 11–34). New York: Haworth Press.

Feldman, S. S., & Nash, S. C. (1984). The transition from expectancy to parenthood: Impact of the firstborn child on men and women. *Sex Roles, 11,* 84–96.

Field, T., Healy, B., Goldstein, S., & Guthertz, M. (1990). Behavior-state matching and synchrony in mother-infant interactions of nondepressed versus depressed dyads. *Developmental Psychology, 26,* 7–14.

Finkelhor, D., with Hotaling, G., & Yllo, K. (1988). *Stopping family violence: Research priorities for the coming decade.* Beverly Hills, CA: Sage.

Framo, J. L. (1981). The intergration of marital therapy with sessions with family of origin. In A. S. Gurman and D. P. Kniskern (Eds.), *Handbook of family therapy.* New York: Bruner/Mazel.

Freud, A. (1965). *Normality and pathology in childhood.* New York: International Universities Press.

Friedan, B. (1963). *The feminine mystique.* New York: Dell.

Garrett, E. T. (1983, August). Women's experiences of early parenthood: Expectation vs. reality. Paper presented at the American Psychological Association Meetings, Anaheim, CA.

George, C., Kaplan, N., & Main, M. (1984). *Attachment interview for adults.* Unpublished manuscript. University of California, Berkeley.

Gilligan, C. (1982). *In a different voice: Psychological theory and women's development.* Cambridge, MA.: Harvard University Press.

Glick, P. C., & Lin, S. (1986). Recent changes in divorce and remarriage. *Journal of Marriage and the Family, 48,* 737–747.

Goldberg, W. A., Michaels, G. Y., & Lamb, M. (1985). Husbands' and wives' adjustment to pregnancy and first parenthood. *Journal of Family Issues, 6,* 483–504.

Gottlieb, B.H., & Pancer, S. M. (1988). Social networks and the transition to parenthood. In G. Y. Michaels & W. A. Goldberg (Eds.), *The transition to parenthood: Current theory and research* (pp. 235–269). Cambridge: Cambridge University Press.

Gottman, J. M. (1979). *Marital interaction: Experimental investigations.* New York: Academic Press.

Gottman, J. M., & Krokoff, L. J. (1989). Marital interaction and satisfaction: A longitudinal view. *Journal of Consulting and Clinical Psychology, 57,* 47–52.

Gottman, J. M., & Levenson, R. M. (1986). Assessing the role of emotion in marriage. *Behavioral Assessment, 8,* 31–48.

Gottman, J. M., & Levenson, R. W. (1989). The social psychophysiology of marriage. In P. Noller & M. A. Fitzpatrick (Eds.), *Perspectives on marital interaction.* San Diego, CA: College Hill Press.

Gough, H. G., Fioravanti, M., & Lazzari, R. (1982). Some implications of self versus ideal congruence on the revised adjective check list. *Journal of Consulting Psychology, 44,* 1214–1220.

Gough, H. G., & Heilbrun, A. B., Jr. (1965, 1980). *The adjective check list manual.* Palo Alto, CA: Consulting Psychologists Press.

Greenberger, E., & Goldberg, W. A. (1989). Work, parenting, and the socialization of children. *Developmental Psychology, 25,* 22–35.

Grossman, F., Eichler, L., & Winickoff, S. (1980). *Pregnancy, birth, and parenthood.* San Francisco: Jossey-Bass.

Haley, J. (1976). *Problem-solving therapy.* San Francisco: Jossey-Bass.

Hanson, S. M. H. (1988). Divorced fathers with custody. In P. Bronstein & C. P. Cowan (Eds.), *Fatherhood today: Men's changing role in the family* (pp. 166–194). New York: Wiley.

Harber, K. (1991). *To work or not to work: The impact on new mothers.* Unpublished doctoral dissertation. Center for Psychological Studies, Albany, CA.

Heinicke, C. M., Diskin, S. D., Ramsay-Klee, D. M., & Oates, D. S. (1986). Pre- and postbirth antecedents of 2-year-old attention, capacity for relationships and verbal expressiveness. *Developmental Psychology, 22,* 777–787.

Heming, G. (1985). *Predicting adaptation in the transition to parenthood.* Unpublished doctoral dissertation, University of California, Berkeley.

Heming, G. (1987, April). Predicting adaptation during the transition to parenthood. Paper presented to the Society for Research in Child Development, Baltimore, MD.

Heming, G., Cowan, P. A., & Cowan, C. P. (1990). Ideas about parenting. In J. Touliatos, B. F. Perlmutter, & M. A. Straus (Eds.), *Handbook of family measurement techniques* (pp. 362–363). Newbury Park, CA: Sage Publications.

Hetherington, E. M., Cox, E. M., & Cox, R. (1982). Effects of divorce on parents and children. In M. E. Lamb (Ed.), *Nontraditional families.* Hillsdale, NJ: Lawrence Erlbaum Associates.

Hetherington, E. M., & Parke, R. D. (1986). *Child psychology: A contemporary viewpoint.* (3rd ed.). New York: McGraw-Hill.

Hinde, R. A., & Stevenson-Hinde, J. (1988). *Relationships within families: Mutual influences.* Oxford: Clarendon Press.

Hobbs, D., & Cole, S. (1977). Transition to parenthood: A decade replication. *Journal of Marriage and the Family, 38,* 723–731.

Hochschild, A. (1989). *The second shift: Working parents and the revolution at home.* New York: Viking Penguin.

Hoffman, L. (1989). Effects of maternal employment in the two-parent family. *American Psychologist, 44,* 283–292.

Hoffman, L., & Hoffman, M. (1973). The value of children to parents. In J. T. Fawcett (Ed.), *Psychological perspectives on population* (pp. 106–151). New York: Basic Books.

Hoffman, L. W., & Nye, F. I. (1974). *Working mothers.* San Francisco, CA: Jossey-Bass.

Holmes, T. H., & Rahe, R. H. (1967). The social adjustment rating scale. *Journal of Psychosomatic Research, 11,* 213–218.

Hops, H., Sherman, L., & Biglan, A. (1990). Maternal depression, marital discord, and children's behavior: A developmental perspective. In G. R. Patterson (Ed.), *Advances in family research: Depression and aggression: Two facets of family interactions* (Vol. 1). Hillsdale, NJ: Lawrence Erlbaum Associates.

Horowitz, M., Schaefer, C., Hiroto, D., Wilner, N., & Levin, B. (1977). Life event questionnaire for measuring presumptive stress. *Psychosomatic Medicine, 39,* 413–431.

Jacobson, N. S., & Gurman, A. S. (1986). *Clinical handbook of marital therapy.* New York: Guilford.

Janis, I. (1958). *Psychological stress: Psychoanalytic and behavioral studies of surgical patients.* New York: Wiley.

Kelley, H. H., Berscheid, E., Christensen, A., Harvey, J. H., Huston, T. L., Levinger, G., McClintock, E., & Peplau, L. A. (1983). *Close relationships.* New York: W. H. Freeman.

Kerig, P. K. (1989). *The engendered family: The influence of marital satisfaction on gender differences in parent-child interaction.* Unpublished doctoral dissertation. University of California, Berkeley.

Kumar, R., & Robson, K. M. (1984). A prospective study of emotional disorders in childbearing women. *British Journal of Psychiatry, 144,* 35–47.

LaRossa, R., & LaRossa, M. M. (1981). *Transition to parenthood: How infants change families.* Beverly Hills: Sage.

Lazarus, R. L. (1991). *Emotion and adaptation.* Oxford: Oxford University Press.

Lazarus, R. L., & Folkman, S. (1984). *Stress, appraisal, and coping.* New York: Springer.

Leifer, M. (1980). *Psychological effects of motherhood: A study of first pregnancy.* New York: Praeger.

LeMasters, E. E. (1957). Parenthood as crisis. *Marriage and Family Living, 19,* 352–355.

Levant, R. F. (1988). Education for fatherhood. In P. Bronstein & C. P. Cowan (Eds.), *Fatherhood today: Men's changing role in the family* (pp. 253–275). New York: Wiley.

Leventhal-Belfer, L. J. (1990). *Child care, parents, and partners: A new perspective.* Unpublished doctoral dissertation, University of California, Berkeley.

Leventhal-Belfer, L. J., Cowan, P. A., & Cowan, C. P. (in press). Child care as a couples' issue: The links between parents' satisfaction with child care decisions, partners' satisfaction, and adaptation to parenthood. *American Journal of Orthopsychiatry.*

Levenson, R. W., & Gottman, J. M. (1985). Physiological and affective predictors of change in relationship satisfaction. *Journal of Personality and Social Psychology, 49,* 85–94.

Lewinsohn, P. H., Steinmetz, J. L., Larsen, D. W., & Franklin, J. (1981). Depression-related cognitions: Antecedents or consequences? *Journal of Abnormal Psychology, 90,* 213–219.

Lewis, J. M., Owen, M. T., & Cox, M. J. (1988). The transition to parenthood: III. Incorporation of the child into the family. *Family Process, 27,* 411–421.

Lewis, R. A., & Spanier, G. B. (1979). Theorizing about the quality and stability of marriage. In W. R. Burr, R. Hill, F. I. Nye, & I. L. Reiss (Eds.), *Contemporary theories about the family* (Vol. 1, pp. 269–294). New York: Free Press.

Lieberman, M. A. (1981). The effects of social support in response to stress. In L. Goldberger & S. Breznitz (Eds.), *Handbook of stress* (pp. 764–781). New York: Free Press.

Locke, H., & Wallace, K. (1959). Short marital adjustment and prediction tests: Their reliability and validity. *Marriage and Family Living, 21,* 251–255.

Loewen, J. W. (1988). Visitation fatherhood. In P. Bronstein & C. P. Cowan (Eds.), *Fatherhood today: Men's changing role in the family* (pp. 195–213). New York: Wiley.

Lowe, L. (1991). *Transition to grandmotherhood*. Unpublished doctoral dissertation, Center for Psychological Studies, Albany, CA.

Lowinsky, N. R. (1990). Mother of mothers: The power of the grandmother in the female psyche. In C. Zweig (Ed.), *To be a woman: The birth of the conscious feminine* (pp. 86–97). Los Angeles: J. P. Tarcher.

Lowinsky, N. R. (1992). *Stories from the motherline: Reclaiming the mother-daughter bond, finding our feminine souls*. Los Angeles: J. P. Tarcher.

Maccoby, E. E., & Martin, J. A. (1983). Socialization in the context of the family: Parent-child interaction. In E. M. Hetherington (Ed.), P. H. Mussen (Series Ed.), *Handbook of child psychology: Vol. 4. Socialization, personality and social development* (4th ed., pp. 1–101). New York: Wiley.

McGuire, J. C., & Gottlieb, B. (1979). Social support groups among new parents: An experimental study in primary prevention. *Journal of Clinical Child Psychology, 8,* 111–116.

McHale, S. M., & Huston, T. L. (1985). The effect of the transition to parenthood on the marriage relationship. *Journal of Family Issues, 6,* 409–433.

Main, M., & Goldwyn, R. (1984). Predicting rejection of her infant from mother's representation of her own experience: Implications for the abused-abusing intergenerational cycle. *Child Abuse and Neglect, 8,* 203–217.

Main, M., & Goldwyn, R. (in press). Adult attachment classification system. In M. Main (Ed.), *A typology of human attachment organization: Assessed in discourse, drawings and interviews*. New York: Cambridge University Press.

Main, M., Kaplan, N., & Cassidy, J. (1985). Security in infancy, childhood, and adulthood: A move to the level of representation. In I. Bretherton & E. Waters (Eds.), *Growing points of attachment theory and research. Monographs of the Society for Research in Child Development, 50* (Serial No. 209, pp. 66–106).

Martin, B. (1975). Parent-child relations. In F. D. Horowitz (Ed.), *Review of child development research* (Vol. 4, pp. 463–540). Chicago: University of Chicago Press.

Markman, H. J., & Kadushin, F. S. (1986). Preventive effects of Lamaze training for first-time parents: A short-term longitudinal study. *Journal of Consulting and Clinical Psychology, 54,* 872–874.

Markman H., & Notarius C. (1987). Coding marital and family interaction. In T. Jacob (Ed.), *Family interaction and psychopathology* (pp. 329–390). New York: Plenum.

Menning, B. (1977). *Infertility: A guide for childless couples*. Englewood Cliffs, NJ: Prentice-Hall.

Michaels, G. Y. (1988). Motivational factors in the decision and timing of pregnancy. In G. Y. Michaels & W. A. Goldberg (Eds.), *The transition to parenthood: Current theory and research* (pp. 23–61). Cambridge: Cambridge University Press.

Miller, N. B., Cowan, P. A., Cowan, C. P., Hetherington, E. M., & Clingempeel, G. (1991, August). Externalizing in preschoolers and early adolescents: A cross-study replication of a family model. Paper presented to the American Sociological Association, Cincinnati, OH.

Miller, W. (1978). The intendedness and wantedness of the first child. In W. Miller and L. Newman (Eds.), *The first child and family formation* (pp. 209–243). Chapel Hill, NC: Carolina Population Center.

Minuchin, S., & Fishman, H. C. (1981). *Family therapy techniques*. Cambridge, MA: Harvard University Press.

Moorehouse, M. (in press). Work and family dynamics. In P. A. Cowan, D. Field, D.

Hansen, A. Skolnick, & G. E. Swanson (Eds.), *Family, self, and society: Toward a new agenda for family research.* Hillsdale, NJ: Lawrence Erlbaum Associates.

Moos, R. H. (1974). *Family Environment Scale.* Palo Alto, CA: Consulting Psychologists Press.

Morgan, S. P., Lye, D. N., & Condran, G. A. (1988). Sons, daughters, and the risk of marital disruption. *American Journal of Sociology, 94,* 110–129.

Mussen, P. H., Conger, J. P., & Kagan, J. (1984). *Child development and personality* (6th ed.). New York: Harper & Row.

Myers-Walls, J. A., & Sudsberry, R. L. (1982). Parent education during the transition into parenthood. In N. Stinnett, J. DeFrain, K. King, H. Lingren, G. Rowe, S. van Zandt, & R. Williams (Eds.), *Family strengths: Positive models for family life* (pp. 49–65). Lincoln: University of Nebraska Press.

Nathanson, S. (1989). *Soul crisis: One woman's journey through abortion to renewal.* New York: New American Library.

Nott, P. N., Franklin, M., Armitage, C., & Gelder, M. G. (1976). Hormonal changes and mood in the puerperium. *British Journal of Psychiatry, 128,* 379–383.

Nuckolls, K. B., Cassell, J., & Kaplan, B. H. (1972). Psychosocial assets, life crisis, and the prognosis of pregnancy. *American Journal of Epidemiology, 95,* 431–441.

Oakley, A. (1980). *Women confined.* Oxford: Martin Robertson.

Oakley, A. (1986). *From here to maternity.* New York: Viking Penguin.

O'Donnel, J. P., & VanTuinen, M. V. (1979). Behavior problems of preschool children: Dimensions and congenital correlates. *Journal of Abnormal Child Psychology, 7,* 61–75.

O'Hara, M. W. (1986). Social support, life events, and depression during pregnancy and the puerperim. *Archives of General Psychiatry, 43,* 569–573.

Olson, L. (1983). *Costs of children.* Lexington, MA: D. C. Heath.

Osofsky, H. (1982). Expectant and new fatherhood as a developmental crisis. *Bulletin of the Menninger Clinic, 46,* 209–230.

Osofsky, J. D., & Osofsky, H. J. (1984). Psychological and developmental perspectives on expectant and new parenthood. In R. D. Parke (Ed.), *Review of child development research: Vol. 7. The family* (pp. 372–397). Chicago: University of Chicago Press.

Parens, H. (1975). Parenthood as a developmental phase. *Journal of the American Psychoanalytic Association, 23,* 154–165.

Parke, R. D. (1979). Perspectives on father-infant interaction. In J. Osofsky (Ed.), *Handbook of infant development* (pp. 549–590). New York: Wiley.

Parke, R. D., & Tinsley, B. (1982). The early environment of the at-risk infant: Expanding the social context. In D. D. Bricker (Ed.), *Intervention with at-risk and handicapped infants.* Baltimore: University Park Press.

Parkes, C. M. (1971). Psycho-social transitions: A field for study. *Social Science and Medicine 5,* 101–115.

Parlee, M. B. (1973). The premenstrual syndrome. *Psychological Bulletin, 83,* 454–465.

Parsons, T., & Bales, R. F. (1955). *Family, socialization, and interaction process.* Glencoe, IL: Free Press.

Patterson, G. (Ed.). (1990). *Depression and aggression: Two facets of family interactions: Advances in family research* (Vol. 1). Hillsdale, NJ: Lawrence Erlbaum Associates.

Pearson, J. L., Cohn, D. A., Cowan, P. A., & Cowan, C. P. (1991). Adults' working models of attachment: Self-defined resiliency and adult adjustment. Unpublished manuscript.

Phillips, D. A., & Howes, C. (1987). Indicators of quality in child care: Review of research. In D. A. Phillips (Ed.), *Quality in child care: What does research tell us?* (pp. 1–20). Research Monograph of the National Association for the Education of Young Children.

Piaget, J. (1967). *Six psychological studies* (D. Elkind, Ed.). New York: Random House.

Pleck, J. (1985). *Working wives/working husbands.* Beverly Hills, CA: Sage.

Powell, D. R. (1987). A neighborhood approach to parent support groups. *Journal of Community Psychology, 15,* 51–62.

Pratt, M., Kerig, P., Cowan, P. A., & Cowan, C. P. (1988). Mothers and fathers teaching three-year-olds: Authoritative parenting and adult scaffolding of young children's learning. *Developmental Psychology, 24,* 832–839.

Pratt, M., Kerig, P., Cowan, P. A., & Cowan, C. P. (in press). Family worlds: Couple satisfaction, parenting style, and mothers' and fathers' speech to young children, *Merrill-Palmer Quarterly.*

Pruett, K. D. (1986). *The nurturing father.* New York: Warner.

Quindlen, A. (May 21, 1991). Speech to National Press Club. National Public Radio.

Quinton, D., Rutter, M., & Liddle, C. (1984). Institutional rearing, parenting difficulties, and marital support. *Psychological Medicine, 14,* 107–124.

Radin, N. (1988). Primary caregiving fathers of long duration. In P. Bronstein & C. P. Cowan (Eds.), *Fatherhood today: Men's changing role in the family* (pp. 127–143). New York: Wiley.

Radloff, L. (1977). Sex differences in depression: The effects of occupation and marital status. *Sex Roles, 1,* 249–265.

Ramey, C. T., Collier, A. M., Sparling, J. J., Loda, F. A., Campbell, F. A., Ingram, D. L., & Finkelstein, N. W. (1976). The Carolina Abecedarian Project: A longitudinal and multidisciplinary approach to the prevention of developmental retardation. In T. Tjossem (Ed.), *Intervention strategies for high-risk infants and young children* (pp. 629–665). Baltimore, MD: University Park Press.

Rapoport, R., Rapoport, R., & Strelitz, Z. (1977). *Mothers, fathers, and society: Towards new alliances.* New York: Basic Books.

Robinson, J. (1977). *Changes in American's use of time: 1975–1976—A progress report.* Cleveland, Ohio: Communications Research Center, Cleveland State University.

Russell, G. (1983). *The changing role of fathers?* St. Lucia: University of Queensland Press.

Rutter, M. (1987). Psychosocial resilience and protective mechanisms. *American Journal of Orthopsychiatry, 57,* 316–331.

Scarr, S. (1984). *Mother care, other care.* New York: Basic Books.

Schaefer, E. S., & Hunter, W. M. (1983, April). Mother-infant interaction and maternal psychosocial predictors of kindergarten adaptation. Paper presented to the Society for Research in Child Development, Detroit, MI.

Schulz, M. (1991, April). Linkages among both parents' work roles, parenting style, and children's adjustment to school. Paper presented at the meetings of the Society for Research in Child Development, Seattle, WA.

Schwebel, A. I., Fine, M., & Moreland, J. R. (1988). Clinical work with divorced and widowed fathers: The adjusting family model. In P. Bronstein & C. P. Cowan (Eds.), *Fatherhood today: Men's changing role in the family* (pp. 299–322). New York: Wiley.

Seligman, M. E. P. (1975). *Helplessness: On depression, development, and death.* San Francisco: W. H. Freeman.

Shapiro, C. H. (1982). The impact of infertility in the marital relationship. *Social Casework, 63,* 387–393.

Shereshefsky, P., & Yarrow, L. J. (Eds.). (1973). *Psychological aspects of a first pregnancy and early postnatal adaptation.* New York: Raven Press.

Sheehy, G. (1976). *Passages: Predictable crises in adult life.* New York: E. P. Dutton.

Skolnick, A. (1991). *Embattled paradise: The American family in an age of uncertainty.* New York: Basic Books.

Snarey, J., Son, L., Kuehne, V., Hauser, S., & Vaillant, G. (1987). The role of parenting in men's psychosocial development: A longitudinal study of early adulthood infertility and midlife generativity. *Developmental Psychology, 23,* 593–603.

Stafford, R., Backman, E., & Dibona, P. (1977). The division of labor among cohabiting and married couples. *Journal of Marriage and the Family, 39,* 43–57.

Steinberg, L., & Belsky, J. (1991). *Infancy, childhood, and adolescence: Development in context.* New York: McGraw-Hill.

Steinglass, P., with Bennett, L. A., Wolin, S. J., & Reiss, D. (1987). *The alcoholic family.* New York: Basic Books.

Szinovacz, M. E. (1977). Role allocation, family structure and female employment. *Journal of Marriage and the Family, 39,* 781–791.

Tannen, D. (1990). *You just don't understand: Women and men in conversation.* New York: William Morrow.

Teachman, J. D., Polonko, K. A., & Scanzoni, J. (1987). Demography of the family. In M. B. Sussman & S. K. Steinmetz (Eds.), *Handbook of marriage and the family* (pp. 3–36). New York: Plenum.

Tinsley, B. J., & Parke, R. D. (1988). The role of grandfathers in the context of the family. In P. Bronstein & C. P. Cowan (Eds.), *Fatherhood today: Men's changing role in the family* (pp. 236–252). New York: Wiley.

Towne, R. D., & Afterman, J. (1955). Psychoses in males related to parenthood. *Bulletin of the Menninger Clinic, 19,* 19.

Trethowan, W. H., & Conlan, M. F. (1965). The couvade syndrome. *British Journal of Psychiatry, 111,* 57–66.

Wainwright, W. H. (1966). Fatherhood as a precipitant of mental illness. *American Journal of Psychiatry, 123,* 40–44.

Wallerstein, J., & Blakeslee, S. (1989). *Second chances: Men, women, and children a decade after divorce.* New York: Ticknor & Fields.

Wandersman, L. P. (1987). Parent-infant support groups: Matching programs to needs and strengths of families. In C. F. Z. Boukydis (Ed.), *Research on support for parents in the postnatal period.* Norwood, NJ: Ablex.

Weissman, M. M., & Klerman, G. L. (1977). Sex differences and the epidemiology of depression. *Archives of General Psychiatry, 34,* 98–112.

Weitzman, L. J. (1985). *The divorce revolution: The unexpected social and economic consequences for women and children in America.* New York: Free Press.

Wenner, N. K., Cohen, M. B., Weigert, E. V., Kvarnes, R. G., Ohaneson, E. M., & Fearing, J. M. (1969). Emotional problems in pregnancy. *Psychiatry, 32,* 389–410.

Werner, H. (1948). *The comparative psychology of mental development.* New York: Follett.

Whelan, E. M. (1975). *A baby? . . . maybe: A guide to making the most fateful decision of your life.* New York: Bobbs-Merrill.

Wile, D. (1981). *Couples therapy: A nontraditional approach.* New York: Wiley.

Wile, D. (1988). *After the honeymoon: How conflict can improve your relationship.* New York: Wiley.

Zajicek, E. (1981). The experience of being pregnant. In S. Wolkind and E. Zajicek

(Eds.), *Pregnancy: A psychological and social study* (pp. 31–56). London: Academic Press/New York: Grune & Stratton.

Zaslow, M., Pedersen, F., Kramer, E., Cain, R., Suwalsky, J., & Fivel, M. I. (1981, April). Depressed mood in new fathers: Interview and behavioral correlates. Paper presented at the Society for Research in Child Development, Boston, MA.

Zilboorg, G. (1931). Depressive reactions related to parenthood. *American Journal of Psychiatry, 87,* 927–962.

INDEX